STEVE PRICE

America's
Best Bass
Fishing

The 50 best places to catch bass

FALCON®

A FALCON GUIDE®

Falcon® Publishing is continually expanding its list of recreational guidebooks. All books include detailed descriptions, accurate maps, and all information necessary for enjoyable trips. You can order extra copies of this book and get information and prices for other Falcon® books by writing Falcon, P.O. Box 1718, Helena, MT 59624 or calling toll free 1-800-582-2665. Also, please ask for a free copy of our current catalog. Visit our website at www.Falcon.com or contact us by e-mail at falcon@falcon.com.

Cover photo: Soc Clay
Back cover photo: Soc Clay
All black-and-white photos by the author unless otherwise noted.

Cataloging-in-Publication Data is on record at the Library of Congress.
  Price, Steve, 1947-
    America's Best Bass Fishing / Steve Price.
        p. cm.
    ISBN 1-56044-775-3
    1. Bass fishing—United States—Guidebooks. I. Title: America's fifty best bass waters.
    II. Title.
    SH 681. P75 2000
    799.1'773'0973—dc21   99-086261

CAUTION

Outdoor recreational activities are by their very nature potentially hazardous. All participants in such activities must assume responsibility for their own actions and safety. The information contained in this guidebook cannot replace sound judgment and good decision-making skills, which help reduce exposure, nor does the scope of this book allow for the disclosure of all the potential hazards and risks involved in such activities.

Learn as much as possible about the outdoor recreational activities in which you participate, prepare for the unexpected, and be cautious. The reward will be a safer and more enjoyable experience.

 Text pages printed on recycled paper.

DEDICATION

This book is dedicated to Patti and Belle, two constant
companions whose faith in me and in this project never wavered.
Would that all writers should be so fortunate.

ACKNOWLEDGMENTS

Although a project of this type often originates with a single person, it invariably involves many others before it can be completed. Such was the case with this book. Assistance came in many ways, most often during countless days on lakes all over the United States and frequently long before this book even became an idea.

Many gave freely of their time and knowledge during hours of interviews at odd times and in unusual places. Denny Brauer and I have talked in too many tournament motel rooms to count; I have taped Guy Eaker as he tended the azaleas around his home; and Davy Hite, Clark Wendlandt, and I have spent hours talking bass fishing while deer hunting on Clark's ranch—to name just a few such occurrences.

Among others whose help played a key role are Terry Baksay, Fred Bland, Randy Blaukat, Mickey Bruce, Johnny Candle, Rick Clunn, Steve Daniel, Woo Daves, Mark Davis, Gary Dobyns, Mike Hawkes, Dennis Hoy, Homer Humphreys, Alton Jones, Ken Marlow, Tommy Martin, Steve McCadams, Richard McCarty, Jim Morton, Larry Nixon, Mitch Ratchford, Skeet Reese, Dean Rojas, John Sappington, Ray Sedgwick, Ron Speed Sr., Ron Speed Jr., Bill Stephens, Harry Stiles, Sam Swett, David Wharton, Jack Wingate, and Scott Wolfe. You are all pros in more ways than one, and to each I say a sincere thank you.

A special note of gratitude also must be directed to Tom Marino, Peggy O'Neill-McLeod, and Brynlyn Lehmann, my editors at Falcon Publishing, whose skill and patience were taxed too many times to count during the writing and production schedule.

TABLE OF CONTENTS

Map Legend

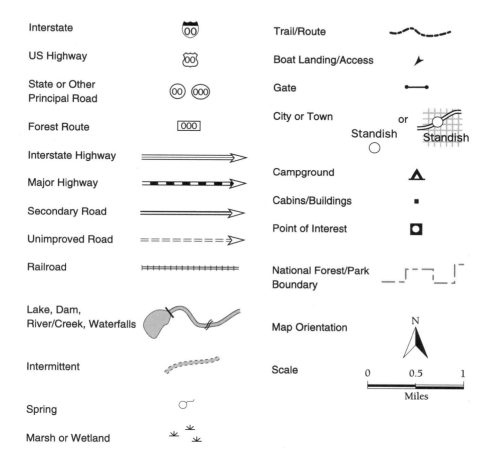

Interstate

US Highway

State or Other
Principal Road

Forest Route

Interstate Highway

Major Highway

Secondary Road

Unimproved Road

Railroad

Lake, Dam,
River/Creek, Waterfalls

Intermittent

Spring

Marsh or Wetland

Trail/Route

Boat Landing/Access

Gate

City or Town   or
                Standish   Standish

Campground

Cabins/Buildings

Point of Interest

National Forest/Park
Boundary

Map Orientation   N

Scale   0   0.5   1
                        Miles

LOCATOR MAP

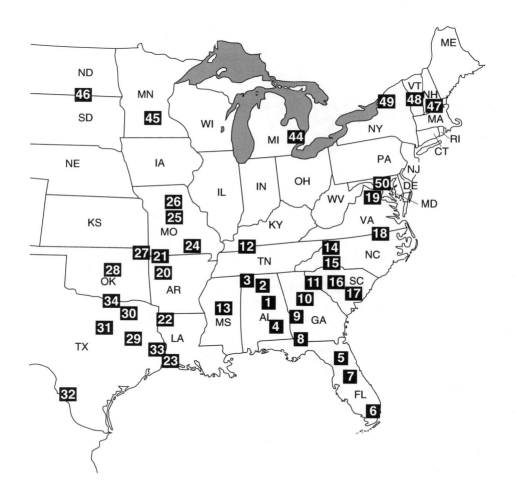

A trophy size bass comes out of the salad at Lake Fork, Texas. In Texas, anglers spend more than $25 billion annually to fish the state's many lakes and rivers. The largemouth bass is by far the state's most popular freshwater gamefish.

INTRODUCTION

What Makes Bass Fishing So Popular

Early on the morning of June 2, 1932, a 19-year old farm boy named George Perry and his close friend Jack Page eased their homemade wooden boat into central Georgia's Montgomery Lake for a few short hours of fishing. They had but one lure between them, and they caught only one largemouth bass that overcast, drizzly day, but it was enough to change not only their lives, but the lives of anglers all across America.

Perry's bass weighed 22 pounds, 4 ounces, and as this is written, stands as the heaviest largemouth bass ever landed. It has become the most hallowed of all freshwater fishing records, and annually draws tens of thousands of fishermen to lakes across the United States in quest of a possible new world record. Many feel the angler who catches that fish will reap more than $1 million in endorsement contracts, and indeed, a number of financial prizes have been posted by various firms for anyone who does catch a new world record bass.

The object of all this interest is a fish that has been evolving in American waters for tens of thousands of years, *Micropterus salmoides,* the largemouth bass. Strangely enough, it is not a true bass, but in reality a sunfish. No matter, because much of the largemouth's appeal is its accessibility. Largemouth bass inhabit lakes, rivers, streams, and creeks in every state except Alaska. Montgomery Lake where Perry caught his world record was hardly more than a large pond.

Another reason the largemouth bass is so popular is its willingness to strike artificial lures. True, the fish can also be caught on a variety of baits such as earth worms, minnows, or crickets, but the fact that bass also charge pell-mell into topwater plugs, diving crankbaits, and bottom-bumping jigs and plastic lizards of all colors, shapes, and sizes has widened its appeal to the masses. Truly, the largemouth bass is "America's fish."

The largemouth has also been successfully introduced into several Central American, African and European countries, is thoroughly established in both Canada and Mexico, and has a strong following in Japan. The heart of bass fishing, however, remains the United States, where many claim bass fishing is not only a sport, it is a lifestyle.

Bass fishing has become so popular that its economic impact to different states, counties, and even cities cannot be denied. In Texas, for example, sportfishermen spent $28 billion on fishing trips and equipment in 1996, according to figures released by the American Sportfishing Association. Sportfishing (the majority of which is bass fishing) created 80,000 fulltime jobs in the state and generated nearly $180 million in state tax revenues in that year alone.

This huge appeal has led to the growing popularity of competitive bass fishing tournaments, which, in turn, have spurred the development of the fishing and boating

Today more than 30 million anglers fish for bass each year on lakes and rivers throughout America. Rods, reels, lures, and boats have all been designed especially for bass fishing.

industries. There are literally dozens of companies across America today that produce hundreds of models of rods, reels, and lures specifically designed to catch largemouth bass.

The boating industry has likewise responded with a new breed of water craft, the bass boat, designed—you guessed it—specifically for bass fishing, although it is certainly suitable for other types of fishing, as well. This, in turn, has led outboard engine manufacturers to design new motors to propel these boats, and other manufacturers to design after-market items, such as trolling motors and electronic sonar (depthfinder) units.

All of this has only helped make the largemouth bass even more popular. Of the approximately 60 million anglers in the United States today, roughly half of them, or 30 million, list the largemouth bass as their favorite. Today there are television shows devoted exclusively to largemouth bass fishing, videos showing prospective anglers the secrets of catching bass, and colleges teaching classes in bass fishing.

Since the late 1960's when bass tournaments began sweeping across the nation, more than a few talented anglers have even been able to turn bass fishing into a lucrative, fulltime profession. Several fishermen have won more than $1 million in prize money simply by catching more bass than their competitors. Basically, bass tournament competitors are allowed to bring in five bass per day comprising a stringer limit to be weighed; competition lasts one to four days, and the angler with the heaviest cumulative weight wins. After being weighed, the fish are released alive back into the water.

Thousands of anglers from throughout the nation now float the Umpqua each year because of the smallmouth.

The goal of the majority of bass fishermen is to catch a trophy fish weighing 10 pounds or more. Numerous lakes throughout the United States have gained reputations for producing fish that big. The world record largemouth, 22 pounds, 4 ounces, was caught in Georgia in 1932, and today it is the most sought-after record in fishing.

Although today the word "bass" commonly refers to the largemouth, the fish has two close cousins that are only slightly less popular among America's anglers. These are the smallmouth bass, *Micropterus dolomieui,* and the spotted bass, *Micropterus punctulatus.* Both are found throughout the nation in many of the same waters inhabited by the largemouth, and in numerous lakes they are actually the dominant species.

The smallmouth does not grow quite as heavy as the largemouth, but many consider it a superior fighter when hooked. A rowdy smallmouth usually goes airborn like a rocketship and seems to spend more time in the air than in the water before it can finally be boated.

The other close cousin, the spotted bass, tends to be slightly smaller than the smallmouth, but its lighter weight certainly does not make it any less ornery. In fact, some feel that "spots" or Kentucky bass, as they are also known, are smarter and more wary than either smallmouth or largemouth, which only adds to their popularity.

Two other "bass," totally unrelated to the largemouth but which are commonly found in the same lakes, include the striped bass (*Morone saxatilis*) and the hybrid striped bass (*Morone saxatilis x Morone chrysops*).

The history of these two species is fascinating. The freshwater striped bass evolved from saltwater fish being accidentally locked in South Carolina's Santee Cooper Lakes (Lakes Marion and Moultrie) after migrating in from the Atlantic to feed on herring. The hybrid striped bass, a cross between the freshwater striped bass and a much smaller white bass, was actually created in fisheries laboratories.

Both fish fight like wet wildcats, grow to over 20 pounds (striped bass attain weights of over 50 pounds), and like the smaller largemouth bass clan, hit a variety of lures and live baits. Fishing for them is every bit as addictive as going after largemouths.

Throughout the nation bass fishing is a year-round sport, too. Only a few states have closed seasons for bass fishing, primarily during the spring. Some of the hottest angling action actually occurs during the months of December, January, and February, particularly in the South where winters are far less severe than in other regions. This is not to say the South does not have cold weather, because it does. Sometimes it actually snows in Miami. But cold temperatures seldom last long in the South and rarely slow the fishing for more than a few days.

Generally speaking, most bass fishing centers around large, man-made impoundments, although there are numerous rivers across America, such as the Columbia in Washington or the St. Lawrence in New York, where bass fishing is every bit as good as lake fishing.

With only a few exceptions, the man-made lakes found across the South are normally larger than in other regions. Many fishermen, making their first visit to the South, are stunned by the awesome size of some of these reservoirs: Alabama's Lake Guntersville has over 69,000 acres, and the largest of all, Lake Okeechobee in Florida, spreads across 450,000 acres.

Striped bass grow much larger than largemouth or smallmouth bass, occasionally reaching weights of 50 pounds in some lakes. At certain times of the year, striped bass can be caught on topwater lures, but more often the fish are caught with live or cut baits.

Because of the immense size of these lakes, some anglers prefer to hire professional guides to take them out for a day or two of fishing. Guides furnish a boat and gasoline, while clients usually provide their own tackle, although not always. Some better-known guides are booked months in advance, and rates may be as high as $250 per day.

Because bass fishing is such big business, the majority of impoundments have motel, cabin, or campground accommodations and restaurants nearby. Even marinas frequently provide these services. In several states, resort parks are located on the water and offer not only lodge and cabin facilities, but also camping, picnicking, golf, tennis, and hiking, as well.

The lakes and rivers described in this book are certainly among the finest in the United States, as most knowledgeable bass anglers will agree. What many probably will not agree on is why certain waters were included andothers omitted. Several factors were considered in the selection process.

Consistent overall productivity ranked first. While it is a given fact that virtually all lakes are cyclic in nature and experience not only long-time aging changes but also short-term "up and down" years, the waters described here have proven productivity records over a long period of time. That means that on any given day an angler's chances of catching fish in that lake are above average.

Overall size of the waterway also ranked very high on the criteria list, and no lake smaller that 10,000 acres was considered, due to possible problems of angling pressure. For this reason, a number of otherwise highly qualified lakes were omitted. Heavy fishing pressure definitely does affect a lake or river. Conversely, none of the five Great Lakes were included because of their huge size. Lake Erie supports one of the finest smallmouth fisheries in the world, but readers will surely realize that fishery cannot adequately be described in a single short chapter. Indeed, entire books have been written about the Lake Erie smallmouth.

Both trophy bass history as well as angling techniques were also part of the criteria. Several lakes that consistently provide above-average size bass were included because that is their primary claim to fame, but at the same time, those fish have to be available to the average angler in above-average numbers and to average fishing techniques.

Other criteria included in the scenic and natural beauty of these waters, as well as the availability of facilities, long-term future potential, and geographical location. Each lake or river had to score high in several of these categories.

And last but no least, the choices were made by the author, gleaned from more than a quarter-century of sharing fishing time on these waters with hundreds of tournament professionals, guides, and just plain fishermen.

When planning a fishing trip to one of the lakes described in this book, contact the Chamber of Commerce or Visitor's Bureau/Tourism Association in the nearest city for additional information describing lodging, restaurants, and other recreational opportunities. Another telephone call or letter to the state game and fish agency will bring additional details on fishing conditions on the lake you plan to visit.

Schedule your trip carefully to correspond with the peak fishing season of the species you're going after. Assemble your tackle and sharpen your hooks before you leave home, and who knows? Perhaps you'll be the one to finally top George Perry's largemouth bass record!

SOUTHEAST

ALABAMA

FLORIDA

GEORGIA

KENTUCKY

MISSISSIPPI

NORTH CAROLINA

SOUTH CAROLINA

VIRGINIA

1 LAKE LOGAN MARTIN

Location: Central Alabama approximately 45 miles east of Birmingham in Talladega, St. Clair, and Calhoun Counties.
Short Take: 15,263 acres; narrow river conditions in the upper end and more open water, pockets, flats, and tributaries in the lower end.
Primary Species: Largemouth and spotted bass.
Best Months: March through May, October, November.
Favorite Lures: Willowleaf spinnerbaits, deep-diving crankbaits, plastic worms and lizards.
Nearest Tourist Services: Pell City, Talladega, Birmingham.

IF EVER AN IMPOUNDMENT DESERVED TO BE described as "two lakes in one," it is Alabama's Lake Logan Martin. One of six reservoirs sandwiched along the Coosa River about an hour's drive east of Birmingham, the upper 16 miles of this lake are little more than the Coosa itself, while the lower 32 miles feature more open-water lake-like conditions, with points, coves, shallow flats, and deeper structure.

Sometimes, it's actually hard to decide which part of the lake to fish, because both areas can offer excellent fishing. Some of the better tributary creeks flow into the river in the upper end, while the lower lake provides excellent action off the deeper points and ridges. Together, both portions total 15,263 acres.

Impounded in 1964, Logan Martin has become, over the years, Birmingham's water playground. Still, despite receiving both heavy recreational boat traffic as well as constant residential construction along the shoreline, the lake continues to produce fine bass fishing. Three Bass Masters Classic world championships have been held here, in 1992, 1993, and again in 1997, with winning weights for the three-day event ranging from 34 to 59 pounds. And at one time, Logan Martin held the record for the state's heaviest largemouth, a 14-pound, 11-ounce giant.

Interstate 20 between Birmingham and Atlanta crosses Logan Martin near Pell City and generally separates the upper and lower portions of the lake. There are two basic fishing patterns for the upper, river-type conditions: fishing the shallow tributary creeks with spinnerbaits or working shoreline stumps, logs, and fallen brush with crankbaits, jigs, or plastic worms.

"The shoreline pattern can be a strong one," notes Birmingham angler Fred Bland, who has fished Logan Martin for two decades, "because there are a lot of stumps along the bank. One of the best stump fields is just above the I-20 bridge on the western shoreline, where the water drops from 10 to about 20 feet. Ten-fish stringers of spotted bass weighing more than 35 pounds have been caught there."

Bland's favorite upper lake tributaries (and everyone else's, too) are Acker, Alligator, and Cane Creeks. All three are spring-fed, have well-defined creek channels, and are filled with stumps and heavy brush, which makes them excellent bass producers year-round. One of the most productive tactics is fishing a spinnerbait very slowly along the bottom, bouncing it off the stumps and logs.

LAKE LOGAN MARTIN
ALABAMA

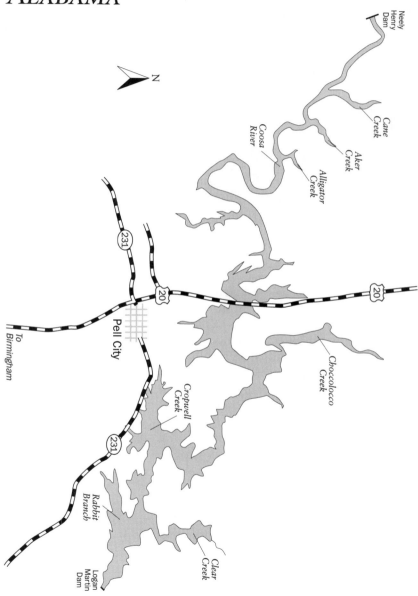

N

Neely
Henry
Dam

Cane
Creek

Coosa
River

Aker
Creek

Alligator
Creek

231

20

20

Pell City

To
Birmingham

Chocolocco
Creek

Cropwell
Creek

231

Rabbit
Branch

Clear
Creek

Logan
Martin
Dam

Located just 40 miles east of Birmingham, Lake Logan Martin continues to be one of the state's premier largemouth and spotted bass fishing lakes. Fishing tributary creeks and boat houses are two of the favorite techniques.

One problem in fishing these creeks is that when the controlling authority, Alabama Power Company, releases water from the next dam upriver, Neely Henry, all three will flood. This allows the bass to spread out and become much harder to find. As a result, many fishermen try to get to the creeks early in the morning before water is released.

At the same time water is released from the Neely Henry Dam, however, it is usually released simultaneously from the Logan Martin Dam, and that helps the lower lake fishing because of the current it produces. Bass move up on points or closer to structures like boat houses, both of which the lower lake has in abundance.

Below the I-20 bridge, the largest and most well-known tributary is Choccolocco Creek, which features a channel depth of more than 20 feet, shallow, stump-covered flats, and a brushy shoreline. Crankbaits and Carolina-rigged lizards produce well on the flats, while jigs are popular around the boat docks.

Two other tributaries worth studying are Clear and Rabbit Branch Creeks near the dam. Both have brush and stumps but more importantly, each is lined with boat houses and piers where most of the owners have made artificial brush piles to help attract bass. It's a great area for skipping worms and jigs under the docks, or working spinnerbaits and jigs along the outside pilings.

Another tributary many anglers enjoy fishing is Cropwell Creek, site of several marinas. The back of the creek is filled with shallow stumps, and not far away is the the old U.S. Highway 231 roadbed, which provides more than a mile of underwater structure.

Anglers on the lower end of the lake certainly don't have to spend all their time fishing creeks, however. This area includes miles of clay and rock points in the main lake, and in between them are shallow bays and coves.

Here jigs, crankbaits, and spinnerbaits will catch largemouth bass in the coves, while plastic worms worked farther out on the points usually attract spotted bass. Virtually every point has a brush pile on it, and the spotted bass hold very close to them in 10 to 12 feet of water.

Among the favorite lures on Logan Martin is a slim, 6-inch green plastic worm, rigged with a 1/8- or possibly 1/4-ounce leadhead and fished with 6- or 8-pound-test line on a spinning rod. The technique used is known as "skipping," and Bland is considered by many to be the originator of the presentation. The lure (plastic jigs can also be used) is literally skipped across the water just like a flat rock to get into areas otherwise unreachable by normal casting.

Another reason anglers enjoy light tackle on this lake is because they usually get more strikes than fishermen who use heavier line and lures. At Logan Martin, with so many bass around, that means they stay busy all the time, regardless of which of the "two" lakes they're fishing.

RESOURCES

Gearing Up: Both baitcasting and spinning tackle can be used here, with lines ranging from as light as 6- to as heavy as 14- or perhaps 17-pound-test. A flipping presentation may require 20- or 25-pound test line. Popular lures include 3/8-ounce spinnerbaits, 1/2-ounce jigs, deep-diving crankbaits, and 6-inch plastic worms and lizards. Light tackle techniques are also very effective.

Accommodations: Complete motel and restaurant facilities are available in Pell City, Talladega, and Birmingham. Camping is also available in the nearby Talladega National Forest. More than a dozen marinas are open around the lake, both on I-20 as well as on U.S. Highway 231 South.

Additional Information: Pell City Chamber of Commerce, Highway 34, Pell City, AL 35125; 205-338-3377.

2 LAKE GUNTERSVILLE

Location: Marshall and Jackson Counties between Guntersville and Scottsboro
in northern Alabama.
Short Take: 69,100 acres; primarily shallow water filled with stumps,
underwater ridges, and several types of aquatic vegetation.
Primary Species: Largemouth bass.
Best Months: March through May, September through November.
Favorite Lures: Spinnerbaits, plastic worms, crankbaits, topwater frogs.
Nearest Tourist Services: Guntersville, Scottsboro, Fort Payne.

ALTHOUGH IMPOUNDMENT OF THIS MASSIVE TENNESSEE RIVER RESERVOIR was
completed in 1939, bass fishermen really did not discover Lake Guntersville until
November 2, 1976. Early that morning a Texas angler named Rick Clunn stunned
the fishing world by boating 24 pounds, 14 ounces of fish in just four casts from a
small grassbed in the mouth of Brown's Creek on the lower end of the lake. It was
the second day of the bass fishing world championship, and sportswriters from
around the country were on hand to report the phenomenal catch.

Clunn went on to win with a then-record three-day total of 59 pounds, 15 ounces,
but the second and third place finishers each also boated more than 50 pounds of
bass. In so doing, these anglers told the fishing world about one of the finest bass
fishing lakes in the nation at that time. Surprisingly, until that tournament, Lake
Guntersville had largely been unnoticed by all but area fishermen.

In the years since, this beautiful 69,100-acre lake, the largest in Alabama, has
undergone a number of changes, the most noticeable being continued attempts by
the Tennessee Valley Authority and other agencies to eradicate the lake's Eurasian
milfoil. This vegetation, somewhat similar to hydrilla in that it can completely cover
shallow water and mats thickly on the surface, was the key to the lake's successful
bass fishery. Through the use of chemicals, mechanical harvesters, and grass-eating
carp, most of the vegetation was eliminated by the early 1990s. Accordingly, the
quality of bass fishing was eliminated, too.

Slowly but surely, however, the vegetation returned, although not to the extent
of the mid-1970s, and so did the fishing. Today, the Big G remains a truly viable and
dynamic bass fishery.

Bass fishing centers around both the vegetation and the lake's numerous underwater stump fields. Both are present along the entire 30-mile stretch between
Guntersville and Scottsboro, and both types of cover hold bass year-round.

Every inch of the cover looks like it holds bass, too, but veteran anglers here tend
to concentrate in a few key areas. Among them are Town Creek and Jones Cove near
Scottsboro, and Brown's Creek near Guntersville. Alabama 69 crosses Brown's Creek,
so it is possible there to study potential fishing conditions before launching a boat.

LAKE GUNTERSVILLE
ALABAMA

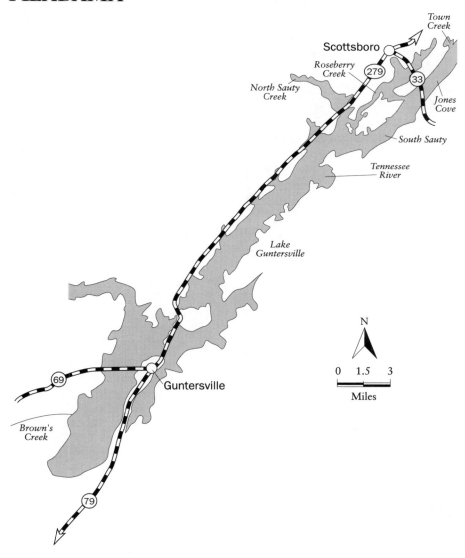

Town
Creek

Scottsboro

Roseberry
Creek

279

North Sauty
Creek

33

Jones
Cove

South Sauty

Tennessee
River

Lake
Guntersville

N

0   1.5   3

Miles

69

Guntersville

Brown's
Creek

79

Lake Guntersville is famous for its Eurasian milfoil. The vegetation was nearly totally eradicated by the Tennessee Valley Authority in the early 1990's but has since re-established itself in many areas of the lake.

Jones Cove, which is a large bay at the mouth of Jones Creek, is probably better known for its boat houses, which all seem to hold fish, than for its milfoil.

Other well-known choices that produce bass nearly as consistently include Roseberry, North Sauty and South Sauty Creeks, and Siebold Branch. North Sauty and South Sauty are huge tributaries on opposite sides of the lake, and each offers miles of varied cover. Roseberry is a smaller creek filled with stumpfields, while Siebold is characterized more as a large flat with scattered stumps, vegetation, and smaller channels.

In each of these places, the secret of finding bass is locating milfoil in three to five feet of water with a nearby drop to six or eight feet. If stumps are anywhere close, the chances of locating fish improve even more.

Isolated islands of milfoil often produce better results than the larger beds— Clunn's big fish spot was a small isolated bed—because they frequently indicate the presence of deeper water nearby. Milfoil does not grow well in greater depths, but it thrives and covers shallow high spots throughout the lake. As such, some of them become magnets for bass. The very best ones tend to be near the mouths of creeks.

For much of its length, and particularly north of the Comer Bridge (Alabama 35 leading into Scottsboro), Lake Guntersville is essentially a river. This should not discourage fishermen, for in addition to the major tributaries, the lake has a number of off-river sloughs and smaller creeks. Because the lake is so large and the major tributaries offer such a variety of fishing choices, most anglers here tend to concentrate in just one or two areas.

Buzzbaits and plastic frogs (they're called "rats" on Guntersville and the technique is "rat fishing"), plastic worms, and spinnerbaits are among the most productive lure choices on Guntersville. Buzzbaits and frogs, especially, tempt autumn bass into explosive strikes through the matted milfoil, and even though many such fish are missed, the experience never fails to leave a heart racing or knees shaking. Just as Clunn's tournament win alerted the world to the lake, it was a national television fishing program on rat fishing that first showed this particular technique to the angling public.

A number of lure companies make these types of lures, which are essentially hollow, floating plastic frog imitations. They're cast over the milfoil, then skittered back across the top with erratic jerks. Rarely are the strikes subtle; most are more like explosions, made all the more dramatic because there is never any indication of when or where a strike will occur. Even missed strikes usually leave an open hole in the milfoil, too.

Other techniques, such as with plastic worms and crankbaits, work best along the outside edges of the milfoil. The outside edge usually marks the beginning of deeper water and frequently holds bass that for some reason don't go into the vegetation itself. Retrieves that yo-yo the lure up and down, or stop-and-go with an erratic motion, work best. Normally, bass are attracted to irregularities along this outside edge, too, such as points or indentations.

Throughout its history, Guntersville has never been known as a true trophy bass lake, although it has produced fish over 10 pounds. Instead, it has gained its reputation by consistently giving up fish in the 4- to 7-pound range. Even though the milfoil will probably never be as widespread as it was when Clunn hit his jackpot, there are still plenty of places on this lake where it could easily happen again.

RESOURCES

Gearing Up: Because most fishing is done in and around heavy cover, medium- to heavy-action baitcasting rods with lines testing 14 to 25 pounds are popular. Large willowleaf spinnerbaits, plastic worms and lizards, medium diving crankbaits, and floating frogs are all productive. Tackle shops are located throughout the area.

Accommodations: Several resorts, including Lake Guntersville State Park, are located around the lake, while both Guntersville and Scottsboro have numerous motels and restaurants. Camping is available at the state park.

Additional Information: Alabama Mountain Lakes Tourist Association, P. O. Box 1075, Mooresville, AL 35649, tel. (256) 350-3500.

3 PICKWICK LAKE

Location: Near Florence and Tuscumbia in northwestern Alabama, and extending through a corner of Mississippi to Counce, Tennessee.
Short Take: 47,500 acres; primarily flooded river with points, gravel bars, stump flats, islands, small tributaries.
Primary Species: Smallmouth and largemouth bass.
Best Months: April, May, September through November.
Favorite Lures: Crankbaits, jigs, plastic grubs, spinnerbaits.
Nearest Tourist Services: Florence, Tuscumbia.

IT'S A PRETTY SAFE BET TO ASSUME THAT WHEN PICKWICK LAKE was impounded in the 1930s, no one dreamed it would become a world-famous smallmouth bass fishery. Famous is hardly the proper word to describe what this lake was like between the late 1960s and early 1990s; staggering is probably more accurate.

During those halcyon years, anglers caught smallmouth bass in the 6- to 8-pound range regularly, sometimes several in a single day. A number of fishermen, including well-known television fishing personality Bill Dance, have hooked but lost world-record fish they saw and estimated to weigh more than 12 pounds.

"I had found a school of smallmouth that were feeding on shad blown up against a rocky bluff," remembers Dance. "I was sculling a flat-bottom johnboat, and I caught several fish on a topwater plug. Then this giant smallmouth hit, jumped five times all around the boat, and finally pulled both treble hooks out of my lure."

Today, this Tennessee River impoundment still produces good smallmouth action, and fair largemouth fishing, as well. Truly big fish are not caught as often, but for consistent mid-size smallmouth action, spiced with an occasional giant, Pickwick remains one of the better destinations in the South.

Several reasons have been given for Pickwick's outstanding productivity. First, the Tennessee River is considered the southernmost natural range of the smallmouth, which means these are the warmest waters the fish inhabit anywhere. The river also forms the basic northern boundary of the threadfin shad, the smallmouth's principal forage, so essentially, the bass are more active and have more to eat here than anywhere else in their range. Finally, Pickwick has not only flow-through river current but also a wide variety of gravel and rock structure that smallmouth love. Biologists think a flow-through system may also help keep the fish more active, which again means they eat more.

A lot of fishing actually begins in the tailrace below Wilson Dam, where, when waterflow conditions are suitable, a controlled, quarter-mile drift downstream can be made. Lure selection for this type of fishing ranges from crankbaits to jigging spoons to plastic grubs.

Live bait fishing is also popular in the tailrace. Shad are dipped up at the base of the dam, then drifted behind the boat along the edge of the fast current. Light

PICKWICK LAKE
ALABAMA

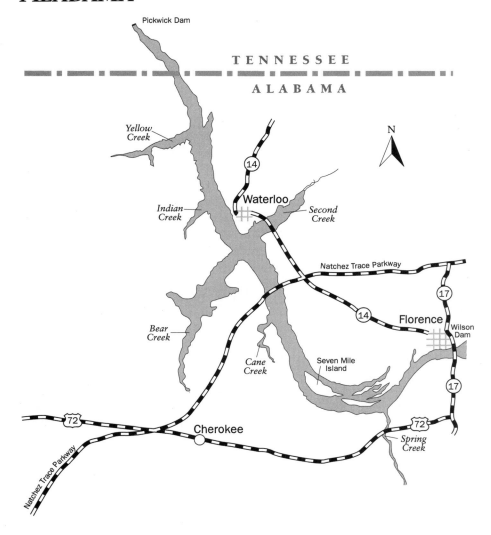

Pickwick Dam

TENNESSEE

ALABAMA

N

Yellow Creek

14

Waterloo

Indian Creek

Second Creek

Natchez Trace Parkway

17

14

Florence

Wilson Dam

Bear Creek

Cane Creek

Seven Mile Island

17

72

Cherokee

72

Spring Creek

Natchez Trace Parkway

spinning tackle is often used, and when a smallmouth hits the bait, the fish is allowed to run with it for a few seconds before the hook is set.

Bouncing small plastic grubs rigged on 1/8- to 3/8-ounce jigheads in current is also practiced in other parts of the lake and certainly has accounted for many trophy fish. One of the most popular areas for this technique is around Seven Mile Island (located about seven miles downstream from Wilson Dam) where the current flows over stumps, rocks, and ditches. This is actually a complex of several long islands, quiet off-river sloughs, and a small but excellent tributary, Spring Creek.

Some anglers fish this area by drifting downstream with the current. Others find a quiet spot out of the current and anchor, then cast upstream and control the grub on a tight line as the current takes it away. As in the tailrace, lines as light as 6- and 8-pound test are often used with this method, and needless to say, a lot of grubs (rigged with an exposed hook) are left snagged on the stumps.

Pickwick is also known for its night fishing, in which 3/8- and 1/2-ounce spinnerbaits are slowly and methodically retrieved across shallow, stumpy flats near the main river channel. Generally, the water depth on these flats is less than 10 feet. Athens, Alabama, angler Bill Huntley was so successful using this technique in the 1970s and 1980s that smallmouth fishermen throughout the nation came to fish with him and learn his secrets.

"The key is finding stumps on a clear, gravel bottom where the fish come up to feed, which isn't hard to do on Pickwick," notes Huntley, whose best single night on the lake included eight smallmouth and two largemouth weighing a total of 64 pounds. "I personally have spent a lot of time around mid-lake near the town of Waterloo because the wide flats there are covered with stumps, but there is also good fishing around the mouth of both Cane and Spring Creeks, too."

Another key is using a yo-yo retrieve in which the spinnerbait rises and falls slowly but continually throughout the retrieve. The reason is that virtually every smallmouth strike occurs while the lure is falling, so increasing the number of times the lure falls automatically increases the potential for a strike.

Largemouth can be taken on the same stump flats as smallmouth, as well as in some of the other Pickwick tributaries like Yellow and Bear Creeks. There is limited vegetation in Pickwick so most largemouth fishermen concentrate on stumps, boat docks, or other shallow shoreline cover. Spinnerbaits, jigs, and crankbaits all produce well.

Pickwick also has a surprising number of flooded roadbeds, particularly on the lower end of the lake and just above Indian Creek. Several of these lead from the shoreline out to the river channel, and they're year-round fish producers. Good lake maps show the locations of some of these structures, while others will have to be pinpointed with electronics, but they're always worth a few casts with crankbaits or Carolina rigs.

Even though Pickwick has perhaps finally begun to show its age and the smallmouth fishing is not what it once was, the lake still produces its share of fine fish. In fact, the word most often used to describe the lake today is "excellent."

RESOURCES

Gearing Up: Both light-action spinning and medium/heavy-action baitcasting rods are used here, depending on style and preference. When fishing 3-inch plastic grubs around the stumps, lighter rods and 6- or 8-pound-test line is preferred. Night fishing, on the other hand, is regularly done with baitcasting gear and 14- to 20-pound-test line. Other lure choices include crankbaits, jerkbaits, jigs, and larger plastic worms, all used on heavier tackle.

Accommodations: Complete motel and restaurant services are available in Florence. Camping is available in Coleman State Park where the lake flows through Mississippi, as well as at Pickwick Dam State Park in Tennessee.

Additional Information: Alabama Mountain Lakes Tourist Association, P.O. Box 1075, Mooresville, AL 35649; 256-350-3500.

4 LAKE MARTIN

Location: Elmore and Tallapoosa Counties on the Tallapoosa River in southeastern Alabama.
Short Take: 39,000 acres; generally clear, deep water with rocky bluffs, islands, underwater reefs.
Primary Species: Largemouth and spotted bass.
Best Months: April, May, October through December.
Favorite Lures: Spinnerbaits, jigs, small plastic worms.
Nearest Services: Alexander City.

THE JOY OF FISHING LAKE MARTIN is not knowing what you've caught until you see it, for this is probably the best lake in Alabama, as well as one of the better lakes in the South, for catching both quality largemouth and spotted bass. In many reservoirs these two species utilize different habitat, but on this clear, 39,000-acre impoundment the fish frequently swim together.

Created in 1926 by a dam across the Tallapoosa River, Lake Martin has long been recognized for its spotted bass action, with fish as heavy as 6 pounds certainly not unheard of. A major professional bass tournament here in 1989, however, in which the winner boated more than 53 pounds of fish, proved just how good the largemouth fishery is, as well.

Anglers always concentrated on spotted bass at Lake Martin because the lake's generally clear water, deeper depths, and rocky shorelines are traditionally the conditions in which that species thrives. The rule was always to use small plastic worms and light lines, which, as often as not, produced enough success to keep anyone happy. Charlie Brewer, for example, developer of the famous Slider light tackle fishing system, has used Lake Martin as one of his testing lakes for many years, and frequently catches 50 to 75 spotted bass a day on his little 4-inch plastic worms and 6-pound-test line.

"I have fished all over the United States," says Brewer, "and I have to rank Lake Martin right at the top of my list of favorite lakes because of the sheer number of fish it has. For many years, I made several extended fishing trips to the lake each fall and winter, regardless of whether or not I had any new products to test."

When the pros came in with their fast-moving spinnerbaits and larger jigs and began catching 7- and 8-pound largemouths, even the Alabama Division of Game and Fish took notice, and today anglers actively go after both fish. The lake has since become an eagerly-awaited stop each year on the professional Bass Anglers Sportsman Society (B.A.S.S.) Tournament Trail, where winning weights for four-day events regularly average more than 50 pounds for a five-fish limit.

The best-known tributaries are Kowaliga, Elkahatchee, Mandy, and Madwin Creeks, which offer both shallow and deep water as well as a mixture of cover and structure that includes fallen timber, rocky points, man-made brush, boat docks,

LAKE MARTIN
ALABAMA

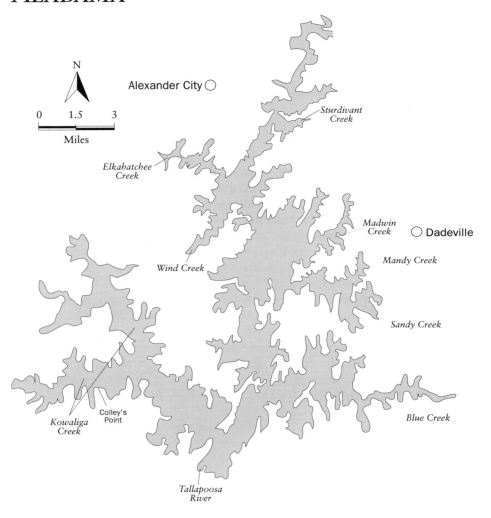

N

Alexander City ○

0   1.5   3

Miles

Sturdivant
Creek

Elkahatchee
Creek

Madwin
Creek   ○ Dadeville

Mandy Creek

Wind Creek

Sandy Creek

Colley's
Point

Kowaliga   Blue Creek
Creek

Tallapoosa
River

and underwater bars. Other tributaries include Sandy, Sturdivant, Coley, Blue, and Wind Creeks.

Kowaliga (pronounced locally as "Ka-LI-ja") is the largest tributary and practically forms the entire lower part of the lake. Easily large enough to keep any angler's attention for days, it includes so much deep, clear, open water that during the summer it also attracts heavy skiing and pleasure boating traffic. As a result, bass fishermen either fish Kowaliga at night during the warm-weather months, or save it for fall and winter.

This lower part of the lake also includes many fishing alternatives, however, such as the pine-clad islands (some have said this part of Lake Martin more nearly resembles a Canadian lake) that provide excellent cool-weather action. Here topwater lures, small plastic worms, and larger Carolina rigs can be worked around the island points where they gradually slope into deeper depths. These are prime areas to locate schools of spotted bass that concentrate here before heading farther back up Kowaliga.

Elkahatchee Creek, located in the upper portion of Lake Martin, is not only fairly narrow but also long, and its reputation as one of the premier year-round fishing areas on the lake is well deserved. Slow-moving buzzbaits rattled through shoreline brush during the autumn months can easily produce a mixed bag of 4- and 5-pounders. Other anglers prefer to concentrate on the sunken roadbed that crosses the mouth of Elkahatchee; it's a good place for deep-diving crankbaits, plastic worms, and Carolina rigs.

Out in the main lake along some of the steeper rock bluffs, fall and winter fishermen like to buzz spinnerbaits as fast as they can right below the surface to catch suspended largemouths. The key is making long casts parallel to and only a foot or so out from the rock faces. It's one of the most exciting ways to fish Lake Martin because the strikes are so explosive.

Brewer's light-tackle Slider worms work equally as well around these bluffs, but usually attract smaller fish. All that's required is making a cast along the rocks, letting the worm sink several seconds, and then slowly swimming it back. The fun part of fishing this way is the sheer number of strikes the little worms get; something always seems to be nibbling on them.

In addition to the large tributaries and the shoreline bluffs, Lake Martin also offers literally thousands of small, rocky coves along its entire length that produce well during the fall and winter months. On the lower part of the lake, especially near Kowaliga Creek, these coves are the first places baitfish seem to congregate if the lake turns muddy or windy. Topwater lures as well as Carolina rigs and small plastics all work well in these places.

Like many lakes in Alabama controlled by Alabama Power Company, Lake Martin's water level is usually drawn down several feet during the winter months. This exposes more of the rocky points and brush piles, and it's a time many lake regulars use to pinpoint specific casting targets after the water rises again in the spring. Despite the colder temperatures, it's also an excellent time for fishing, for either largemouth or spotted bass.

RESOURCES

Gearing Up: Because of the clear water here, most anglers prefer either spinning outfits with 6- and 8-pound-test line, or light- to medium-action baitcasters with 10- and 12-pound-test line. Spinnerbaits, small plastic worms, jigs, and Carolina rigs are favorite lure choices.

Accommodations: Complete motel and restaurant services are available in Alexander City. Camping is offered at Wind Creek State Park, located on the lake.

Additional Information: Alexander City Chamber of Commerce, P.O. Box 926, Alexander City, AL 35011; 256-234-3461.

5 RODMAN RESERVOIR

Location: Putnam and Marion Counties, approximately 15 miles southwest of Palatka, in northeast Florida.
Short Take: 10,000 acres; standing timber, stump flats, some hydrilla and other vegetation, river channel.
Primary Species: Largemouth bass.
Best Months: November through February, but can be good any month.
Favorite Lures: Plastic worms, soft jerkbaits, topwater plugs, shallow crankbaits.
Nearest Tourist Services: Palatka.

OF ALL THE LAKES IN FLORIDA that consistently produced trophy bass of over 10 pounds in the 1970s and 1980s, Rodman Reservoir was perhaps the most famous. For nearly two decades, this 10,000-acre lake on the Oklawaha River ranked at or near the top on everyone's list of premier big bass waters.

Today, Rodman (also known as Lake Oklawaha) might still be listed by some as a trophy lake, but more importantly perhaps, it remains a consistently good lake for overall quality fishing. Trophy fish in the 10- to 12-pound range continue to be caught each year, but it is not the lake it once was. Age, changes in the habitat, and other factors have simply reduced the number of double-digit fish here.

Rodman was created as part of the ill-fated Cross Florida Barge Canal, and as such, connects to the famous St. Johns River to the east through Buckman Lock and six miles of dredged canal. From Buckman Lock, the lake extends about 13 miles up the Oklawaha River to Eureka Dam; the Oklawaha itself begins near Leesburg and flows northward and eventually meets the St. Johns River near Welaka. The Rodman Dam is located south of the Buckman Lock and the barge canal.

Like nearly all Florida lakes, Rodman is basically shallow and filled with standing timber as well as varying amounts of marsh-type vegetation. Periodically the lake is drawn down several feet by the U.S. Army Corps of Engineers and the Florida Game and Fresh Water Fish Commission to control the spread of hydrilla and also to expose more of the bottom to sunlight; this dries out the mud and stimulates other types of plant growth that become habitat for smaller organisms in the food chain. This, in turn, always improves the bass fishing.

Historically, the best fishing has been and continues to be in the area between the canal and Rodman Dam, to Orange Springs. Much of the open water in front of the dam is a fairly shallow stump field, and from this stump field anglers can look up the lake to a forest of flooded cypress. The Oklawaha channel winds through these stumps and trees, and is where some of the lake's largest bass are taken.

Former professional fishing guide Billy Peoples, whose clients have taken bass weighing more than 14 pounds from Rodman, remembers one fishing day that typifies just how good the lake can be. In just four hours of fishing with two clients, they

RODMAN RESERVOIR
FLORIDA

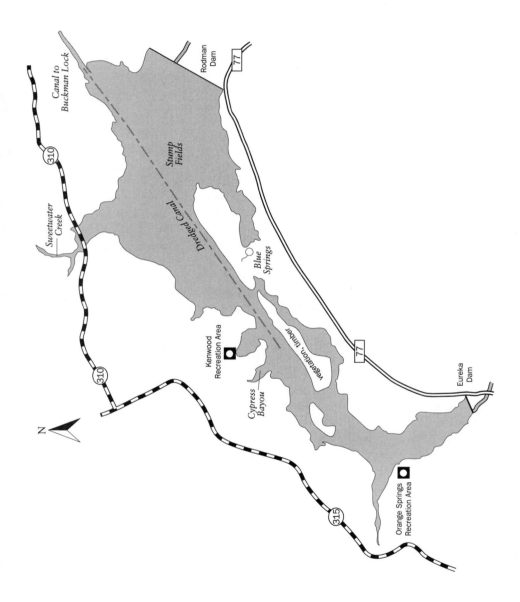

put two bass over 10 pounds in the boat and lost two more, including one that probably weighed about 15 pounds. In addition, they talked to another guide whose clients had two fish over 9 pounds—all before lunch.

That particular day, Peoples was using live golden shiners as bait. These forage fish are used as bait for big bass throughout Florida, and the technique has evolved into an art form. It is certainly the most reliable way to catch a big bass, and for the uninitiated, it truly can be a memorable experience. For one thing, shiners as long as 12 inches and weighing nearly a pound are sometimes used. For another, the shiners are often fished under a cork, so that it becomes a very relaxing, watchful way of fishing—until the cork disappears. Slack line is reeled in, the rod is pointed down, and then the hook is set with a hard, strong upward swing, just like it's done with a plastic worm or jig.

If a truly big bass has taken the shiner, the hook-set usually ends before the rod is fully raised, for it's like yanking on a load of bricks. Big bass don't get moved as easily as smaller ones do. Even after being hooked, a lot of giant bass get free when they first come to the surface, simply because the angler has never seen a bass so large! Golden shiners are available at bait and tackle shops throughout the area.

In the stump fields and around the timber, plastic worms, soft jerkbaits, and topwater lures (especially early and late in the summer) also work well. The Oklawaha bends and turns throughout its length, and anywhere it does is a good place to fish.

Sweetwater Creek flows in from the northeast to join the Oklawaha in the stumps and timber, and it certainly has produced its share of quality bass. The bay leading into the creek is shallow and filled with vegetation and is a good place to try either plastic worms or topwater poppers.

Two other popular fishing spots are Cypress Bayou, a large tree- and grass-filled bay on the northern shore of the lake west of the Kenwood Recreation Area; and Orange Springs, where anglers can fish weedy shoreline cover fed by clear spring water. In years past, the Orange Springs area produced as many trophy bass as any part of the lake because of the heavy vegetation. Golden shiners were literally fished underneath the greenery, much of which was simply floating along the shoreline.

Normally, Rodman's biggest bass are caught during the spawning season between November and February, but big bass can come at any time. Autumn and winter on the lake can be extremely pleasant weather-wise, but during the summer months there is some school bass action on the lake, and it's worth experiencing, too. Big bass, including 10 pounders, are sometimes lurking underneath the smaller, more active fish.

Studies have been ongoing for a number of years by certain groups to have Rodman drained, a plan vigorously opposed by bass fishermen throughout the United States. Proponents want the river restored to its original channel, believing the resulting mud and stump flats will quickly turn back into the wildlife habitat it was before the barge canal project. Anglers, of course, can point to the multi-million dollar economic impact the lake has on the surrounding counties, as well as the fact that Rodman itself has become home to both bald eagles and ospreys. By late 1999, the issue was far from settled, and until it is, anglers can still enjoy the challenge of one of Florida's most exciting fisheries.

RESOURCES

Gearing Up: Because of the heavy cover as well as the chance to hook a truly big bass, most visitors here use medium/heavy- to heavy-action rods with lines testing at least 20 pounds. Some do use lighter tackle, but they are not hunting trophy fish. Popular lures include large plastic worms and lizards, shallow running crankbaits, and topwater chuggers and poppers.

Accommodations: Complete motel and restaurant facilities are available in Palatka. Camping is available at both the Rodman and Kenwood Recreation Areas as well as in the nearby Ocala National Forest.

Additional Information: Putnam County Chamber of Commerce, P.O. Box 550, Palatka, FL 32077; 904-328-1503.

6 LAKE OKEECHOBEE

Location: Southern Florida between Ft. Myers and West Palm Beach.
Short Take: 467,000 acres (second largest lake wholly within U.S. boundaries); shallow, abundant vegetation, some rocks.
Primary Species: Largemouth bass.
Best Months: November through May, but lake open all year.
Favorite Lures: Lipless crankbaits, plastic worms, spinnerbaits, topwaters.
Nearest Tourist Services: Clewiston, Moore Haven, Belle Glade, Pahokee, Okeechobee City.

WHENEVER THE WORDS "BASS FISHING" AND "SOUTH FLORIDA" are mentioned in the same sentence, the subject is likely to be Lake Okeechobee, the 467,000-acre mini-ocean at the mouth of the Kissimmee River. Not only is the lake huge, it has bass fishing to match; Okeechobee unquestionably ranks as one of the finest fishing lakes in the United States.

And whenever a visitor wants to fish Lake Okeechobee, only three other words need to be remembered: "water level" and "vegetation." Bass here relate to vegetation, which grows primarily around the shoreline, and when the water level is high, additional vegetation gets flooded and the fishing improves even more.

"It's almost ironic that we have more than 460,000 ares of water to fish, but we probably really only utilize about 75,000 acres," laughs Steve Daniel, a Clewiston-based guide who has been fishing Okeechobee since 1984. "The simple truth is that the best way to catch bass here is by staying close to some type of vegetation, and that means working around the shoreline or in the Rim Canal."

Lake Okeechobee is known for producing numbers of fish as well as trophy fish, and either can come on any given cast. Even tournament anglers who normally fish too fast to catch many trophy-sized bass catch big fish on this lake.

As such, a number of areas around the shoreline have become well-known bass producers over the years. Overall, the western shoreline between Okeechobee City in the north and Clewiston in the south probably sees the most fishing action because the vegetation is thickest along this side of the lake. Not only has hydrilla become established in the north around Okeechobee City, but eel grass, pepper grass, bullrushes, and other types of marsh greenery cover literally thousands of acres of shallow water.

Anglers fishing the northern end of the lake often launch in Okeechobee City or in the nearby Kissimmee River, Okeechobee's largest tributary, and head to either King's Bar, a hydrilla-lined high spot near the mouth of the river; or to Eagle Bay, a small bay behind the rim canal where anglers can explore marsh, creek, or hydrilla options around Eagle Bay Island.

The key here, as well as anywhere else hydrilla grows, is fishing along its outside edge with plastic worms, lizards, and perhaps topwaters, and concentrating on small irregularities along that edge. In some years the hydrilla may be more scattered than

LAKE OKEECHOBEE
FLORIDA

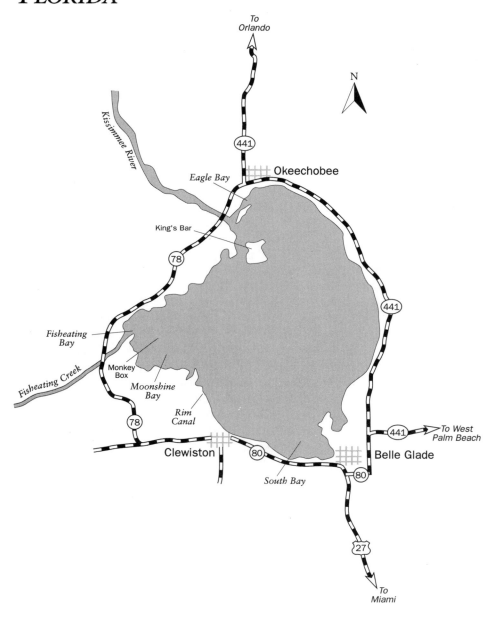

in others, and in these situations, pitching or flipping lures into the open water around the vegetation can also produce good results.

Fisheating Creek, Okeechobee's second largest tributary, flows into Okeechobee along the lake's western shoreline about 20 miles below the Kissimmee, and is another well-known area. Fisheating Bay where the creek enters, is characterized not only by shallow marsh with scattered vegetation but also by several reefs that may or may not be fishable, depending on water levels. Area tackle shops can give specific, updated information on how to navigate through this area, as it can be treacherous in low water.

The same conditions apply south of Fisheating Bay in an area known as the Monkey Box, certainly one of Okeechobee's most famous fishing spots. Part of a much larger section of marsh known as Moonshine Bay, the water here is filled with eel and pepper grasses, bullrushes, and other vegetation that is totally unfishable in low water, but good to excellent in high water. When it is fishable, anglers often let the wind drift them through the vegetation while they pitch plastic worms and lizards to open spots.

The scattered marsh of Moonshine Bay extends all the way to Clewiston, and is accessible through several dredged boat lanes. In some places this scattered vegetation extends more than 10 miles into the lake before open water is reached. First-time visitors here should never travel on the lake without a good map and compass or GPS unit, because all of it looks alike to the untrained eye and venturing away from the boat lanes can lead to disorientation.

South of Clewiston there is more open water, and while the vegetation may not be as thick, the fishing can still be productive. South Bay, located on the southern tip of Okeechobee near the city of Belle Glade, is one of the better known fishing spots on this side of the lake. Again, one of the better fishing techniques is drifting across with the wind and casting to the scattered grass.

There is often some schooling bass action in South Bay in the winter months, most of it taking place along the outside edges of the vegetation. Lipless crankbaits and weedless surface spoons are good lure choices when surface-feeding bass are encountered.

The Rim Canal, a dredged canal around the lake, offers fast access to many different areas without having to navigate the open water. It also provides protected water if the wind is blowing, and surprisingly, bass fishing in the canal can be quite good. Most concentrate around the various canal entrances to the lake, or at bends and corners where rocks have have been piled during dredging. Plastic worms are generally the most productive lures.

Fishing for trophy bass with live golden shiners, as is done on a number of other Florida lakes, is popular on Okeechobee, and guides like Daniel do it regularly. Most of the time they fish north of Clewiston along the edges of the vegetation in Moonshine Bay, or even farther north around the hydrilla beds.

"On most days, there are probably several different lures and techniques that can catch fish on this lake," says Daniel, "and certainly, there are plenty of places to

The key word to remember when fishing Lake Okeechobee is vegetation, and this huge south Florida lake offers thousand of acres of greenery for bass anglers.

try them. Even when you tell a fisherman all he has to remember about Okeechobee is to fish the vegetation, he still has a lot to consider."

RESOURCES

Gearing Up: Most anglers here use medium- to medium/heavy-action baitcasting equipment and lines testing 14 to 25 pounds, due to both the heavy vegetation and the opportunity to hook big bass. Favorite lures include large topwater plugs, weedless surface spoons, plastic worms and crawfish, lipless crankbaits, and large willowleaf spinnerbaits for possible use in scattered vegetation.

Accommodations: Complete motel and restaurant facilities are available around the lake in the cities of Belle Glade, Clewiston, Moore Haven, and Okeechobee City. Numerous marinas and fish camps in these cities also offer accommodations as well as campgrounds.

Additional Information: Okeechobee Chamber of Commerce, 55 South Parrott Ave., Okeechobee, FL 34974; 800-871-4403.

7 KISSIMMEE WATERWAY

Location: Central Florida near Kissimmee and extending southward 97 miles to Lake Okeechobee.
Short Take: Numerous lakes plus river/canals; basically shallow, heavy vegetation, canals lined with riprap.
Primary Species: Largemouth bass.
Best Months: October through March.
Favorite Lures: Plastic worms, lipless crankbaits, topwaters, spinnerbaits.
Nearest Tourist Services: Kissimmee, St. Cloud.

FEW, IF ANY, OF AMERICA'S LAKES AND RIVERS HAVE EVER EVOKED as many mixed emotions as has central Florida's Kissimmee Waterway, a series of lakes connected by the Kissimmee River and man-made canals. If you're an environmentalist, you may deplore the channelization done by the Corps of Engineers that changed the natural dynamics of the river, but if you're a bass fisherman, you may love the Waterway for the fishing action it can provide.

The Kissimmee Waterway in its entirety embraces nearly two dozen lakes between the city of Kissimmee and Lake Okeechobee, a distance of about 97 miles. The majority of these lakes are actually much closer to Kissimmee, and in this chapter, only two are being considered: Tohopekaliga and Kissimmee, which are the two best-known bass fisheries in the chain. A series of navigable locks, spillways, or canals separate all of the lakes, so it is possible to fish anywhere in the system with a minimum of effort. Launching ramps are located throughout.

Tohopekaliga (sometimes called West Tohopekaliga, other times simply Toho) and Kissimmee are both similar in that they are extremely shallow bodies of water filled with different types of vegetation, including hydrilla, Kissimmee grass, eel grass, lily pads, maiden cane, and floating hyacinths. Each lake has several islands as well as a deep water channel, although this channel is not maintained for navigation. Toho encompasses about 18,000 acres, Kissimmee 44,000 acres.

Although bass may be anywhere in either of these two lakes, a number of specific areas seem to produce consistently good results. On Tohopekaliga, Paradise and Cypress Islands in the lake's upper end are favorite areas. Because of differences in the vegetation growth each year, however, as well as the periodic water manipulation projects conducted by the Florida Game and Fresh Water Fish Commission, anglers here will often do best simply by concentrating along any type of edge they may find in the vegetation, be it an open boat canal, a deeper water drop, or even a change from one type of vegetation to another.

The same general rule of thumb also applies on Lake Kissimmee. While Brahma and Bird Islands in the lake's lower end seem to produce well on a regular basis—the water depths change rapidly along the southern ends of both islands—it is the edge effect that often proves to be the most reliable place to look for fish.

KISSIMMEE WATERWAY
FLORIDA

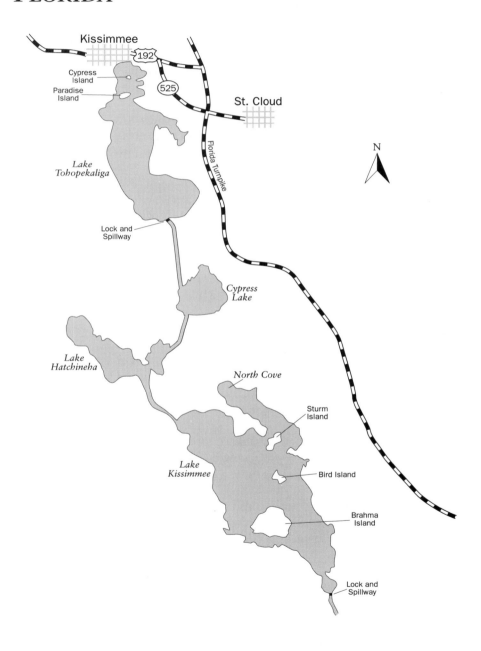

The North Cove area of Lake Kissimmee provides this very option, as the shoreline is covered with vegetation but the water drops very quickly down to 10 or 12 feet all along the northeastern shoreline and around Sturm Island at the entrance to the cove.

In years past, one of the favorite big bass lures on both Toho and Kissimmee was a weedless topwater spoon, which, when adorned with a plastic worm trailer, could be sashayed through the weeds and across the water without much danger of snagging. This lure caught untold numbers of bass in the 10-pound class—Kissimmee has produced fish up to 16 pounds—but it has since been replaced in popularity by plastic worms, which are either fished on the surface without a weight, or with a weight and presented vertically through the vegetation.

Much of the shoreline on either lake is lined with maiden cane, and one favorite fishing tactic is pitching and flipping worms and occasionally jigs into these reeds. Where the reeds are more scattered and grow farther out into the water, floating worms or soft plastic jerkbaits can be fished through them.

Like most Florida lakes, the bottoms of both Toho and Kissimmee are soft and mucky, a condition that grows continually worse each year and which adversely affects bass spawning success. For that reason, Florida biologists periodically draw down different lakes to expose this muck so it can be bulldozed out. The drawdowns usually last several months, during which time literally tons of old decaying vegetation, mud, and silt are removed and new vegetation sprouts.

These drawdowns have been performed several times on Toho, and each time the results are the same: the new grass and the "new" hard bottom have produced much improved bass fishing. At Toho, the lake rebounded so well that by 1998 local marina operators and guides were comparing the fishery to that of the early 1980s when the lake was judged to be at its peak.

No matter how spectacular the fishing may be in either Tohopekaliga or Kissimmee, however, the fact remains that, like virtually every Florida bass lake, a sudden cold front all but shuts down the fishing. Those cold fronts, unfortunately, usually begin hitting in January just when the lake's largest bass are preparing to move to spawning beds.

The other lakes in the Kissimmee Chain, as well as the canals joining them, all contain fish. Some of the deepest water, ranging from 15 to 17 feet at times, is actually found in the rock-lined canals. If there is any particular area like this that provides better fishing, it is probably in the canal several miles (and another lock) below Lake Kissimmee. Here the water simply is not fished by as many anglers and the bass have not been pressured. This is a long run that takes about two hours, including lock time, from Lake Toho.

RESOURCES

Gearing Up: The presence of heavy cover combined with the possibility of truly big bass dictate the use of medium/heavy- and possibly even heavy-action rods and lines testing 17 to 30 pounds. Lure choices range from six and eight-inch plastic worms and shallow-running crankbaits to lipless swimming plugs and large willowleaf spinnerbaits.

Accommodations: The cities of Kissimmee and St. Cloud offer a wide range of accommodations and restaurant choices. Camping is offered at several public parks throughout the area. This is an extremely popular vacation destination area.

Additional Information: Kissimmee-St. Cloud Convention & Visitors Bureau, P.O. Box 422007, Kissimmee, FL 34742-2007; 800-327-9159.

8 LAKE SEMINOLE

Location: Seminole County in southwestern Georgia, along the Florida state line.

Short Take: 37,500 acres; shallow stumps, timber, hydrilla, hyacinths, flats, islands, natural springs, two river channels.

Primary Species: Largemouth bass.

Best Months: March through June, September through November.

Favorite Lures: Topwater plugs, plastic worms, crankbaits.

Nearest Tourist Services: Bainbridge.

IF EVER A SINGLE IMPOUNDMENT could be called synonymous with southern bass fishing, it would be Lake Seminole, the 37,500 acre impoundment on the Chattahoochee and Flint Rivers along the Georgia/Florida state line. Seminole has it all: acres of standing timber, vegetation, stumps, trophy bass, old fishing camps, and legendary fishermen. Every southern bass lake has its tales of grandeur, but at Seminole, they're usually true.

Over the years the lake has produced at least two bass over 16 pounds and countless more over 10 pounds. Today, Seminole is not known as a trophy bass lake, but rather, as solid fishing water that might produce a giant or two. In 1994, during a four-day national bass tournament here, the winner boated 20 bass weighing 91 pounds, 3 ounces, an average of more than 4 pounds per fish.

"The bass fishery here owes its success to the habitat," explains Jack Wingate, who has operated a fishing camp on the lake since a year after its impoundment in 1957 and who has become as famous as the lake itself. "There are thousands of acres of standing timber, weeds, hyacinths, and mossbeds, 250 separate islands, dozens of natural flowing springs, and miles of hard-bottom flats.

"If the bass don't like one particular area, they've got plenty of choices to go somewhere else."

Plenty of choices, indeed. There are so many oak- and cypress-lined sloughs and clear-water ponds hidden at the ends of narrow, winding waterways that it's easy for a first-time visitor here to get lost. Surprisingly, there are only two tributaries here, Spring Creek and Fish Pond Drain, both of which are stunningly beautiful. Spring Creek is by far the largest, and since it is spring-fed, often has exceptionally clear water.

All of this shallow-water habitat has contributed to making Seminole an excellent topwater bass lake. Although the bass hit surface plugs from March through October, May and June rank as two of the best months. Key areas include spots like Saunders Slough, Chimney Island, and Hole-in-the-Wall, as well as the boat channel through the stumps known as I-75. None of these are marked on any map, but all are well known locally.

LAKE SEMINOLE
GEORGIA

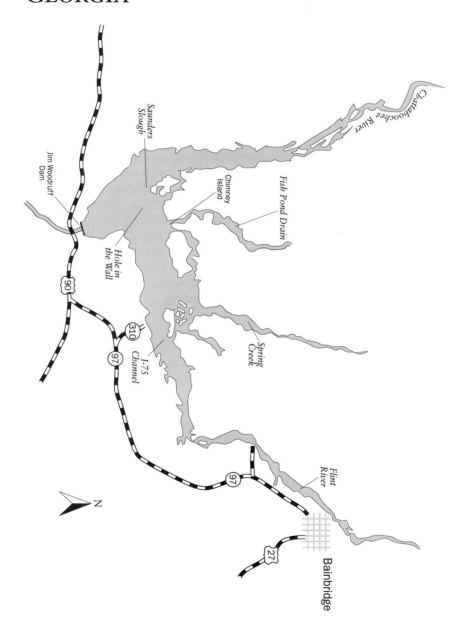

Most of the time the water here is fairly clear, which means making long casts and working lures slowly past the cover. Wingate has done it so often and caught so many fish he automatically lapses into a lure retrieve cadence of pops and pauses and can practically tell when and where a strike will occur. Small poppers and surface lures with rear propellers are among his favorites.

Because of its location in the Deep South, summer fishing takes place very early in the morning until perhaps 9 A.M., then stops until 4 or 5 P.M. and continues until dark. Because of the widespread stumps, little night fishing is done on Seminole.

There is also some summer fishing here for both striped and hybrid striped bass. The fish are occasionally taken on topwater lures, but at this time of year, the fish are located more often in some of Seminole's deeper springs where the water is cooler. There are many such springs up and down the lake; in fact one of the most reliable is directly across the lake from Wingate's lodge, and there's another just half a mile farther down the lake. Maps pinpoint their exact location, and jigging spoons are the most effective lures.

In the autumn after the water begins to cool, schooling bass action begins, and one of the best areas for this is in the open water near the junction of the Chattahoochee and Flint Rivers. One moment the water may be absolutely calm, the next moment it will turn into a wild frenzy of boiling fish, including not only largemouths but also white bass, striped bass, and even hybrid stripers. Practically any sinking/swimming plug will draw a strike at times like this, and once the bass submerge, they can still be tempted with small bucktail or plastic jigs or spoons.

At other times of the year, bass fishing centers around either shoreline cover or scattered vegetation around the islands. In many areas, along the Flint River particularly, the shoreline is littered with blown-down trees and other debris where the bass regularly hit spinnerbaits, buzzbaits, and small crankbaits. Around the grassbeds and islands near the mouth of Fish Pond Drain, Carolina-rigged plastic worms and lizards often produce well, while in the more open water spinnerbaits can be used.

Another fishing opportunity at Seminole that is worthy of mention is fishing the Flint River for redeye bass (*Micropterus coosae*). The Flint is one of only a few waterways in the United States where this bass, which looks and acts much like a smallmouth but seldom grows as large, lives. The world record, caught from the Flint, weighed just over 8 pounds.

Because these fish are found most often around rocks, the normal fishing strategy is to motor up the Flint River for several miles, then gradually fish back downstream, concentrating on the numerous rock and boulder formations in the water. Small crankbaits and minnow-imitation plugs are probably the most productive lures, but jigs and plastic worms also take fish.

Along the way, fishermen are just as likely to catch largemouths, especially if it's early and they work buzzbaits around the shallow stumps and blown-down trees. Later in the day, plastic worms and jigs also produce well.

Ten-pound bass do not come nearly as regularly as they did a decade or two ago, when one of Wingate's guides led his clients to a 10-pounder each day for a week, but stories like that keep fishermen returning year after year. They come to visit Wingate himself, too, who still sells plastic worms out of cut-down milk jugs, or to eat barbeque in his camp restaurant. It's all part of the history and the lore of one of the nation's most famous bass lakes.

RESOURCES

Gearing Up: Because virtually all bass fishing is done around heavy cover, medium- to medium/heavy-action baitcasting rods are used, along with 14- to 25-pound-test line. Primary lures include topwater plugs, buzzbaits, willowleaf spinnerbaits, jigs, plastic worms and lizards. Heavier jigging spoons work best for striped and hybrid striped bass.

Accommodations: Complete motel and restaurant facilities are available in Bainbridge as well as at several lcations around the lake. Camping is available at Seminole State Park and at numerous Corps of Engineers parks nearby.

Additional Information: Bainbridge and Decatur County Chamber of Commerce, P.O. Box 736, Bainbridge, GA 31718; 912-246-4774.

9 LAKE EUFAULA

Location: Approximately 160 miles southwest of Atlanta on the Chattahoochee River near Eufaula, Alabama and Georgetown, Georgia, forming the boundary between both states.
Short Take: 45,000 acres; channels and ledges, large tributaries, very little vegetation.
Primary Species: Largemouth bass.
Best Months: February through May, October, November.
Favorite Lures: Plastic worms, crankbaits, Carolina-rigged lizards.
Nearest Tourist Services: Eufaula.

OLD-TIMERS IN THE TACKLE SHOPS AROUND EUFAULA still talk about the day 25 years ago when Tom Mann and his fishing partner, David Lockhart, broke the bank. On a warm July day in 1972, the two anglers brought in 25 bass weighing just under 155 pounds—an amazing average of more than 6 pounds per fish.

Lockhart's 13-pound, 2-ounce fish took big bass honors, but he's sure he lost an even larger fish that broke his 25-pound-test line.

Officially named Walter F. George Reservoir but more commonly known as Eufaula because of its location in the beautiful city of Eufaula, this southeastern Alabama impoundment probably enjoys one of the most storied histories of any lake in America. Mann's and Lockhart's day came during its peak when big bass and heavy stringers were the norm; today, nearly half a century after construction began on the two-and-a-half-mile-long dam across the Chattahoochee, Lake Eufaula still offers visiting anglers an occasional reminder of what those glory days were like.

In the past decade, however, Eufaula has tended to be cyclic in that it produced good fishing for several years, then seemingly turned fallow. Following several poor seasons, the action picked up again. Regardless of which cycle the lake may be in, it still attracts heavy angling pressure, especially during the spring and autumn months when fishing is usually the best.

"Overall, we classify Eufaula as a structure lake," notes Tom Mann, the famous Eufaula lure-maker and co-author of that 155-pound catch with Lockhart. "Even though there are several very good tributary creeks up and down the lake, the bass really seem to congregate more along the main river dropoffs.

"One reason may be that the lake also has long, shallow flats that seem to stretch for miles. The bass can feed up in the shallow water, then drop right back into the channel without having to move very far at all."

Some of the better-known hotspots feature not only flats and river channel but also tributary creek channels where the creek cuts through flats to empty into the main Chattahoochee.

Cheneyhatchee, White Oak, Thomas Mill, Barbour, and Cowikee Creeks each offer this type of structure.

Lake Eufaula
Georgia/Alabama border

Plastic worms come in a wide variety of styles, sizes, and colors, but overall, they remain one of the most effective of all bass lures. They've been in use for nearly half a century, and are especially popular at Lake Eufaula.

Of these, Thomas Mill Creek, located on the Alabama side of the lake about halfway between the city of Eufaula and the dam, is particularly noteworthy because the Chattahoochee channel swings in near the mouth of the creek to produce almost classic stair-stepping structure close to the bank. For this reason, it's always a good idea to stay within the buoys when running up and down the lake; on the flats the water becomes very shallow very quickly.

"When we talk about ledges and structure on Eufaula," says Mann, "we're basically talking about fishing this type of depth change, where the water gradually falls from two to 10 to 15 and on down to 30 feet or so. From Thomas Mill Creek southward for several miles, the river channel stays fairly close to the Alabama side and offers these type of ledges."

Another popular area, especially in the spring, but liable to produce a good fish anytime, is Georgetown Flats, located south of the U.S. Highway 82 bridge between Eufaula and Georgetown. Here along the Georgia side of the lake there are hundreds of acres of water generally less than 10 feet deep. It's an excellent place to hop a Carolina-rigged lizard or tube bait, or work a bottom-bumping crankbait.

In the tributary creeks, anglers concentrate primarily on shoreline brush, stumps, and fallen trees. There is some vegetation along the main lake shoreline north of Eufaula and also in some of the tributaries, but nowhere is there really enough of it to keep a serious fisherman busy for long.

The largest and perhaps best-known of all of Eufaula's tributary creeks is Cowikee (locally pronounced as kai-AG-gie), which winds into the Alabama countryside for several miles before splitting into north, middle, and south forks. In both the spring and fall all three branches can produce good fishing, due to the variety of cover available. This can be good spinnerbait water as well as a productive place to pitch plastic worms or jigs.

Muddy water caused by spring rains can be a problem on Eufaula, although some of the lower lake tributaries and the deep water by the dam occasionally remain clear. By the same token, however, a strong north-northwest wind any time of year quickly turns Eufaula rough and dangerous, due to its north-south orientation. The roughest water will be at the dam, but fortunately, nearby Hardridge and Sandy Creeks offer shelter.

Because there is such a variety of depths to be fished on this part of the lake, the most productive lures range from shallow-running spinnerbaits to bottom-bumping plastic worms and Carolina-rigged lizards, with crankbaits covering every depth in between. Many fishermen also like using heavy 3/4- and 1-ounce spinnerbaits they slow-roll over the edges of the ledges; it's a difficult technique to learn but very effective when done properly. Another lure that receives virtually no publicity here is a 3/4-ounce white bucktail jig, which also produces well in deep water when allowed to sink several feet, then retrieved in short, erratic jerks and pauses.

When Mann and Lockhart caught their big stringer they were using one of the first lures Mann designed, the Little George, a small, compact lead-bodied lure with a rear blade, named after then-Governor George Wallace. It remains an effective lure today, in the lake's deeper water. The technique most often used is to cast toward shallow water, allow the lure to sink, and then bring it back with a series of rod-pumping motions that lets the lure rise and fall progressively deeper as it clears a ledge.

Today, Mann remembers his day with Lockhart, along with a lot of other big bass experiences during those long-ago years, and he knows they'll never be repeated. That doesn't stop him from fishing the lake on a regular basis, however, because he and legions of other anglers know Eufaula can still provide a lot of excitement when conditions are right.

RESOURCES:

Gearing Up: Medium- to medium/heavy-action baitcasting rods with lines testing 12 to 20 pounds are standard here, although medium and medium/heavy spinning outfits can certainly be used. Primary lures include 3/8-ounce white/chartreuse spinnerbaits, crawfish-colored crankbaits, tailspinners, and large, grape-colored plastic worms. Fishing tackle shops are located throughout the area.

Accommodations: Complete motel and restaurant services are available in Eufaula as well as in Phenix City and Columbus, Georgia. Several offer boat launching as well as boat docking facilities. Camping is available at numerous locations along both shores, including Lakepoint Resort State Park on the Alabama side and Bagby State Park in Georgia.

Additional Information: Eufaula Chamber of Commerce, 102 North Orange Street, Eufaula, AL 36027; 334-687-6664.

10 LAKE LANIER

Location: About 35 miles north of Atlanta near the cities of Gainesville and Buford.

Short Take: 38,000 acres; very deep, clear water with abundant underwater structure, islands, little shoreline cover except in tributaries, no vegetation.

Primary Species: Spotted, largemouth, and striped bass.

Best Months: March through May, October, November; striped bass good January, February.

Favorite Lures: Jigs, spoons, plastic worms, crankbaits, spinnerbaits.

Nearest Tourist Services: Atlanta, Gainesville.

MICKEY BRUCE NEVER WANTED TO CATCH THE BASS, but the fish gave him no choice. He and friend Cliff Craft were practicing for a tournament, and another boat had just pulled up behind them in the same cove. The largemouth had swallowed Bruce's jig and was heading home.

"I don't really know exactly how much the bass actually weighed," laughs Bruce as he recalls the day, "but after I landed it we measured it as best we could. The bass was exactly as long as the inseam on my pants, which is 30 inches, and its open mouth matched my cap size, which is 7 3/4."

Because of the upcoming tournament, Bruce released the fish, which he estimated would weigh at least 12 pounds, in hopes of catching it again later during competition. Of course, he's never seen the fish since, but he did learn later that someone had caught a 14-pounder in that same area.

Fish that size are caught each spring in Lake Lanier, says Bruce, who grew up on the shores of the 38,000-acre impoundment. At least three bass over 17 pounds (the largemouth record is 17-9) have been caught in the lake, and he can verify two of them.

Lanier, however, is not known as a trophy largemouth lake. Among fishermen its fame lies in its spotted bass action, where both the number and quality of the fish is remarkable. The largest spotted bass on record from the lake weighed 8 pounds, 5 ounces, but numerous fish over 7 have been caught. Lanier is also popular for its striped bass fishing, especially during the winter months when 20-pounders can occasionally be taken on minnow-imitation crankbaits.

The lake is even more popular with non-fishermen, however, including sailboaters, pleasure cruisers, and water-skiers. The Corps of Engineers ranks Lanier as one of the most heavily visited lakes it operates. It's easy to understand why, not only because of its proximity (35 miles) to Atlanta but also for its clear, wide-open water and scenic islands.

Overall, Lake Lanier can be divided into four different areas for fishing. These include the lower lake around Lanier Islands with its more open water but still with large tributaries (Six Mile, Baldridge, and Big Creeks); the mid-section around

LAKE LANIER
GEORGIA

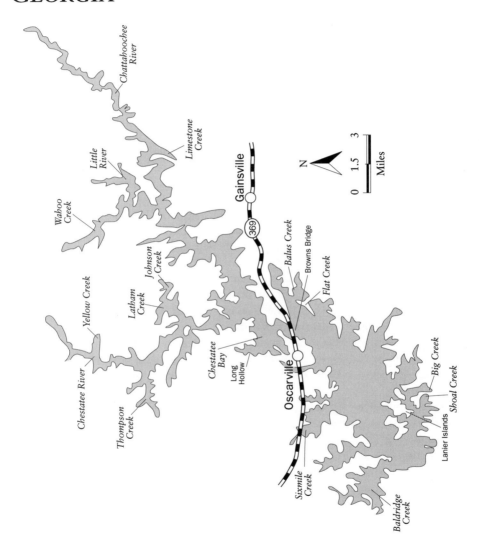

Browns Bridge (Georgia Highway 369) where the lake finally narrows and the Chestatee and Chattahoochee Rivers meet; and then both of the two rivers themselves, with their own tributaries.

Spotted bass are most common in the lower lake and are often caught off fast-falling points where the depth changes quickly and where local fishermen often put out their own brush piles. Jigs and small plastic worms probably catch more fish than any other lures. Shoal Creek, which runs between the southern shoreline and the Lanier Islands resort complex, offers miles of excellent structure fishing of this type.

Farther out on the points, anglers often drift larger worms through the flooded timber. When the Corps of Engineers impounded Lanier they topped all the timber at a height of about 30 feet, then finished filling the lake. Today those trees, submerged under 15 feet or more of water, still provide excellent habitat and often produce some of the lake's largest spotted bass.

The Browns Bridge area offers both spotted bass and the beginning of largemouth fishing. Within a five-mile radius of the bridge, bass fishermen can work the mouths of several large bays (they're known as "hollows" in Georgia) with flats, ridges, smaller channels, and some shoreline cover. The best-known of these are Long Hollow (Chestatee Bay) on the northern side of the lake, and another spot known locally as Dead Water, just across from Long Hollow.

The Chattahoochee and Chestatee Rivers meet several miles above Browns Bridge, and each offers miles of prime largemouth habitat. Not only is the overall depth more shallow; both rivers and their tributaries have more off-color water, ditches, flats, sunken roadbeds, boat docks, and shoreline brush than anywhere else on Lanier. With such conditions, this is the first area of the lake where spinnerbaits can be used effectively.

Bruce caught his monster bass in Wahoo Creek, a huge, winding tributary of the Chattahoochee where the water is nearly always stained. The back end of the creek has wide, shallow flats tailor-made for jigs and crankbaits, and annually produces big bass in February and March. Other well-known Chattahoochee creeks include Limestone and Little River, both similar to Wahoo but smaller.

In the Chestatee River, Thompson, Yellow, Latham, and Johnson Creeks are the best known. All are characterized by numerous small bays and points and excellent shallow-water/deep-water drops. As in the Chattahoochee tributaries, jigs, crankbaits, and soft plastics produce well here.

Because Lake Lanier receives so much boating traffic, many fishermen enjoy night fishing here during the summer months. There is no shortage of boat houses in the various creeks, but some excellent fishing also takes place around the various marinas and sailboat clubs. The floating docks, with their maze of underwater anchoring cables, seem to be magnets for fish. Small finesse-type plastic worms and light line are extremely popular in this type of fishing.

Striped bass fishermen occasionally find their quarry in these two rivers during the spring when the fish are migrating upstream to spawn, but the most reliable action takes place during the coldest time of year, December through February. At this time the truly dedicated striper pros fish at night, with Flat and Balus Creeks among the favorite locations. Long, minnow-type crankbaits produce well; fish over 45 pounds have been taken here.

Bruce and other Lanier regulars do fairly well on largemouths and spotted bass during the winter months, but it's generally tough fishing in deep water. Really, he says, he uses the wintertime simply as a tune-up for spring, when he can go back up to Wahoo Creek and try for another bass as long as his pants leg.

RESOURCES

Gearing Up: Smaller finesse-type plastic worms and 6- and 8-pound-test lines are often the order of the day in the lower lake's clear water; in the upper lake tributaries, medium- and medium/heavy-action baitcasting rods with larger 3/8-ounce jigs and 1/2-ounce spinnerbaits are standard. Deep-diving crankbaits and some topwater lures also work well. Striped bass fishermen use larger minnow-type crankbaits.

Accommodations: Full motel and restaurant facilities are available in Gainesville and Atlanta. In addition, facilities abound around the lake itself, including the large resort at Lake Lanier Islands. Camping is offered at more than a dozen Corps of Engineers recreation sites.

Additional Information: Greater Hall County Chamber of Commerce, P.O. Box 374, Gainesville, GA 30503; 770-532-6206; U.S. Army Corps of Engineers, P.O. Box 567, Buford, GA 30515; 770-945-9531.

11 J. Strom Thurmond Lake

Location: Georgia/South Carolina border near Augusta, Georgia.
Short Take: 70,000 acres; two major river tributaries, rock and/or clay points, hydrilla.
Primary Species: Largemouth and hybrid striped bass.
Best Months: March through May, September.
Favorite Lures: Topwaters, plastic worms and lizards, jigs, crankbaits.
Nearest Tourist Services: Augusta.

ALTHOUGH J. STROM THURMOND LAKE HAS occasionally suffered through an identity crisis due to both name changes as well as incorrect spelling—originally named Clark Hill, often spelled Clarks Hill (the name of a town at the dam), and then given a federal name change to J. Strom Thurmond Lake to honor the South Carolina Senator—the lake's fishing has had no such problems.

The 70,000-acre Savannah River impoundment has been known for both its largemouth and hybrid striped bass fishing for many years, and the largemouth fishing has actually improved due to the spread of aquatic vegetation like hydrilla and elodea. The lake is the largest Corps of Engineers project east of the Mississippi River and one of the 10 most visited Corps lakes in the nation.

Located just a short distance from Augusta, Thurmond Lake offers a quiet change from the fast-paced life of the city. The Sumter National Forest covers much of the eastern (South Carolina) side of the lake, and along the Georgia side very little shoreline development has been allowed, factors that combine to give the reservoir a truly rustic appearance. The rolling countryside also contributes to the lake's appearance, for impoundment-filled long, winding valleys and covered small hilltops have resulted in literally thousands of wooded points, coves, and small islands throughout the length of the lake.

The primary tributary is the Savannah River, which flows out of Richard B. Russell Lake immediately to the north. The other major tributary is the Little River, which flows in from the Georgia side on the lake's lower end. At full pool the water covers a lot of shoreline brush, which makes for excellent spring spinnerbait action, but for much of the remainder of the year the banks are largely bare rock and red clay.

Although the hydrilla is now widespread, it is more well established in the lower end of the lake, which is why many fishermen prefer to spend their time there. Keg Creek and Big Branch, portions of the Little River, and the lower end of the Savannah River all provide a myriad of fishing opportunities. Farther up the Savannah arm Soap Creek, another tributary also named Little River (this one flowing in from the South Carolina side), and Fishing Creek each offer additional fishing choices.

Like several other lakes with similar configurations, the key to successful fishing here is often in thinking "points," regardless of whether they're covered with brush

J. Strom Thurmond Lake
Georgia/South Carolina border

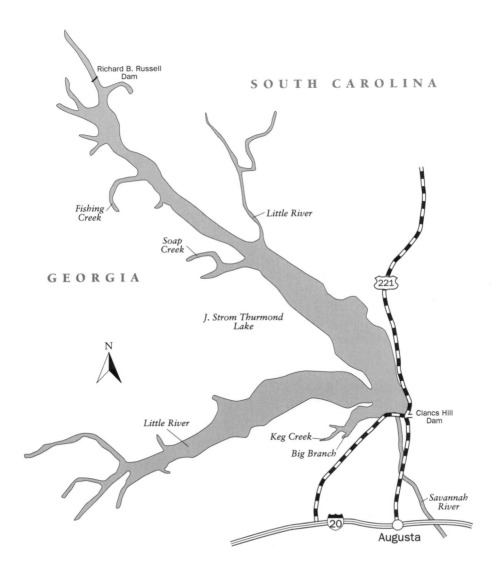

SOUTH CAROLINA

Richard B. Russell
Dam

Fishing
Creek

Little River

Soap
Creek

GEORGIA

221

J. Strom Thurmond
Lake

N

Clancs Hill
Dam

Little River

Keg Creek

Big Branch

Savannah
River

20

Augusta

or are exposed clay. Crankbaits are favorite lure choices in March, while Carolina-rigged lizards take over in May and June. All that's usually required is casting shallow and working the lures down into deeper water until a productive depth range is established.

Most Thurmond Lake regulars rate May as the best month of the year here, because this is when topwater lures produce so well. It is hard to imagine finding schools of 4- to 7-pound largemouths anywhere, but it does happen on this lake. The bass are feeding on blueback herring, a small migratory fish that seems to excite the bass even more than threadfin or gizzard shad, which are also present.

One reason for this may be because the herring, which first appeared in the lake in 1983, spawn in May, which corresponds to the post-spawn season of the largemouths. The bass have regained their energy as well as their appetites by then and absolutely gorge themselves on the herring.

Frequently, the best places to encounter one of these feeding sprees is where water is funneled or pinched between the end of a point and an offshore island. In these "flow-throughs" (as they are known locally), the bass use the rocks and clay to help trap the herring. These types of places are common up the Savannah River arm of the lake, and when such conditions are encountered a variety of lures including topwater poppers, bucktail jigs, soft plastic jerkbaits, and crankbaits all take fish.

The techniques for fishing the hydrilla are the same here as on other lakes. Slow-rolling spinnerbaits over the top of the greenery produces well early in the spring, while Carolina rigs fished along the outside edges do better in the summer. Night fishing is also popular in the summer, with both topwaters and plastic worms producing well around island points.

In the autumn months, topwater action begins again in the lower end of the lake, while spinnerbaits can be used around shallow wooded cover in the creeks in the upper end. Schooling activity, which may have started as early as July in some areas, also offers another possibility.

In the 1970s and 1980s Thurmond Lake's main claim to fame rested largely on its hybrid striped bass fishing, which, indeed, is still a sight to behold. Thurmond Lake was the first reservoir in the United States to be stocked with hybrids (1966), and the fish, a cross between the striped bass and white bass, quickly established itself as an angler favorite not only because of its fierce fighting ability but also because of its somewhat predictable schooling activity between August and late October.

Anglers would motor into a quiet cove near the dam just before daybreak and never make a cast. All they did was wait, watch the sun rise, and occasionally check their watches. Then, almost as if following a written script, the calm, slick water would erupt as thousands of hybrids began feeding on schools of baitfish they had pushed to the surface. Practically any lure, but especially topwaters and jerkbaits, tossed into the foaming water would catch a fish. Hybrids of nearly 20 pounds have been caught in the lake, and even larger fish have been taken in the river below the dam.

Hybrids can also be caught between February and April far up the Savannah River near the Russell Dam as they attempt to spawn. Here, bucktail jigs produce extremely well. By mid to late April the fish have moved back down the river where they usually spend the summer months suspended 12 to perhaps 15 feet deep near the mouths of the large tributaries. Anglers fish live herring or use jigging spoons to catch them at that time.

RESOURCES

Gearing Up: For nearly all largemouth and hybrid fishing, anglers use medium- to heavy-action rods with lines testing 12 to 14 pounds, although some choose stronger lines when fishing around heavy cover in spring. Favorite lure choices include tandem willowleaf spinnerbaits, 3/8-ounce jigs, jigging spoons, plastic worms and lizards, topwater chuggers and poppers, and medium- to deep-diving crankbaits.

Accommodations: A wide selection of motels and restaurant facilities are available in Augusta. Camping is offered at more than a dozen Corps of Engineers parks and private campgrounds around the lake in both Georgia and South Carolina.

Additional Information: U.S. Army Corps of Engineers J. Strom Thurmond Project, Route 1, Box 12, Clarks Hill, SC 29821; 800-533-3478. Augusta Convention and Visitors Bureau, 1450 Greene Street, Suite 110, Augusta, GA 30901; 706-823-6600.

12 KENTUCKY LAKE

Location: Tennessee River impoundment approximately 20 miles southeast of Paducah, Kentucky and extending into Tennessee.
Short Take: 160,000 acres; shallow, stump-filled flats, boat docks, rocky points, major creek and river tributaries, some vegetation.
Primary Species: Largemouth and smallmouth bass.
Best Months: April through October.
Favorite Lures: Spinnerbaits, shallow crankbaits, jigs, plastic worms and tube jigs.
Nearest Tourist Services: Paris, Springville, Camden, Gilbertsville.

ONE OF THE LARGEST MAN-MADE LAKES IN THE UNITED STATES, Kentucky Lake has long enjoyed a reputation for its truly remarkable crappie fishing. That has suited the bass fishermen just fine, because for many years it probably lessened the fishing pressure on both largemouth and smallmouth that are found here.

Even after word began circulating about Kentucky Lake's continuous catches of 4- to 7-pound largemouths and 5-pound smallmouths, however, it was still often difficult to visualize more anglers on the water simply because this lake is so big. Technically, Kentucky Lake stretches completely across Tennessee, beginning at the Pickwick Lake Dam in Counce and continuing all the way to Gilbertsville in Kentucky. In reality, for more than 60 miles between Counce and Camden the lake is simply the Tennessee River.

Even from here, the lake is huge, and is made even larger by its biggest tributary, the Big Sandy River, which flows in from the south near the U.S. Highway 79 bridge; Big Sandy itself is larger than many lakes and has numerous tributaries of its own.

All of which bodes well for the largemouth and smallmouth bass. There is an awesome amount of cover and structure for them to use, including stump flats, boat docks, rocky shorelines, extended points, sandy channels, and ditches.

Interestingly, some of the productive largemouth habitat has turned out to be the artificial cover put in place to attract crappie. Because crappie fishing has been such an important economic factor in the area, many of the marina/resorts have put out what are known as stake beds to keep the crappie more accessible to their guests. These same beds, which consist of dozens of boards or stakes attached to a base so they stand up vertically from the bottom, are always worth a cast with a jig or plastic worm because bass like this type of structure, as well.

The majority of Kentucky Lake's largemouth fishermen, however, concentrate along the many primary and secondary points and shallow flats of the coves and tributaries, especially where they may find either a field of shallow stumps extending out into the water, flooded willows and buck bushes (especially in spring), or gravel banks.

KENTUCKY LAKE
KENTUCKY/TENNESSEE BORDER

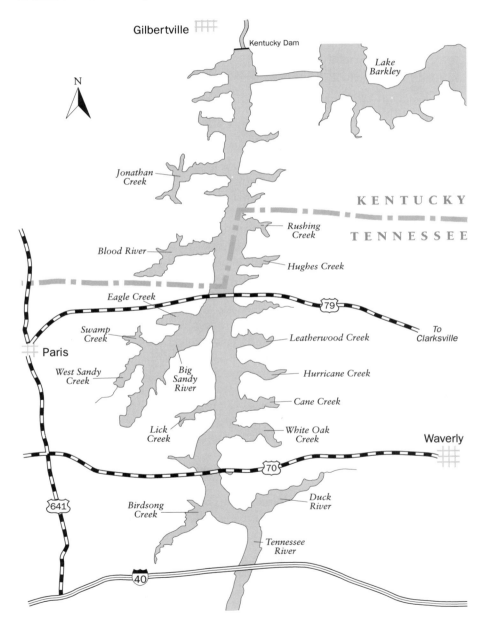

Gilbertville

Kentucky Dam

Lake
Barkley

N

Jonathan
Creek

KENTUCKY

Rushing
Creek

TENNESSEE

Blood River

Hughes Creek

Eagle Creek

79

To
Clarksville

Swamp
Creek

Leatherwood Creek

Paris

West Sandy
Creek

Big
Sandy
River

Hurricane Creek

Cane Creek

Lick
Creek

White Oak
Creek

Waverly

70

641

Birdsong
Creek

Duck
River

Tennessee
River

40

Among the places known for this type of cover are Eagle Creek, located near the mouth of the Big Sandy River; and Swamp Creek and West Sandy Creek, both in the Big Sandy. Farther up the lake, Lick and Birdsong Creeks, and the Blood River are also favorite areas.

In each of these places, shallow- to medium-running crankbaits are among the most productive lures. If fish are particularly aggressive, spinnerbaits may also be used in the spring around the flooded brush, and in the fall, topwaters produce well.

There is some Eurasian milfoil in the lake but not nearly as much as in the early 1990s. During those years much of this part of the state suffered through a severe drought that allowed the water to become more clear than normal and allow the milfoil to spread rapidly. As the grass spread, the bass population boomed. When the drought ended and normal rainfall again created the generally turbid conditions common in the lake, the milfoil died (with some help from herbicide spraying), and the fishing has declined, at least by the standards set during those low rainfall years.

Regardless of water or weather conditions, Kentucky Lake's smallmouth have always lived in the shadow of the largemouth and crappie here. They simply do not grow as large as in other nearby Tennessee impoundments. Still, the lake does have a strong population, primarily along the eastern side where more gravel and rocky banks are present. Key areas include Leatherwood, White Oak, and Hurricane Creeks. Farther north in Kentucky, Hughes and Rushing Creeks are among the best known.

Steve McCadams, a guide who has fished Kentucky Lake for more than 25 years, recommends that smallmouth anglers use both silicone and plastic jigs, hopping them around the rocks or over the gravel down to depths of about 15 feet. Slow-rolling heavy 3/4- and 1-ounce spinnerbaits also works well, depending on conditions. The best time to catch smallmouth, he believes, is early spring when the fish move back into the creeks and can be pinpointed more easily in pockets around the current.

"One thing visitors should remember about Kentucky Lake is that the best fishing takes place in the spring when high water floods shoreline cover," says McCadams. "Later in the year when the lake is down, that same cover will be completely out of water and the bass are much harder to locate.

"This is an old lake and most of the original cover is gone, but overall, the fishing is still very good if you concentrate in the main creeks."

RESOURCES

Gearing Up: Medium- and medium/heavy-action baitcasting rods are the most popular among bass fishermen here, because of the cover. Most will also use lines testing 12 to 20 pounds. Favorite lures include 3/8- and 1/2-ounce jigs, 1/2-ounce willowleaf spinnerbaits, medium-running crankbaits, buzzbaits, and plastic worms.

Accommodations: Complete motel and restaurant facilities are located in Paris, Paducah, Springville, and Camden, as well as at numerous full-service resorts around the lake. Many of these resorts also have campgrounds.

Additional Information: Paris/Henry County Chamber of Commerce, P.O. Box 8, Paris, TN 38242; 800-345-1103. Marshall County Tourist & Convention Center, P.O. Box 129, Gilbertsville, KY 42044; 270-362-4128.

13 ROSS BARNETT RESERVOIR

Location: Jackson, Mississippi.
Short Take: 30,000 acres; shallow, stumps, vegetation, two primary tributary creeks.
Primary Species: Largemouth bass.
Best Months: February through June, October, November.
Favorite Lures: Spinnerbaits, plastic worms, jigs.
Nearest Tourist Services: Jackson.

EVER SINCE 1966 WHEN ROSS BARNETT RESERVOIR FILLED, anglers have seemingly had a love/hate relationship with the lake. It is an extremely shallow impoundment (the average depth is about five feet), and there are vast areas of stumpy flats, which are generally good for bass fishing.

On the other hand, heavy rains will make this lake extremely muddy and very difficult to fish. In the winter months, sudden cold fronts will also affect fishing success on the lake because it is so shallow.

Nonetheless, Ross Barnett ranks as a favorite bass fishing spot for many fishermen throughout the South. The Bass Masters Classic world championship was contested here in 1978, and a number of top-level professional fishing events have been conducted on the lake in recent years. Some local anglers who know Ross Barnett well actually prefer to fish when the weather is at its worst because they say it tends to position bass very specifically around stumps and in the pockets of standing timber and thus narrows their search considerably.

On other days, these same anglers argue, the fish are more likely to be roaming, and with all the stumps, lily pads, and other cover available, the bass are extremely hard to find.

It's a far cry from some of the growing pains this lake has endured over the years. Because of the abundant habitat, excellent water quality, and strict pollution control measures enforced by the Pearl River Authority, fishing in the late 1960s and early 1970s could only be described as excellent. As the timber rotted and many of the shallow coves were taken over with vegetation, the fishing declined sharply. Some even began to describe Ross Barnett as a "Dead Sea."

In September, 1978, the lake level was drawn down in an attempt to expose and eradicate some of the vegetation. Once the drawdown was complete, the Mississippi Department of Wildlife Conservation initiated a protective slot limit of 15 to 20 inches for bass (any largemouth within that size had to be released immediately). These two management techniques worked remarkably well, and Ross Barnett rebounded quickly.

Most anglers who visit Ross Barnett describe it as two distinct lakes, a common description on many impoundments throughout the United States, but probably more accurate here than on most. The lower end of the lake, which extends 13 miles

ROSS BARNETT RESERVOIR
MISSISSIPPI

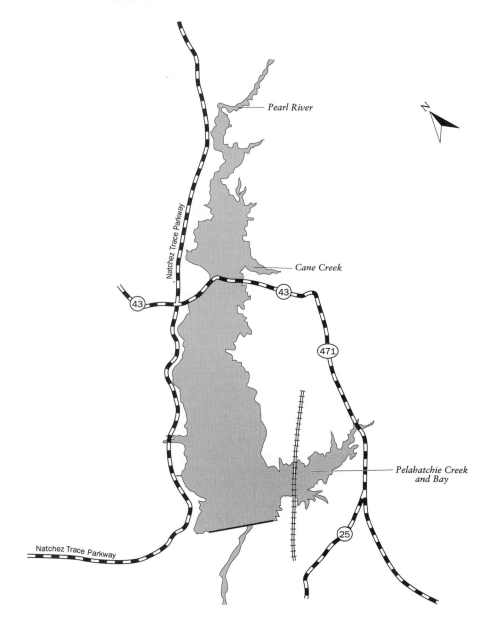

Pearl River

Cane Creek

Natchez Trace Parkway

43

43

471

Pelahatchie Creek
and Bay

Natchez Trace Parkway

25

from the dam up the lake to the Mississippi Highway 43 bridge, is characterized by open-water flats and the lake's largest tributary, Pelahatchie Creek.

Above the bridge, the lake is largely contained within the winding channel of the Pearl River. There are a number of small oxbow pools here as well as some vegetation. The primary tributary in this part of the lake is Cane Creek, but it is actually quite small in comparison to Pelahatchie. Both sides of the creek channel are shallow and stumpy, but the channel does offer several sharp bends that are always worth a quick cast or two.

Much of the fishing takes place on the lower part of the lake. In spring, Pelahatchie Creek and Bay (where the creek enters the main lake) offer numerous options, ranging from shallow flats, stumps, vegetation, riprap, bridge pilings, and the winding channel of the creek itself.

In the summer, the lower lake also produces good schooling bass action. If there happens to be an early hatch of both gizzard and threadfin shad, the schooling activity often gets into full swing by June. The area around the railroad trestle in the mouth of Pelahatchie Creek is one of the best places to look for schooling fish.

Schooling action also occurs in the river north of the Mississippi 43 bridge. Key places to look are along the river bends and the edges of the stumps and timber. The baitfish move up and down the edges of the stump rows, and the bass follow close behind.

For schooling bass, topwater poppers and chuggers may produce, especially if the bass are really feeding well, but early in the season a spinnerbait may out-perform a chugger. Ross Barnett has always been known for its huge shad populations, but at certain times of the year, matching lure size to bait size is extremely important here.

One of Ross Barnett's trademarks over the years has been its vast fields of lily pads. They're present both above and below the bridge, and they're always worth fishing, no matter what month you're on the water. In some places, the lily pads are as big as small card tables.

Spinnerbaits, floating worms, and weedless spoons are among the favorite lures, which are simply retrieved close to the surface right through the vegetation. With spoons and plastic worms, the lures are even pulled up on top of the pads and then eased off slowly and deliberately back into the water. Strikes are sudden and violent, and as often as not, come from a fish in the 4- to 6-pound class.

During that 1978 Bass Masters Classic, a weedless topwater spoon with a small spinner blade attached in front caught the winning stringer. Practically all the contestants were fishing the lily pads that year, and the bass were extremely aggressive, sometimes moving 10 feet to hit a spoon. Winner Bobby Murray, who brought in a total of 14 bass weighing 37 pounds, 9 ounces, remembers losing three bass in 15 minutes that probably could have added another 20 pounds to his catch.

Located just outside Jackson, Ross Barnett Reservoir offers a mixture of shallow cover and structure, including stump fields, lily pads, and ditches.

RESOURCES

Gearing Up: Because of the generally dingy water color as well as the heavy cover, most bass fishermen here prefer to use medium- and medium/heavy-action rods with lines of 15- to 25-pound test. Productive lures include 3/8- and 1/2-ounce willowleaf spinnerbaits, 1/2-ounce jigs, and plastic worms fished on a Texas or Carolina-rigged.

Accommodations: Complete motel facilties and a wide choice of restaurants are available in Jackson. Camping is permitted at several parks operated by the Pearl River Authority around the lake.

Additional Information: Metro Jackson Convention & Visitors Bureau, P.O. Box 1450, Jackson, MS 39215-1450; 601-960-1891.

14 Lake Norman

Location: Catawba River impoundment north of Charlotte near Mooresville, North Carolina.
Short Take: 32,500 acres; large tributary creeks with points and coves, boat docks, underwater ridges, good upriver cover with current.
Primary Species: Largemouth and striped bass.
Best Months: March, April, October, November.
Favorite Lures: Spinnerbaits, medium-running crankbaits, plastic worms, jigs.
Nearest Tourist Services: Mooresville, Charlotte.

IF THE BASS FISHERMEN ON LAKE NORMAN SEEM to fish faster than usual, don't be alarmed. It's simply because they're accustomed to going fast—many drivers and crew members from the NASCAR auto racing circuits have homes around the lake, and more than a few of them enjoy bass fishing.

The largest of 10 lakes along the Catawba River, Lake Norman is administered to and controlled by Duke Power Company. Because the water is used to produce electricity for much of North Carolina, the lake level fluctuates frequently. During the winter months, the lake may be drawn down eight to 10 feet.

"It really is an amazing lake, to produce such good fishing and to be so close to a large metropolitan area," notes professional angler Guy Eaker, who has fished Lake Norman for more than 25 years. "It offers a lot of different types of water and cover and has been a good training lake for a number of tournament anglers over the years."

Many area anglers, including Eaker, describe Lake Norman as a "point and pier" lake, meaning that two of the easiest ways to fish here are simply to run as many points as possible using a crankbait that covers depths down to perhaps 20 feet, or fish piers with spinnerbaits and jigs. One of these patterns will produce fish throughout most of the year.

The best fishing months overall for largemouths are March and April when the bass are beginning to move shallow to spawn. Two excellent areas to fish are Lucky Creek on the lower end of the lake near the Cowans Ford Dam, and Mountain Creek in the upper end where North Carolina Highway 150 crosses the lake.

The bass seem to begin moving into Lucky Creek sooner than into other tributaries, and readily hit spinnerbaits, jerkbaits, and jigs. Mountain Creek, which is full of piers and also riprap from the NC 150 bridge, tends to be slightly off-color; it's a good spinnerbait area. This is one of the largest tributaries on Lake Norman, and because of its many points it is also a good place to fish a Carolina-rigged lizard or imitation crawfish.

Another excellent tributary is Davidson Creek, located along the eastern shoreline in the lower part of the lake. Some of the best fishing takes place around the Interstate 77 bridge where the water is usually dingy and baitfish concentrations are heavy. Spinnerbaits and Carolina rigs both produce good results.

The Catawba River itself offers excellent summer fishing because of its current

LAKE NORMAN
NORTH CAROLINA

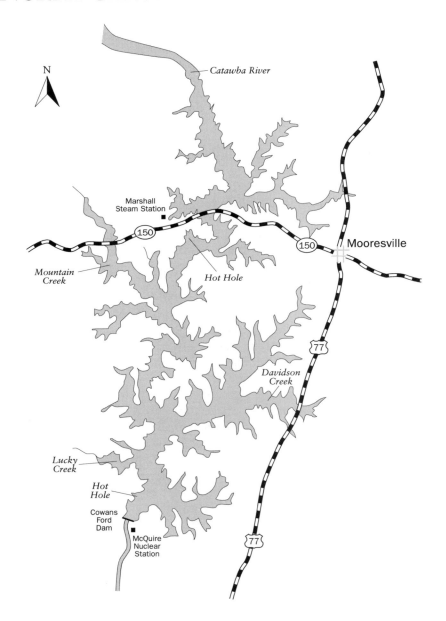

N

Catawba River

Marshall
Steam Station

150

150 Mooresville

Mountain
Creek

Hot Hole

77

Davidson
Creek

Lucky
Creek

Hot
Hole

Cowans
Ford
Dam

McQuire
Nuclear
Station

77

and shoreline cover. Spinnerbaits and small topwater lures work well around the many small shoreline cuts and pockets; if the current is strong, crankbaits and plastic lizards can be fished around points.

In the autumn months, bass begin moving back onto the points and then into the creeks. The key to finding these fish, advises Eaker, is first locating schools of shad. If the baitfish are present, they'll probably be breaking the water because bass are feeding on them; a lipless crankbait or a topwater popper can sometimes produce a five-bass limit in as many casts.

Pier fishing is good on Lake Norman because so many homeowners enjoy fishing and put extra brush around their piers to attract and keep fish close. Spinnerbaits and jigs are two of the best pier fishing lures on Lake Norman, but crankbaits and plastic worms should also be tried. Because the piers do receive a lot of fishing pressure, however, skipping jigs and soft plastic lures far underneath the structures may be required to get a strike.

Two other areas of Lake Norman deserve special mention for both largemouth and striped bass anglers. These are the famous hot holes where warm water is discharged back into the lake by Duke Power Company. One is located just south of Marker 17 below the NC 150 bridge where the Marshall Steam Station is located, and the other is along the western shoreline just above the dam. Here, warm water is pumped back into the lake from the McGuire Nuclear Station located just below the dam. Both hot holes attract baitfish, bass, and stripers during the autumn, winter, and early spring because the water in them may be 10 to 15 degrees warmer than in the rest of the lake.

Several lures can be used in these places, which are about the size of a football field and 20 to 25 feet deep. Suspending jerkbaits work well at times, as do crankbaits and jigging spoons. Both largemouth and striped bass hit all three lures. Duke Power has steel cables across the water that limit access very far back to these two areas for safety purposes, but there is still plenty of warm water to fish.

At the Marshall Steam Station outlet, for instance, the warm water flows down the lake's western shoreline, creating excellent cold weather fishing opportunities on the points and in the coves nearby. When water is not being released at the dam to power the generators there, this warm-water discharge will actually move upstream, and create the same good fishing opportunities above the NC 150 bridge.

RESOURCES

Gearing Up: Medium- to medium/heavy-action baitcasting rods with lines testing 10 to 20 pounds are standard here. Favorite lures include 3/8- and 1/2-ounce spinnerbaits, plastic worms and lizards, jerkbaits, and medium- to deep-diving crankbaits. Spoons can be used to fish the deep water in the winter months.

Accommodations: A wide choice of motel accommodations and restaurants is available in Mooresville, especially along NC 150. Camping is also available at several family campgrounds around the lake as well as at some of the marinas.

Additional Information: Mooresville Chamber of Commerce, P.O. Box 628, Mooresville, NC; 704-664-3898.

15 LAKE WYLIE

Location: Catawba River impoundment extending from just south of Charlotte, North Carolina to Rock Hill, South Carolina.
Short Take: 12,455 acres; river-type lake filled with underwater stumps, boat docks, long points, excellent structure, no vegetation.
Primary Species: Largemouth bass.
Best Months: March, April, November.
Favorite Lures: Deep-diving crankbaits, jigging spoons, plastic worms, jigs.
Nearest Tourist Services: Charlotte, Rock Hill.

IF THERE IS A "MYSTERY LAKE" IN THE SOUTH, the title should probably be given to Lake Wylie, a 12,455-acre impoundment on the Catawba River in North and South Carolina. The mystery is why this lake, first impounded in 1904 and then enlarged by a new dam in 1924, continues to produce as many bass as it does.

Part of the mystery might be answered by the fact Lake Wylie has a tremendous shad population, so the largemouths certainly have plenty to eat. The question then can be asked why this particular Duke Power Company lake, the oldest in their Catawba River system, has the baitfish when others just upriver do not.

The answer to that question is still unknown, and even deepens the mystery, since Wylie does not contain any aquatic vegetation, considered by many to be one of the keys to any successful bass/forage fishery. The lake instead is lined with boat docks and private piers, and is characterized by large, winding tributary creeks with pockets, long points, underwater stump fields, and basically dingy water.

In addition to the main Catawba River and the various creeks, another important tributary is the South Fork of the Catawba River. One of the better-known fishing areas on the lake, in fact, is at the junction of these two rivers where a long rocky point is formed. It's especially productive in the fall and winter when fished with crankbaits or jigging spoons.

The South Fork of the Catawba offers another attraction for cool-weather fishing, a warm-water discharge "hot hole," in which heated water from the Allen Steam Station on the main Catawba River is piped across to the South Fork. This warm water gradually flows down the river and helps make this entire area a good fall/winter fishing choice.

Several tributary creeks have gained attention over the years for producing excellent bass catches, including some eight-bass stringers of just under 50 pounds. The two best-known creeks are Big Allison and Little Allison, the first two creeks above the Wylie Dam along the western shoreline. As with the South Fork and main Catawba Rivers, the junction of these two creeks forms a long underwater point that dips and then rises to form a small high spot under the surface. Deep-diving crankbaits or Carolina-rigged plastic worms are among the most popular and productive lure choices for this area.

LAKE WYLIE
NORTH CAROLINA/SOUTH CAROLINA
BORDER

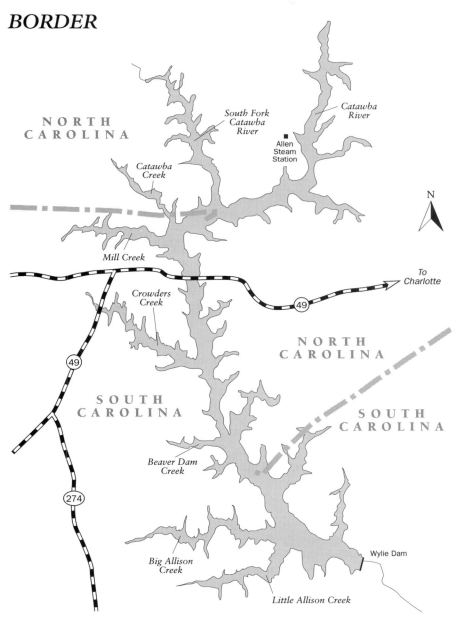

NORTH
CAROLINA

South Fork
Catawba
River

Catawba
River

Allen
Steam
Station

Catawba
Creek

N

Mill Creek

Crowders
Creek

To
Charlotte

49

NORTH
CAROLINA

49

SOUTH
CAROLINA

SOUTH
CAROLINA

Beaver Dam
Creek

274

Wylie Dam

Big Allison
Creek

Little Allison Creek

Mill Creek and Crowders Creek are two other tributaries that deserve attention. Mill Creek, in particular, may have more baitfish in it than anywhere else on the lake, so bass also tend to gather there. This particular tributary also offers some excellent depth changes with gentle ridges that stair-step down 30 feet or more. Still another reason Mill Creek is productive is because it empties into the main Catawba channel along the outside of a bend, resulting in classic underwater points and dramatic shallow-water/deep-water configurations.

Both Crowders and Mill Creeks also offer miles of boat dock fishing which is usually most productive with either crankbaits or jigs. Some use the crankbaits not so much to catch bass but to locate the brush, which they then fish more carefully with a jig. One reason the dock fishing is so good on Wylie is because the large majority of owners put brush out to help attract crappie, and while this brush is seldom visible from the surface, it can occasionally be found by noting the direction of the rod holders on the dock itself (if you don't want to use the crankbait method). In most cases, the brush is directly beneath the rod holder.

Lake Wylie's points and channel edges are lined with underwater stumps, which is one more reason this is such a good crankbait lake. Most bass are caught at depths between two and 10 feet, which is the prime crankbait range; the lures can be fished either up or down the points and will still catch bass. With the exception of the hot summer months when most bass are caught off main lake points, the tributary creeks produce best, and they're full of stumps, too.

The best overall months for Lake Wylie bass fishing are probably March and April when the bass are moving from the deeper river channel up to main lake points en route to the creeks to spawn. This is an excellent time to fish crankbaits and jigs. November is also a favorite month among local anglers because this is when the bass have migrated back into the creeks and are feeding heavily on baitfish. Again, it's a good time to fish small crankbaits.

Another fishing technique popular at this time, which actually originated on Lake Wylie in the 1950s, is Carolina rigging. In fact, it was the lake's stumpfields that led to the now-standard swivel/leader/plastic-worm combination. The angler most often credited with the Carolina-rig innovation, Lloyd Deaver of nearby Gastonia, North Carolina, wanted a more efficient method of crawling his small plastic worms through the thick cover, and using a length of leader after a weight accomplished just that. Today, Carolina-rigging is one of the most popular of all techniques and is used by bass fishermen around the world.

RESOURCES

Gearing Up: Medium- and medium/heavy-action baitcasting rods are standard for Lake Wylie because of the stumps and underwater brush around the boat houses. Line choices range from 12-pound test for crankbaits to 20-pound test for jigs. Other popular lures include four- to six-inch plastic worms and 3/4-ounce jigging spoons. Both deep- and medium-running crankbaits are also effective.

Accommodations: Complete motel and restaurant facilities are available in Charlotte and Rock Hill. Camping is also available near the lake.

Additional Information: South Carolina Department of Natural Resources, Division of Wildlife & Freshwater Fisheries, P.O. Box 167, Columbia, SC 29202; 803-734-3886.

16 Lake Murray

Location: Lexington, Saluda, and Newberry Counties in central South Carolina near Columbia.
Short Take: 50,000 acres; large tributaries, deep and shallow water, vegetation, boat docks, fallen timber.
Primary Species: Largemouth and striped bass.
Best Months: March through May, September, October.
Favorite Lures: Spinnerbaits, jigs, plastic worms and tube baits, Carolina-rigged lizards; bucktail jigs, crankbaits for stripers.
Nearest Tourist Services: Columbia, Lexington, Chapin.

LIKE A NUMBER OF SOUTHERN BASS LAKES NOW WELL INTO MIDDLE AGE, Lake Murray frequently gets by-passed by traveling anglers, even though it's located just a few miles off Interstate 20 near South Carolina's capital city. This 50,000-acre impoundment is well-deserving of a closer look, however, for under the right water conditions, bass fishing here can be excellent.

This is a lake that produced one of the heaviest tournament winning stringers in recent years, 28 fish (seven bass per day limit) weighing more than 87 pounds. Even now with a five-bass-per-day limit, local tournament angler Davy Hite emphasizes that 20- and 25-pound one-day stringers are still caught.

One of America's most accomplished and well-known bass fishermen, Hite attributes his national success to his years of fishing experience on Murray, for the lake offers a wide variety of cover and water conditions not always found on a single body of water. Big tributaries feature well-defined channels with both deep and shallow water, shoreline brush, shallow vegetation, boat docks, and stained water. At the same time, the main lake has clear water, submerged vegetation, long points, and underwater islands.

On the average, the lower half of the lake produces better bass fishing. The vegetation, before the state's eradication efforts began, was heavier here and thus provided more habitat. Even with little or no aquatic greenery, however, the tributaries of Bear, Beards, Beaver Dam and Hollow Creeks continue to provide the lake's largest bass. Cedar Creek is also a local favorite.

What makes these tributaries, especially Hollow and Bear Creeks, such good fishing spots are their size and the variety of cover they offer. In either creek fishermen can choose from such options as inside/outside hydrilla lines, boat docks with brush piles, rocky points, shallow flats, fallen timber, bridge pilings and riprap. If these choices aren't enough, both also have underwater islands, deep channels, and even other tributaries flowing into them.

Historically, the first type of cover to look for is hydrilla, because it tends to hold bass most of the year. When the greenery is still several feet below the surface, a

Lake Murray
South Carolina

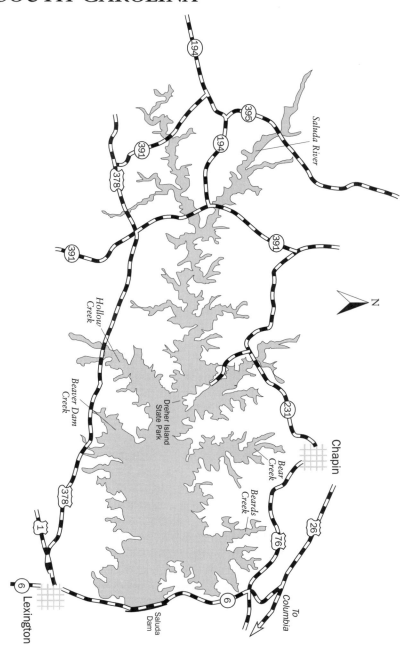

spinnerbait technique known as slow-rolling, in which the lure is retrieved just over the top of the grass, often produces very well. Carolina-rigged lizards fished along the edges of the hydrilla can also be effective.

In the spring, Bear and Beards Creeks, both located on the northeastern side of the lake, will have slightly warmer and protected water, so this is where spawning activity traditionally begins. After a mild winter, this could be as early as February, but more often the top spring fishing doesn't begin until late March. Later in April and May, Hollow and Beaver Dam Creeks, located on the southern shore, produce better fishing.

"Water temperature is really the major key to spring fishing on Murray," says Hite. "If we have a cold winter, the spawning activity can be delayed for weeks. Because this lake has a lot of deep water even in the tributary creeks, the bass will stay deep even though they're very close to their actual spawning flats."

Because of that, most anglers here rely on two primary lures, a spinnerbait for the shallow-water cover and a jig for deeper depths, with a crankbait in reserve for anything in between.

While the lower-lake tributaries are large and varied, some prefer to fish the far upper end of Lake Murray where the Saluda River is still basically contained within its original channel. This is especially true during the summer months when the lower lake is both clear and crowded with pleasure boats. The Saluda River shoreline is characterized by hundreds of coves, points, and small creeks, and the water is usually dingy. With brush, stumps, and rocks all readily available, the bass here are shallow and much easier to locate.

This is where much of the spinnerbait fishing takes place. Fishermen can literally move down any stretch of chosen shoreline and see a constant supply of casting targets. The river also provides some current, which helps position bass even more definitively. When a spinnerbait doesn't produce, jigs often will.

Striped bass were first put into Lake Murray in 1961 and have been stocked on a regular basis ever since. They do not reproduce naturally here. With fish weighing more than 45 pounds taken in years past, the lake at one point was better known for its striper fishing than for its largemouth action, but today the average size of the stripers is around 5 pounds.

One of the most enjoyable striped bass fishing techniques is "jump fishing," which can be done in the autumn when striped bass are schooling on the surface. The stripers drive swarms of baitfish to the surface where flocks of gulls join in the feeding frenzy, and it is these diving birds that show anglers where the fish are.

Often there's only time for a few casts with either a topwater plug or a jig before the stripers become spooked and return to deeper water. Veteran striper fishermen then use binoculars to scan the lake for another flock of feeding gulls and "jump" over to it as quickly as they can. On cloudy, dreary days, it may be possible to race back and forth across the lake for hours, fishing different schools like this.

RESOURCES

Gearing Up: Medium- to medium/heavy-action baitcasters see the most action here, due to the amount of cover. Favorite lure choices include 3/8- and 1/2-ounce white/chartreuse spinnerbaits, black/blue jigs, and firetiger crankbaits. For striped bass, shad-colored bucktail jigs or small, shallow-running minnow-imitation crankbaits can be used.

Accommodations: Complete motel and restaurant facilities are available in and around Columbia and Lexington. Camping is offered at numerous sites around the lake, including Dreher Island State Park.

Additional Information: Greater Columbia Chamber of Commerce, P.O. Box 1360, Columbia, SC 29202; 803-733-1110.

17 SANTEE COOPER

Location: Southeastern part of South Carolina approximately 60 miles southeast of Columbia near the cities of Sumter, Manning, Summerton, and Santee.

Short Take: 160,500 acres total; two separate lakes, Marion (100,500 acres) and Moultrie (60,00 acres), joined by a seven-mile canal; generally shallow, stumpy water and standing timber (Lake Marion); more open water with some hydrilla (Lake Moultrie).

Primary Species: Largemouth and striped bass.

Best Months: February through May, September through November. Stripers best in October.

Favorite Lures: Spinnerbaits, plastic worms, crankbaits for largemouths; topwaters, jigs, spoons best for schooling striped bass.

Nearest Tourist Services: Summerton, Santee, Manning.

THE SANTEE COOPER LAKES OF MARION AND MOULTRIE rank as two of the most famous bodies of water in the South, but mainly because of a total accident. In 1942 when the Santee Dam closed and began impounding Lake Marion, a number of saltwater striped bass that had migrated up the Santee River to spawn were inadvertently trapped in the lake. Unnoticed by anglers during the years of World War II, the big silvery fish with dark lateral stripes not only spawned but thrived—and in the process created an entirely new fishery for anglers all over America.

In the nearly half century since the discovery of those freshwater striped bass, the fish have been propagated in hatcheries and stocked in lakes all across America. Not only that, but the Santee Cooper striped bass also later laid the foundation for the scientific creation of another fish, the hybrid striped bass (a cross between striped bass and the white bass), which has also been stocked throughout much of the United States.

Today, the Santee Cooper lakes (so named because of the Santee and Cooper Rivers) continue to turn out large numbers of striped bass, but their average size has diminished considerably from the heyday of the 1960s and 1970s. In those days an angler and his guide could each keep as many as 15 stripers per day, and most did, because the fish are good to eat. Years and and years of heavy fishing pressure simply took their toll on the overall population.

The pressure on striped bass, however, may have resulted in less pressure on the largemouth, which also thrived in the swampy, stump-filled impounds. Among the great largemouth lakes of the South, Marion and Moultrie always ranked near the top, producing fish over 10 pounds with astonishing regularity. By the late 1990s, however, largemouth numbers appeared to be on the decline (by Santee Cooper standards, anyway) as water quality management officials continued an aggressive program of hydrilla and elodea removal by stocking grass-eating Chinese carp. This

SANTEE COOPER
SOUTH CAROLINA

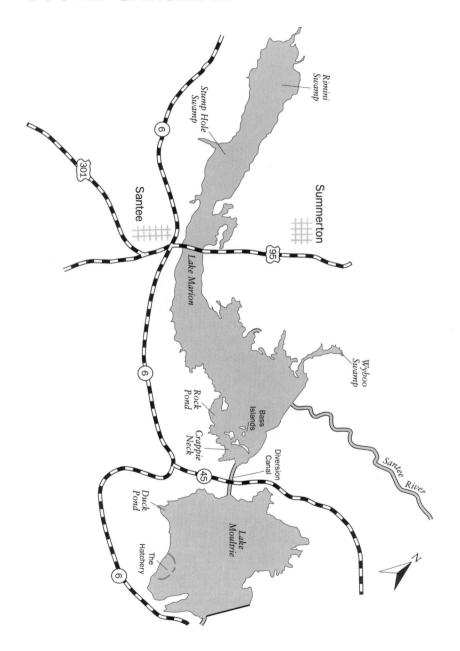

The Santee Cooper Lakes of Marion and Moultrie initially gained their fame for striped bass, but today they're also known for excellent largemouth fishing.

is a familiar story on numerous southern impoundments today; as the carp eat up the bass habitat, the population goes down.

Nonetheless, it is still possible to enjoy very good fishing for either largemouths or stripers on the two lakes. A number of fishing spots stand out for both species in both Marion and Moultrie.

In Lake Moultrie, the most famous largemouth area is probably the Hatchery, a large, shallow, stumpy area known for its big bass. A high earthen dike surrounds most of the Hatchery, but it is open in several places to fishing access. Often, the best fishing takes place in these cuts, especially when wind creates a current blowing water either in or out of the Hatchery. When this occurs, crankbaits and jigs are excellent lure choices.

Another well-known area on Moultrie is the Duck Pond. This is a large, shallow flat with scattered lily pads and cypress trees standing in three to four feet of water. On cloudy days, there's hardly a better buzzbait area on either lake.

The Diversion Canal itself can be good for bass fishing, although it does not see a lot of bass fishing pressure because there is so much better water nearby. One of those spots is where the canal enters Lake Marion, in an area known as Crappie Neck. Here there are several large islands, plenty of standing timber, and several submerged roadbeds. Jigs and spinnerbaits work well around the cypress, while crankbaits can be used on the roadbeds.

Just out from Crappie Neck is a group of islands known as the Bass Islands, which are famous for producing excellent largemouth catches on spinnerbaits. Nearby is another area named the Rock Pond, also with flooded cypress and equally as well known. Eutaw Creek, itself a maze of flooded cypress, is still another excellent largemouth producer in this area of the lake.

Above the Interstate 95 bridge, Lake Marion begins to look much more like a swamp, and, indeed, several areas of the lake are designated as such. Among them are Wyboo Swamp, Stump Hole Swamp, and Rimini Swamp. In all of these areas, the lake resembles a flooded forest (which it actually is), and careless fishermen do get lost here.

Much of the striped bass fishing in the two lakes is done with live herring or cut bait, which is drifted down the river channels or into the deeper holes. Artificial lures, especially jigs, spoons, and occasionally topwater lures work the best during September and October when the fish school near the surface. Guides sit in the open water scanning the horizon with binoculars, looking for diving gulls. Once a flock is seen, fishermen race to the spot as quickly as possible to make a few casts before the stripers submerge.

Although submerged stripers can often still be caught on deep jigs, it's much more fun to catch them on top, so when the fish do go down, the waiting/watching game begins again. On really good days, the action may remain fairly constant for several hours. And when the stripers are hitting well, it's just a reminder of the role the Santee Cooper lakes have played in fishing history.

RESOURCES

Gearing Up: Medium- to medium/heavy-action baitcasting rods with lines testing 14 to 25 pounds are standard for most fishing, although striped bass anglers using live baits may opt for heavier tackle. Favorite lures include 3/8- and 1/2-ounce willowleaf spinnerbaits, 1/2-ounce jigs, buzzbaits and chugger-type topwater lures, and shallow-running or lipless crankbaits.

Accommodations: Complete motel and restaurant facilities are available in Summerton, Santee, and Manning, as well as at a number of fishing camps around the lake. Camping is available at Santee State Park along the lake near Santee.

Additional Information: Santee Cooper Counties Promotion Commission, P.O. Drawer 40, Santee, SC 29142; 803-854-2131.

18 KERR RESERVOIR

Location: North Carolina/Virginia border near the cities of Henderson, North Carolina and South Hill and Clarksville, Virginia.
Short Take: 48,900 acres; brush-lined tributaries, long, wooded points, sunken roadbeds, shallow coves.
Primary Species: Largemouth and striped bass.
Best Months: March through May, September, October.
Favorite Lures: Plastic worms, crankbaits, spinnerbaits, topwaters.
Nearest Tourist Services: Clarksville, South Hill.

A FEW YEARS AGO when professional bass angler Jack Hains won the Bass Anglers Sportsman Society's national tournament on Virginia's Kerr Reservoir, he brought in 15 bass weighing more than 57 pounds, an average of nearly 4 pounds per fish. The 286 other anglers competing against Hains added more than 7,680 total pounds of bass of their own—if ever a lake needed any validation for its bass fishery, Kerr received it that week.

Kerr Reservoir, however, really did not need such validation. It has been a stellar bass fishery practically ever since the Corps of Engineers completed their dam across the Roanoke River in 1953. With some 800 miles of irregular and lightly developed shoreline, an abundance of both deep and shallow water, rock and gravel bottom, and several large tributaries (including both the Dan and Hyco Rivers), it has continued to be one of the Southeast's premier impoundments.

Perhaps the lake's major problem is that it is known by two different names. The Corps of Engineers named the lake after then U.S. Congressman John H. Kerr, who heavily promoted the project, but a more popular name among bass fishermen has long been Buggs Island, a familiar landmark in the river below the dam.

Although bass fishing can be good throughout the year at Kerr, the two primary seasons are spring and fall when fish migrate into shallow coves and points for spawning or pre-winter feeding. Spinnerbaits and medium-running crankbaits work well in the spring (Hains won his tournament in the month of May), while topwater lures produce well in September and October.

"One of the reasons Buggs Island is such a popular lake among bass fishermen is that a variety of lures work well during these two seasons," explains angler Woo Daves, who grew up fishing the impoundment. "It's large enough, and there are enough different types of cover and structure that a fisherman can practically choose the lure he wants to use, and then find a place where that lure works."

Daves himself prefers fishing plastic worms, and he rigs either with a standard slip sinker (Texas style) or on a short leader (Carolina-rigged), and sometimes in spring he leaves the weights off entirely and floats them as weedless surface lures around heavy shoreline brush.

KERR RESERVOIR
VIRGINIA/NORTH CAROLINA BORDER

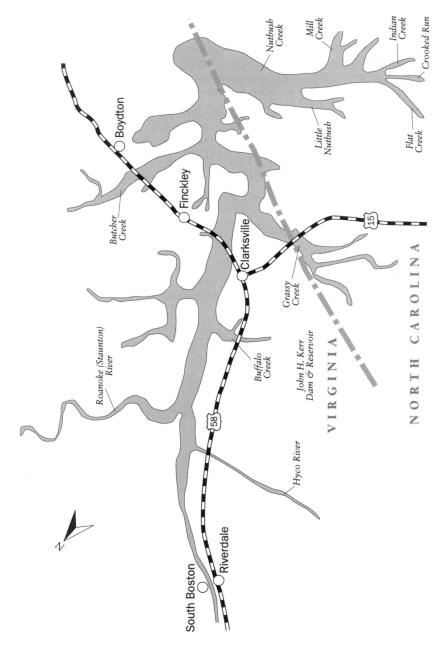

The floating worm technique has become increasingly popular in recent years, especially on lakes like Kerr that have thick shoreline cover. Because floating worms are rigged weedless as well as weightless, they can be cast into the heart of sticks and bushes and then eased back out without fear of snagging. The most popular colors for topwater worms are pink, yellow, and white—not because bass necessarily like those shades, but because fishermen can see the lures more easily as they work them through the thick tangles.

Autumn can be an awesome topwater season here as bass hit a variety of poppers, chuggers, and even buzzbaits on the points. High-water conditions help the fall topwater action since it floods trees and brush that might ordinarily be high and dry. Daves and other anglers often get the best results by retrieving their surface plugs as fast and with as much noise as possible—a sure recipe for pure fishing fun. Interestingly, when bass want topwaters really churning across the surface, a more normal slow retrieve will draw far fewer strikes.

Without doubt, the best-known fishing area of the entire lake is Nutbush Creek, located on the lower end of the lake across from the dam. One look at a map shows the reason: it is the largest tributary on the entire lake and has several smaller tributaries of its own. The shoreline is irregular with hundreds of small, wooded coves, gently tapering points, several flooded roadbeds, and excellent stair-stepping structure.

The smaller tributaries of Nutbush include Burroughs Mill Branch, Little Nutbush, Flat Creek, Crooked Run, and Indian Creek. While each offers excellent shoreline cover and well-defined channels, the very backs of these creeks are quite shallow. All told, however, within the main creek as well as in these tributaries, there are miles of water and shoreline to fish.

Some anglers never go anywhere else except to Nutbush because it is so large, but there are some other areas, particularly Butcher, Grassy, and Buffalo Creeks, that are worth a look. They're not nearly as big, but they have a lot of the same type of coves and points as Nutbush.

If anyone wants to fish crankbaits or Carolina-rigged plastic worms, Grassy Creek has a winding creek channel that runs against the bank in several places that is tailor-made for diving plugs or deep worms, while Butcher has patches of flooded timber and a lot of deep-water drops that make it good for both largemouths and stripers.

Striped bass fishing is good in May when the fish migrate up the Dan River in an attempt to spawn. During this time they'll strike plastic grubs, spoons, bucktail jigs, and occasionally a big topwater plug. During much of the summer the fish roam the lake's deep water chasing gizzard shad and are extremely difficult to catch; local guides often troll live bait along the channels for them. While fish in the 25- to 30-pound class have been caught here, most average much smaller.

As the largest impoundment in Virginia, Kerr Reservoir certainly draws its share of anglers, especially in the spring when they remember the totals put up by Hains and the other bass pros in that national tournament. The lake's winding configuration helps keep them well spread out, however, even in the most popular creeks.

Kerr Reservoir, more commonly known as Buggs Island, is characterized by points, coves, and brush-covered shoreline, making flipping a popular technique. Nutbush Creek is the most well-known tributary, and attracts a lot of anglers.

RESOURCES

Gearing Up: Most fishermen prefer medium- or medium/heavy-action rods with lines testing 8 to 14 pounds, as the water can be fairly clear. Striped bass fishermen may use heavier rods and line, especially when trolling live bait. Favorite lures include medium-running crankbaits, plastic worms, willowleaf spinnerbaits, and topwater plugs.

Accommodations: Major motel chains and numerous restaurants are available in South Hill, a city that prides itself on its friendliness to bass fishermen. Campgrounds are located at several Corps of Engineers parks around the shoreline.

Additional Information: South Hill Chamber of Commerce, 201 South Mecklenburg Avenue, South Hill, VA 23970; 804-447-4547.

19 James River

Location: Richmond, Virginia southeast to Jamestown.
Short Take: More than 60 miles of fishable water; numerous tributary creeks, abundant shallow cover, tidal influence.
Primary Species: Largemouth bass.
Best Months: May through September.
Favorite Lures: Plastic worms, spinnerbaits, crankbaits, topwaters.
Nearest Tourist Services: Richmond.

PERHAPS NOWHERE ELSE IN THE UNITED STATES CAN ANGLERS mix American history and bass fishing as easily as on the James River south of Richmond, Virginia. Both the Colonial era as well as the Civil War are well represented along the river, including not only several magnificent antebellum plantations but also Jamestown, site of the first permanent American settlement.

The bass fishing is as rich as the history, too. This is essentially a shallow-water fishery with an abundance of cover, and rarely will any bass be caught deeper than about six feet. Flooded cypress trees, lily pads, rocks, shell beds, duck blinds, piers and pilings, and laydown logs are all abundantly present.

Although the James River can be fished for miles above Richmond, it is a totally different fishery there than below the city. That's because right in Richmond the river crosses a "fall line," a series of ledges and waterfalls marking the end of the Piedmont and the beginning of the coastal plain region of the state. Above the fall line the river is best known for its smallmouth while below it largemouth dominate.

Southeast of Richmond the river not only widens and slows, but is also affected by tides. There are numerous tributary creeks and even two tributary rivers, the Appomattox and the Chickahominy, that offer additional miles of fishable water; in fact, most bass fishermen prefer to concentrate in one of these tributaries rather than along the main river shoreline. Below Jamestown, the water is normally considered too salty for bass fishing.

Among the best-known tributaries are Herring, Powell, and Upper Chippokes Creeks. Herring probably receives the most fishing pressure of any tributary on the river due to its easy access from U.S. Highway 5 between Richmond and Williamsburg. It's full of lily pads, fallen timber, and several meandering ditches. The Berkeley Plantation is also located along this creek; one night during the Civil War, Confederate and Union troops blew sad bugle notes back and forth at each other across the river, resulting in what is now known as the hymn *Taps*.

Upper Chippokes Creek is the largest tributary creek of the James, and like the others is filled with laydowns, duck blinds, cypress trees and vegetation. Plastic worms, spinnerbaits, and some topwater action can always be found here, especially around the duck blinds which invariably seem to hold at least one bass. Veteran professional bass angler Woo Daves, who lives in the area and has fished the James

James River
Virginia

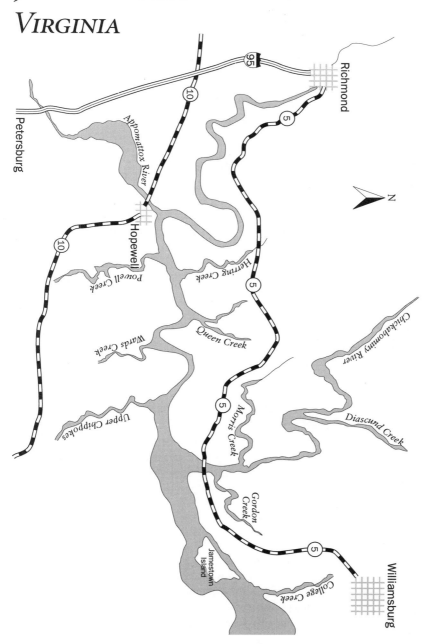

N

Richmond

Petersburg

Appomattox River

Hopewell

Powell Creek

Herring Creek

Wards Creek

Queen Creek

Upper Chippokes

Morris Creek

Chickahominy River

Diascund Creek

Gordon Creek

Jamestown Island

College Creek

Williamsburg

for more than 30 years, stages an annual one-day bass tournament for NASCAR racing drivers and their crews each spring after their Richmond race, and in most years the tournament is won in Upper Chippokes.

Daves also spends much of his fishing time in the Chickahominy River, just a few miles downstream from Chippokes. Not only is the fishing excellent, the natural scenery is gorgeous, with grassy flats, flooded cypress, miles of shoreline lily pads, abundant bird life, and minimal shoreline development. Here fishermen have some 25 miles of shallow, winding river to fish, and every single spot looks like it should hold a bass. Key tributaries of the "Chick" include Gordon, Morris, and Diascund Creeks, each of which offers similar cover and excellent fishing.

The Appomattox River flows into the James near the city of Hopewell and also receives a lot of fishing pressure, but in contrast to the Chickahominy, the Appomattox has a slightly deeper channel that drops to as deep as 20 feet in places. This depth, plus the fact the water is constantly moving with the tides, keeps the overall fishing in the James good throughout the hot summer months.

The last tributary most bass fishermen fish is College Creek, located just downriver from Jamestown Island. It is a small, winding creek with shallow grassy flats, some lily pads, and a little flooded cypress. By the time an angler launches near Richmond and gets here, he has made an extremely long run and already passed a lot of excellent fishing; thus, College Creek receives much less pressure because it is fished most often only by those who launch nearby.

On the average, a tidal fluctuation in the James is about two feet. The water takes six hours to come in, remains high for 45 minutes, then takes another six hours to recede. The best fishing normally takes place as the high tide goes out and continues through the first hour of the incoming tide. During this time, both baitfish and bass are pulled out of the thick shoreline vegetation and become more active and more accessible.

As with most American river systems, bass do not grow as large in the James as they do in nearby reservoirs. Each spring several fish in the 7- and 8-pound range are caught, but on the average a 6-pounder is a big fish here. Those fish can come at any time of year, however, and on a wide variety of lures.

The overall quality of fishing in the James River can be documented by the fact that three Bass Masters Classic world championships were conducted here in 1988, 1989, and 1990, the only time the event has been contested on the same water three consecutive years.

RESOURCES

Gearing Up: Medium-action rods are probably used most often here, with lines testing 12 to perhaps 17 pounds. Favorite lures include six-inch plastic worms, medium-running crankbaits, single-spin Colorado blade 1/4-ounce spinnerbaits, and topwater poppers.

Accommodations: Complete motel and restaurant facilities are available in Richmond and Williamsburg. Camping is also permitted in several areas.

Additional Information: Virginia Tourism Corporation, 901 East Byrd Street, Richmond, VA 23219-4048; 804-786-4484. Virginia Department of Game and Inland Fisheries, 4010 West Broad Street, Richmond, VA 23230; 804-367-1000.

SOUTHCENTRAL

ARKANSAS

LOUISIANA

MISSOURI

OKLAHOMA

TEXAS

20 Lake Ouachita

Location: West-central Arkansas near Hot Springs.
Short Take: 48,000 acres; rocks, gravel, major river and creek tributaries, abundant vegetation, undeveloped shoreline.
Primary Species: Largemouth and striped bass.
Best Months: April through November.
Favorite Lures: Spinnerbaits, jigs, topwaters, Carolina-rigged lizards.
Nearest Tourist Services: Hot Springs.

IT WAS 10:30 AT NIGHT AND MARK DAVIS HAD ALREADY CAUGHT ABOUT 30 BASS since the moon had come out, but this time when he threw his black spinnerbait around the stumps on the rocky point and a fish struck, it felt different. It was different, for it weighed an even 12 pounds, the largest bass Davis—a former Lake Ouachita guide—had ever caught anywhere, and one of the largest ever caught on the lake.

The lake is Lake Ouachita, a beautiful, island-filled impoundment on the Ouachita River that is gaining more and more attention as a quality largemouth fishery. Eurasian milfoil and elodea now cover much of the lake's shallow-water habitat, so bass fishing will probably continue to improve in the years ahead. Spotted bass are also present, and stocking efforts have been initiated to establish smallmouth, as well.

Located along the edge of the Ouachita National Forest, the lake has virtually no shoreline development, which adds to its scenic appeal. The primary river feeding the lake is the Ouachita, but it is joined by three other rivers, the South and North Forks of the Ouachita and the Iron Fork River, which flows into the North Fork. Primary creeks include Big and Little Blakeley, Cedar Creek, and Rabbit Tail.

Overall, the lake might be characterized as deep, clear, and rocky, but this is only part of the picture. There are literally hundreds of rocky, tree-filled coves, and numerous islands with points and flats, that provide a lot of fairly shallow fishing. And too, the vegetation usually provides some shallow fishing throughout the year. For the most part, the productive bass fishing depths here range between 12 and about 25 feet.

To aid in navigation, numbered markers have been placed along the shoreline. Beginning at the dam with Marker 1 and making a loop down one shore and around the opposite side, there are 49 different markers by which to navigate. Davis, by the way, who has caught probably a dozen Lake Ouachita bass in the 10-pound class over the years, caught his 12-pounder at Marker 15.

Markers 15, 16, and 17, are located toward the western end of the lake and are known as the Mountain Harbor area. It is characterized by a lot of gravel and rock points that often have additional stumps or vegetation on them. They're favorite spring fishing areas.

LAKE OUACHITA
ARKANSAS

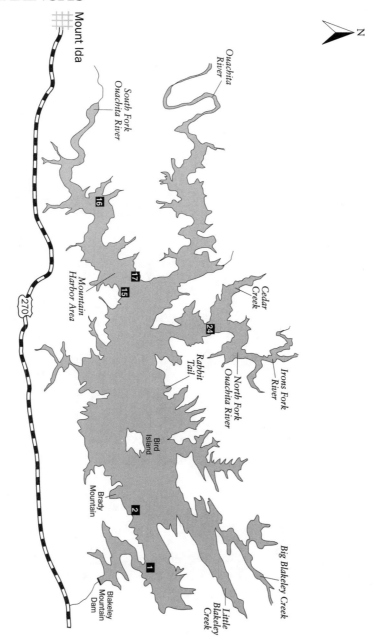

Mount Ida

Ouachita
River

South Fork
Ouachita River

270

16

17

15

Mountain
Harbor Area

Cedar
Creek

24

Rabbit
Tail

Irons Fork
River

North Fork
Ouachita River

Bird
Island

Brady
Mountain

2

1

Blakeley
Mountain
Dam

Big Blakeley Creek

Little
Blakeley
Creek

N

91

Lake Ouachita offers excellent bass fishing because of its mixed habitat of rocks and vegetation. It is also one of the most scenic lakes in the state.

Other well-known spots include the Brady Mountain area around Markers 2 and 3, which is deep, open water where bass regularly school on the surface during the summer; and Cedar Creek near Marker 24 where the creek comes very close to the main river channel. In the middle of the lake Bird Island offers a lot of shallow flats for spring and fall fishing.

"The lake is best known for schooling largemouths, because the bass begin schooling in May and usually continue schooling as late as November," says Davis. "The water is clear, so you can catch a lot of fish on topwater lures, and the fish may be as heavy as 3 or 4 pounds. Ouachita is also a great night fishing lake, especially between May and July. That's when I've caught the majority of my biggest fish here."

Were a bass fisherman limited to a single lure on Ouachita, the choice would likely be a three-inch smoke-colored plastic grub, fished on a 1/4-ounce leadhead and 8 to 10-pound-test line. It was Davis' bread-and-butter lure during his guiding years here, and it remains a favorite for other guides still working the lake.

In the spring another favorite fishing technique for the rocky points and flats is working a six- or eight-inch plastic lizard on a Carolina-rigged along the inside edge of the grassline. For springtime night fishing, which is best during the full moon, big, single-blade spinnerbaits produce excellent results.

Because Lake Ouachita may fluctuate as much as 15 feet during the year (it is drawn down during the winter months), the milfoil does not necessarily play as heavy a role in the fishing as one might think. It is most important when the water is high, which is normally from late spring to early fall. In early spring, anglers fish the inside edge, then as the season progresses they fish over the top of it, and later in the summer they concentrate on the outside edge.

When the water is low during the cold-weather months, anglers concentrate more on the lake's humps, points, and channels. Jigging spoons are excellent winter lures here, along with Carolina rigs and even deep-diving crankbaits. One of the attractions for anglers coming to Lake Ouachita, in addition to the chance of possibly hooking a really big bass, is the fact so many varied techniques can be used.

Striped bass fishing here is excellent, especially in the early spring. At least two fish topping 50 pounds have been recorded, and numerous others in the 30- to 40-pound class have been caught. In the spring the fish migrate up the Ouachita River and are most often caught with live baits. The fish also school on the surface in the fall and can be taken on large topwater or shallow-running jerkbaits.

Smallmouth were first stocked in 1996 in the deeper water near the Lake Ouachita dam. As this is written, regulations still require any smallmouth caught to be released immediately, but the fish are beginning to spread throughout much of the rest of the lake. Carolina rigs, tube jigs, and occasionally spinnerbaits are the most productive lures for them.

RESOURCES

Gearing Up: Lake Ouachita bass fishermen can choose between light-action rods and 10-pound-test line or medium/heavy-action tackle and lines of 17- or 20-pound test, depending on the type of fishing being done. Most opt on the lighter side. Striped bass fishermen use heavier rods and lines, especially when fishing live baits in spring. Lure choices for largemouths range from 3/8- and 1/2-ounce jigs for use on the bottom to big topwater chuggers that can be fished on the surface. Other choices include 1/2-ounce and heavier spinnerbaits, medium- to deep-diving crankbaits, and plastic lizards and grubs.

Accommodations: Motel and restaurant facilities are available in Hot Springs. Camping is available at Lake Ouachita State Park as well as throughout the adjoining Ouachita National Forest.

Additional Information: Arkansas Game & Fish Commission, Fisheries Division, #2 Natural Resources Drive, Little Rock, AR 72205; 501-223-6300.

21 BULL SHOALS LAKE

Location: Northwestern Arkansas and southwestern Missouri near the city of Mountain Home, Arkansas.
Short Take: 45,400 acres; clear water, rocky shorelines and cliffs, gravel points, numerous tributary creeks and coves, no vegetation.
Primary Species: Largemouth, smallmouth and spotted bass.
Best Months: March through May.
Favorite Lures: Plastic tube jigs and worms, crankbaits, topwaters.
Nearest Tourist Services: Mountain Home.

WITH THE EXCEPTION OF TOLEDO BEND RESERVOIR IN TEXAS AND LOUISIANA, it is doubtful any lake in the United States has created as many bass fishing legends as has Bull Shoals Lake in northwestern Arkansas. The number of bass fishermen who learned their trade here and went on to become prominent in the sport or industry—personalities like Virgil Ward, Charlie Campbell, and Forrest Wood to name just three—is amazing, but there's a good reason why it happened. Shortly after impoundment in 1951, Bull Shoals began producing truly awesome catches, and anglers from far and wide traveled here to take part in the action.

Those were the halcyon days of American bass fishing, of course, but today, nearly half a century later, this 45,400-acre lake on the White River continues to produce excellent fishing. The lake can be extremely challenging due to the generally clear water, but largemouths weighing more than 13 pounds have been caught here, as have smallmouths topping 7 pounds.

Overall, Bull Shoals is a winding river-type lake with dozens of tributary creeks and an uncountable number of smaller coves along its more than 700 miles of shoreline. Depths tend to fall rapidly along much of the shoreline, increasing the importance of depthfinder readings. Many fish, particularly smaller spotted bass, may be caught at depths of 50 feet or more.

Among the favorite fishing areas are Howard, Jimmie, Sister, and Gulley Spring Creeks, all located on the lower half of the lake. Each features shallow flats and gravel points where the bottom does not fall away quite so quickly. These are also very large tributaries where fishermen could literally spend days fishing all the points and coves available to them.

A number of different techniques work well, depending on the season of the year. Due to its location in northern Arkansas, Bull Shoals experiences a water "turnover" in late May and again in November. By far the most popular time on the lake is between March and May when bass move shallow to spawn. During this time, topwater lures attract a lot of largemouth bass, while small plastic tube jigs and crankbaits catch smallmouth and spotted bass.

The topwater fishing is what most visiting anglers tend to remember about Bull Shoals. The very idea of tossing a Zara Spook, Chug Bug, or some other surface lure

Bull Shoals Lake
Arkansas/Missouri border

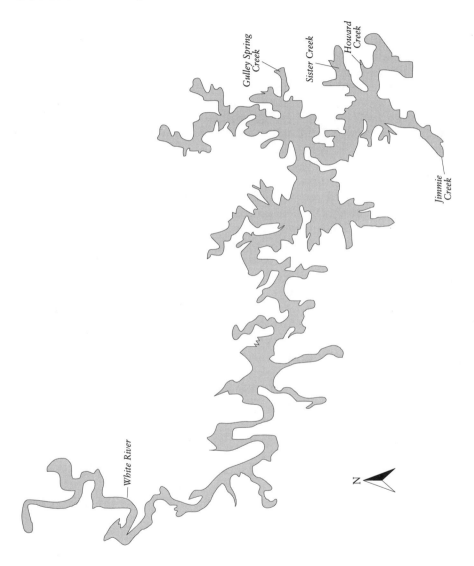

out over water 50 feet deep seems preposterous, but at Bull Shoals big largemouths rocket up out of the depths and clobber the lures with a vengeance. This is how the aforementioned Charlie Campbell became legendary as a topwater angler; his years of experience on this lake basically rewrote the book on topwater bass fishing.

Small plastic jigs and spinnerbaits work equally well at Bull Shoals—this is where Virgil Ward developed the famous Beetle Spin lure—especially when worked slowly and methodically down the gravel points and around the rocks.

Summer fishing is generally slow on Bull Shoals, leading many anglers to do their fishing at night. Plastic worms or jigs are favorite lures then because the fish are often holding off the edges of the points and bluffs at depths of 20 feet or more. In the winter, jigging spoons can be productive when fished along channel banks and the cliffs.

The extremely clear water in Bull Shoals generally dictates the use of light lines (with the exception of topwater lures), especially when fishing plastic tube jigs and spider grubs. Underwater visibility is generally 10 feet or more. The lake level does fluctuate as much as 50 feet annually, due to rainfall, and when it does rain, some of the tributaries turn dingy very quickly.

Typically, the smallmouth at Bull Shoals inhabit slightly deeper water than largemouths, although both species normally can be found in the same tributary creeks and even on the same rocky points. Small plastic tube jigs are among the most productive smallmouth lures, although the bronzebacks will also hit both topwaters and crankbaits.

In 1989, the Arkansas Game and Fish Commission, assisted by local businesses and sportsmen's clubs, began one of the largest fish habitat enhancement programs ever undertaken on a freshwater lake The project took four years to complete, and the resulting improvement in fish catches is still being felt today. More than 40,000 trees were sunk in 20 to 25 feet of water, creating 400 different sites along some 23 miles of shoreline. The sites are marked with shoreline signs, and are maintained on a rotational basis by the addition of more trees every few years.

Because Bull Shoals is maintained by the U.S. Army Corps of Engineers and the lake level fluctuates so much, there is virtually no shoreline development around the lake. A wooded buffer zone surrounds the lake, and while fishing and hunting are allowed from the shore, no motorized vehicles are permitted. Even the marina operators lease their facilities from the Corps.

There is no shortage of Corps-maintained public use areas, and camping is popular all around the lake. There are also more than two dozen resorts in the area, all catering to fishermen. With so much available, it's no wonder Bull Shoals has produced the legendary anglers it has.

RESOURCES

Gearing Up: Most anglers prefer light- or medium-action rods for Bull Shoals, and lines testing 6 to 8 pounds. Slightly heavier lines may be used for topwater fishing. Favorite lure choices include plastic tube jigs, medium- and deep-diving crankbaits, large topwater plugs, and jigging spoons.

Accommodations: More than two dozen resorts are open in the area, virtually all providing cabin and/or lodge accommodations and restaurant facilities. Camping is offered at numerous Corps of Engineers parks around the lake.

Additional Information: U.S. Army Corps of Engineers, P.O. Box 369, Mountain Home, AR 72653-0369; 501-425-2700.

Because largemouth bass are commonly found in thick cover, anglers do not hesitate to put their lures into log jams and brush like this. Pitching and flipping jigs and soft plastic lures are the most popular techniques.

22 LAKE BISTINEAU

Location: Northwestern Louisiana approximately 30 miles east of Shreveport near Minden.
Short Take: 17,280 acres; shallow, flooded cypress, islands, sloughs, hydrilla, and coontail moss.
Primary Species: Largemouth bass.
Best Months: March through October.
Favorite Lures: Plastic worms, jigs, topwaters, jerkbaits.
Nearest Tourist Services: Minden, Shreveport.

UNLESS YOU'VE SPENT MUCH TIME BASS FISHING in the Deep South, places like Snake Island, Cowfight Slough, Sawmill Flats and Hay Meadow don't necessarily sound like places to launch a boat. On Louisiana's Lake Bistineau, however, they're but a few of the many colorfully named landmarks on this unusual 17,280-acre impoundment east of Shreveport—and in this case they're the names of excellent bass fishing hotspots.

Created in 1938 by a dam across Bayou Dorcheat, Bistineau is a shallow lake (average depth is about six feet) filled from end to end with flooded cypress trees and to some extent, hydrilla and coontail. The water is clear, but it has a blackish tint due to tannin produced by the cypress. At first glance, everything on the lake looks the same, but the sloughs, bayous and various open water ponds all have distinct characteristics as well as their own names. Practically every inch of the 25-mile-long lake has been named by local anglers, and those names appear on most lake maps.

Because the lake is so shallow and the flooded timber so extensive, successful bass fishing here often centers around locating depth changes formed by ditches or small channels, or concentrating along points and edges of the vegetation and timber. On this lake, vast areas both with and without timber can easily be classified as flats, so it's important to look for some feature that breaks up the monotony of those flats.

Veteran timber fishermen have learned to look at the trees themselves to try to pattern bass. For example, the fish may be around only the largest trees, or beside small clumps of trees, or on the points of a larger cluster of trees. Any tree out of line along a row of flooded trees may be the key spot, while at other times only those trees along the edge of a deeper channel will hold fish.

Others concentrate on the small openings or ponds inside the timber. Some of these are only a couple of casts wide, but they frequently have a slight depth change (perhaps a foot or so) that can be enough to attract bass. The lack of trees in these places also allows more direct sunlight on the water, which gives them a different temperature from the surrounding areas.

LAKE BISTINEAU
LOUISIANA

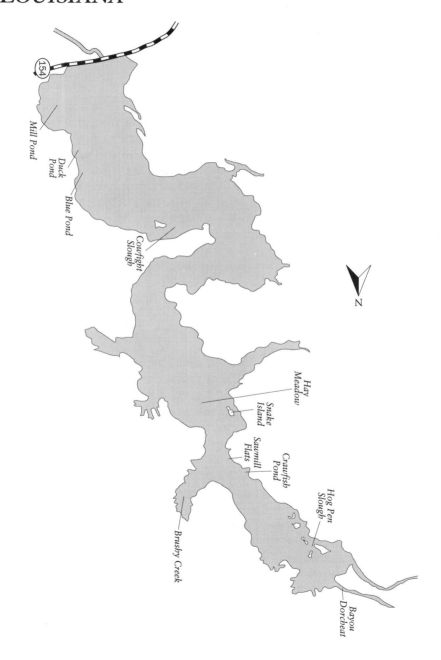

Mill Pond

Duck Pond

Blue Pond

Cowfight Slough

154

N

Hay Meadow

Snake Island

Sawmill Flats

Crawfish Pond

Hog Pen Slough

Brushy Creek

Bayou Dorcheat

The lower part of Lake Bistineau offers more open water, although flooded cypress is abundant along the shorelines and is especially thick near the dam. Hydrilla and coontail are prominent in this part of the lake, notably in places like Blue Pond, Duck Pond, and Mill Pond—all open-water pools in the timber. Most of the fishing, particularly in spring and winter, is by pitching jigs or plastic worms to the trees and working through the vegetation.

Cowfight Slough, located along the western shore four miles north of the dam, is a similar area filled with both flooded cypress and vegetation. Here the hydrilla often grows all the way out to the Bayou Dorcheat Channel itself, which provides that magical combination of depth and cover simultaneously.

Farther up the lake the Hay Meadow, which was actually a meadow before the lake flooded, is a large flat with seven- to 10-foot depths and scattered cypress. It's a good spring spawning area, as well as a place to possibly find schooling bass in the fall. This is one of the few lakes anywhere where schooling fish may all be 5-pounders.

Sawmill Flats and Crawfish Pond, both along the western side of Bistineau, are two of the better-known fishing areas in the upper part of the lake. At Crawfish Pond the Bayou Dorcheat Channel makes a sharp bend to the east but current continues flowing straight, thus giving Sawmill Flats constantly moving water. Not only is the water moving, it's also cooler, which makes this an excellent spring and summer fishing area. The water is so cool, in fact, that bass on Lake Bistineau spawn first in the lower end of the lake rather than the upper end; the difference is about two weeks in March and April.

Directly across the lake from Sawmill is one of Bistineau's larger tributaries, Brushy Creek. The 10- to 12-foot channel here is very well defined, making it an excellent early spring spot. In the summer, however, the creek usually fills with hydrilla and is not that productive.

One additional area, Hog Pen Slough in the far upper end of the lake, is worth mentioning as a spring fishing area. Located between several small islands and a large timber flat, it receives water from the small tributary of Boone Creek. This constant flow produces the same moving water/cooler water condition as at Sawmill Flats and makes this an excellent spring and summer area.

Throughout the year, the most productive lures throughout the lake are jigs and plastic lizards and worms, since virtually all casting is to specific targets. More and more fishermen are using the soft plastics on short-leader Carolina rigs, due to the brush and tree roots along the bottom, while jig fishermen have never stopped using the famous green/white bucktail that has been a Texas/Louisiana favorite for more than three decades. Topwater lures with front and/or rear propellers are excellent summer lures for fishing around the timber with a stop-and-go retrieve, and some use topwaters for autumn schooling bass, too.

Needless to say, any first-time visitor to Lake Bistineau needs a good map, not only to show the location of the main channel but also to pinpoint the sloughs, flats, ponds, and islands by which the local anglers describe the lake. After all, when you ask directions to the Hay Meadow and someone says to follow Cockle Burr Slough north to the Plum Orchard, ease through the cut to Bird Island, then continue up Mud Slough to Half Moon, you've got to know where you're going.

RESOURCES:

Gearing Up: Medium-action rods are standard here, with lines testing 12 to about 20 pounds. Favorite lures include 1/2-ounce bucktail and silicon jigs, 10-inch plastic worms, and topwater prop lures.

Accommodations: Motel and restaurant facilities are available around the lake at various marinas as well as in Minden and Shreveport. Cabins and camping are offered at Lake Bistineau State Park.

Additional Information: Minden Chamber of Commerce, 110 Sibley Road, Minden, LA 71055; 318-377-4240.

23 Louisiana Delta

Location: South, east, and west of New Orleans, stretching to the Gulf of Mexico.
Short Take: Hundreds of square miles in area; shallow bayous, ponds, bays, canals, flooded marsh, hyacinths, hydrilla, flooded cypress, fallen timber.
Primary Species: Largemouth bass.
Best Months: March, April, October, November.
Favorite Lures: Plastic worms and tube jigs, spinnerbaits, jigs.
Nearest Tourist Services: New Orleans, Houma.

WHEN A FISHERMAN THINKS OF SOUTHERN LOUISIANA, his thoughts generally drift to inshore saltwater species like speckled trout, flounder, and redfish. After all, the Bayou State's saltwater fishing is legendary and attracts anglers from around the world.

Freshwater and largemouth bass do not get much consideration unless the angler has already experienced the bounty that swims in the canals, bayous, and bays near New Orleans. Those who have sampled the bass fishing here—the area is known simply as the Delta—have described it as the finest in the nation.

"The Delta is an area that is difficult to describe, simply because it's so large and has so many different types of water," explains veteran bass fisherman Sam Swett, who has fished the region for years. "It includes hundreds of square miles of swamp and canals all the way to the Gulf, and it even extends eastward across the Mississippi River.

"It is basically a marsh filled with grass and water. Many of the canals lead to ponds and lakes that may be as much as five miles across. East of the Mississippi, it's more like a prairie because there aren't that many trees. There are miles of winding canals that suddenly open into a lake that in turn leads right into another lake.

"It's okay if you get confused, because the Delta can be a confusing place."

The best part about the bass fishing in the Delta is that nearly all of it relates to shallow shoreline cover, both in the canals as well as most of the lakes. Water hyacinths are one of the dominant forms of vegetation, and they may line the edges of a canal or lake for miles. The places that seem to attract bass most often are around small ditches or cuts where water drains into the canal from the adjoining marsh.

Fishermen pitch or flip plastic worms and tube jigs, or cast spinnerbaits along the edges of these hyacinths and/or hydrilla. Normally, the water is less than four feet deep. In some canals where the hydrilla is not as dominant, small crankbaits can also be used.

Descriptions of Delta fishing locations are rarely specific. Instead, the best way to gain a basic understanding of the entire region is to study four large, well-known sections of the Delta. These are Bayou Black, Des Allemands, Venice, and Delacroix/Caernavon.

Louisiana Delta
Louisiana

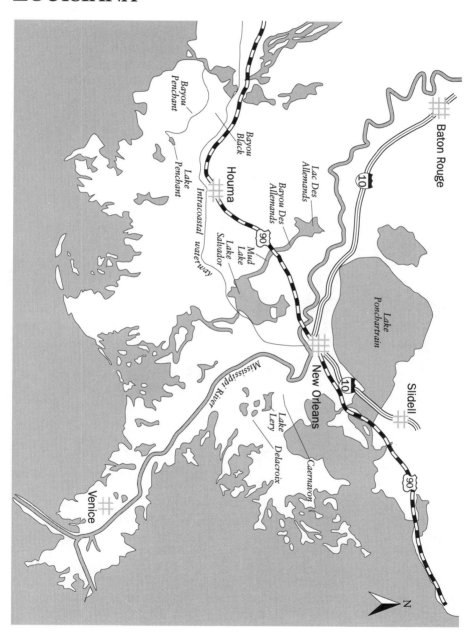

More than 300 square miles of canals, open water ponds, and flooded marsh chacterize the Louisiana Delta. It ranks as one of the south's finest bass fisheries, primarily because of the shallow cover and abundant forage.

Bayou Black, as the crow flies, is about 60 miles southwest of New Orleans, but of course you can't get there that way. It's actually easier to drive down U.S. Highway 90 to the city of Houma and launch into the Intracoastal Waterway. Even then, you still have about a 20-mile run to the west. Bayou Black is far more than a single bayou; it is a large complex of canals that includes Lake Penchant. Many of the canals lead directly off the Intracoastal Waterway and were constructed years ago for oil exploration. Now, most of them are lined with vegetation.

The Des Allemands area includes Bayou Des Allemands, Mud Lake, and Lac Des Allemands; US 90 crosses the area between Mud Lake and Lac Des Allemands about 20 miles southwest of New Orleans. This is a popular waterfowl hunting area, and duck blinds dot the open water. In the spring, summer, and early autumn, these blinds make excellent bass fishing spots, too. The western shoreline of Mud Lake has several small drainage ditches leading out of the marsh, as well as a lot of shoreline hydrilla that is fishable, as does Lac Des Allemands.

The Venice area is basically at the end of the Mississippi River, and for years it took top billing as the best bass fishing area in the Delta. Canals, flats, pools and beautiful tropical-like water consistently produced excellent catches. In 1998, Hurricane Georges lashed this area and the resulting saltwater intrusion killed thousands of largemouths. A year after Georges, the area had certainly recovered enough to again be listed as one of the Delta's top four spots, but bass fishermen today usually spend more time in Bayou Black or head east of the Mississippi to the Delacroix/Caernavon prairies.

Caernavon is only 17 miles southeast of New Orleans, but it looks totally different from most of the rest of the Delta. Here, trees are largely absent, and in their place are thousands of acres of gently waving marsh grass. Lake Lery is a popular open-water fishing area here, but many prefer to stay in the winding canals themselves. This region of the Delta has been enhanced by a special diversion canal that brings in water directly from the Mississippi, as well as by the stocking of fast-growing Florida bass. The river water has helped the spread of vegetation, which in turn has increased the habitat for forage. The result is that the largest bass in the entire Delta (now over 10 pounds) generally come from this area.

Tides also influence much of the Delta fishing. There is only one high and one low tide each day, but the water level may fluctuate two feet each time, especially in the lower part of the Delta. Another possible problem in fishing here is summer weather. It is hot and humid. The best fishing, by far, occurs in the spring and again in the fall. In the summer, some of the canals, especially in the Caernavon area, are totally choked with vegetation that makes boat navigation difficult.

All in all, however, the Louisiana Delta offers one of the nation's most fascinating and rewarding fishing experiences, regardless of which time of year an angler can visit.

RESOURCES:

Gearing Up: Because virtually all the fishing is done in and around thick vegetation and other cover, medium- to heavy-action baitcasting rods are preferred. Lines testing 14 to 25 pounds are normally used, since pitching and flipping are the primary presentation techniques. Productive lures include plastic worms, lizards, and tube jigs; willowleaf spinnerbaits, and 1/2-ounce jigs. Some topwater lures, including buzzbaits and plastic frogs, also work at times.

Accommodations: New Orleans, of course, offers a wide choice of accommodations, and the restaurant selection is equally as varied. Camping is permitted at nearby Bayou Segnette State Park, where anglers can launch and begin fishing immediately.

Additional Information: New Orleans Metropolitan Convention & Visitors Bureau, 500 Natchez Street, Suite 300, New Orleans, LA 70130; 504-525-8877.

24 TABLE ROCK LAKE

Location: Southwestern Missouri in Stone County near Kimberling City.
Short Take: 43,000 acres; deep, generally clear water with rocky points, bluffs, coves, channels, some flooded timber, numerous tributaries, no vegetation.
Primary Species: Largemouth, smallmouth, and spotted bass.
Best Months: March through June, October, November.
Favorite Lures: Plastic spider jigs, Carolina-rigged lizards, topwater chuggers, minnow-imitation crankbaits.
Nearest Tourist Services: Kimberling City.

AMONG BASS FISHERMEN, the words "deep, clear lake" immediately bring thoughts of tough, difficult fishing, ultralight lines, and small fish. Such is not the case at Table Rock Lake, a 43,000-acre impoundment along the White River in southwestern Missouri that often fishes more like an impoundment in the Deep South.

There is clear, seemingly bottomless water here, of course, but also stained water, as well. Deep coves and river channels rise to stair-stepping ledges that lead to shallow gravel flats filled with boulders, standing timber, and flooded brush. Table Rock has been so productive over the years that special fishing techniques have been developed here, and the bass are not always small, either. There are three distinct fisheries for largemouth, smallmouth, and spotted bass, with largemouths over 10 pounds and smallmouth over seven having been recorded.

Looking at a map of Table Rock leaves any visiting angler in total confusion because of all the arms and creeks snaking in different directions. The lake has nearly 750 miles of shoreline, and none of it goes in a straight line. Countless coves, cuts, bays, and lesser tributaries weave through rolling, wooded hillsides for more than 50 miles in some places, making on-the-water fishing choices difficult at best.

That's why it is imperative to divide Table Rock into distinct sections. The primary tributary is the White River, flowing in from Beaver Lake in northern Arkansas. The White has extremely clear water, but its two major tributaries, the Kings and James Rivers, are slightly stained and thus attract more bass fishermen than the White itself. Among the well-known fishing areas of the White River are Big Indian Creek, Shell Knob, Viney Creek, and Owl Creek. All offer shallow gravel flats adjacent to deeper water as well as rocky points and coves with flooded timber.

Both the Kings River, which enters the White 36 miles from the dam, and the James River, flowing into the White 18 miles above the dam, have slightly stained water, although often only in comparison to the clear water of the White. The Kings River is more famous as a float-fishing river, especially in its upper reaches where both largemouth and smallmouth may be taken. The James, on the other hand, offers several excellent tributaries of its own, including Aunts, Bearden, and Piney Creeks.

TABLE ROCK LAKE
MISSOURI

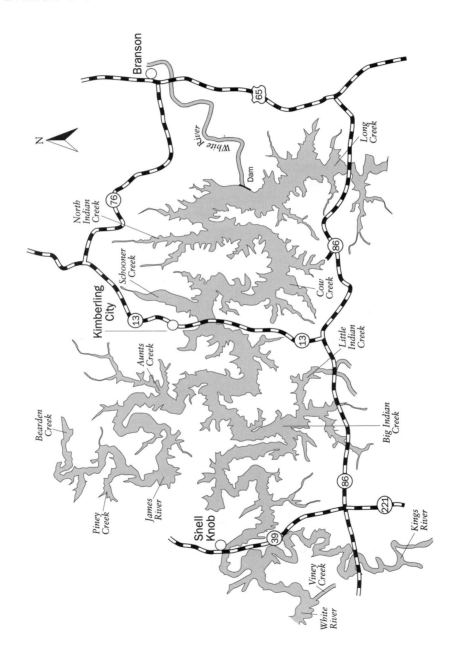

N

Branson

65

White River

Dam

Long Creek

76

North Indian Creek

86

Schooner Creek

Cow Creek

Kimberling City

13

13

Little Indian Creek

Aunts Creek

Big Indian Creek

Bearden Creek

86

James River

Piney Creek

Shell Knob

39

221

Kings River

Viney Creek

White River

Fishing any of these areas can be difficult unless local expertise is available, for the simple reason that every tributary offers dozens and dozens of rocky points and coves, and there truly isn't any way to determine which might be better than another on any particular day.

The mid-section of the lake, extending roughly between the Missouri Highway 13 bridge in Kimberling City down to Indian Creek, is perhaps the best place to start fishing Table Rock. This nine-mile stretch includes bluffs, flats, standing timber, coves, small creeks—it's a microcosm of the entire impoundment—and it doesn't involve miles and miles of boat travel. In this area, Schooner, North Indian, Little Indian, and Cow Creeks are certainly top fishing spots to consider.

Lure choice depends largely on the season of the year. In early spring, many bass will suspend in the deeper coves as they wait for the water to warm. They will sometimes hit a big, slow, wobbling jerkbait fished on the surface and simply reeled across the open water or across deep points. This technique was developed by local guides here on Table Rock and nearby Bull Shoals Reservoir years ago, and has become a standard bass fishing tactic.

When the bass move shallow in March, they're susceptible to a spider jig, a twin-tail plastic grub rigged with a 1/4-ounce leadhead, that is simply crawled along the gravel bottom in the backs of coves. If baitfish are observed in these coves, try shad-colored jerkbaits. A third choice might be to fish small plastic worms rigged Texas-style with a sliding sinker along the edges of the bluff banks around standing timber. The sheer numbers of bass that move shallow and can be observed on spawning beds here is phenomenal, and provides a prime example of just how many bass this lake holds.

After the water temperature reaches about 60 degrees and spawning has been completed, topwater lures produce well throughout the lake until mid-June. Fishing can be in these same coves, only slightly farther out over deeper water.

Throughout the remainder of the summer, Carolina-rigged worms and lizards can be fished off deeper bluffs in about 25 feet of water, but one tactic that's usually more fun is catching spotted bass out of the flooded timber. The timber, generally found in deep coves and perhaps 60 feet below the surface, is located by studying electronic depthfinders. Once the trees are located, all that's needed is a four-inch finesse worm, which is fished vertically just like a spoon. At times, as many as 40 or 50 spotted bass can be caught this way without ever moving the boat.

Later in the autumn months, spinnerbaits and crankbaits can be worked in the backs of the larger tributaries. While those creeks in the mid-section of the lake will produce fish with these lures, a larger tributary on the lower end of Table Rock, Long Creek, will be worth checking. Long Creek itself has a number of smaller creeks entering it, including Brushy and Yocum Creeks; the key to this pattern is locating schools of baitfish in these areas. Long Creek is also known as one of the better smallmouth areas.

Although Table Rock may seem intimidating at first glance, it really is not that difficult to solve the puzzle of locating bass. There are a lot of fish here, and they're biting throughout most of the year.

RESOURCES

Gearing Up: Spinning and baitcasting tackle are both popular on Table Rock, although lighter rods and lines for each are used. Light- and medium-action rods with lines testing 8 to 12 pounds are the norm, due to the clear water. Lure choices include shad- and crawfish-colored crankbaits and jerkbaits, spider jigs with 1/8- to 1/2-ounce leadheads, topwater chuggers, and small green plastic finesse worms.

Accommodations: Complete motel and restaurant facilities are available in Kimberling City as well as in nearby Branson. Campgrounds are also located in the Kimberling City area.

Additional Information: Table Rock Lake/Kimberling City Area Chamber of Commerce, P.O. Box 495, Kimberling City, MO 65686; 417-739-2564.

25 LAKE OF THE OZARKS

Location: Morgan and Camden Counties in central Missouri near Osage Beach and Camdenton.
Short Take: 58,500 acres; winding river arms with coves, rocky bluffs, boat docks, deep, generally clear water, springs, no vegetation or standing timber.
Primary Species: Largemouth and spotted bass, hybrid striped bass.
Best Months: March through May, September through November.
Favorite Lures: Jigs, plastic worms and grubs, crankbaits.
Nearest Tourist Services: Osage Beach, Camdenton, Gravois Mills.

IF THERE TRULY IS A LAKE THAT COULD BE TERMED MID-AMERICA'S PLAYGROUND, it would be Lake of the Ozarks, the 58,500-acre impoundment on the Osage River in central Missouri. More than a dozen communities surround this winding lake, each offering a wide variety of vacation options that attract visitors from throughout the United States.

Somewhat surprisingly, perhaps, this added recreation pressure probably serves to reduce the number of anglers who come here, which could be one reason the fishing is so good. Another is the fact that in 1976 the Missouri Department of Conservation imposed a 15-inch minimum length limit for largemouth bass, which generally allows the bass one additional spawning season before they can be legally harvested.

Lake of the Ozarks was formed by a dam across the Osage River in 1931, and at that time it became the largest man-made reservoir in the world. The largest tributaries are the Niangua and Little Niangua Rivers, but two creeks, Grand Glaize and Gravois, are large enough to be considered rivers. In addition, there are dozens of smaller creeks; in all, the lake has over 1,000 miles of shoreline and more than 40 miles of tributaries.

All of which could make for very confusing fishing, except for the fact one singular bass pattern ties it all together because it works anywhere on the lake. That pattern is fishing boat docks, for there are literally thousands of these structures around the lake in every cove and corner. Lake of the Ozarks is known far and wide as a boat dock lake, and if an angler has no idea of where or how to fish here, all he has to do is start fishing a row of docks.

That isn't all that's fishable, of course. Limestone bluffs form much of the lake's shoreline, and in many places local anglers have made their own brush piles. When the lake level is unusually high, some natural shoreline brush and fallen timber gets flooded in the backs of coves, and for structure fishermen there are miles of channel breaks.

Well-known professional bass angler Denny Brauer has lived near the lake for more than two decades, and his philosophy of fishing here is to divide the water into sections according to the season of the year. In the spring, for example, because

LAKE OF THE OZARKS
MISSOURI

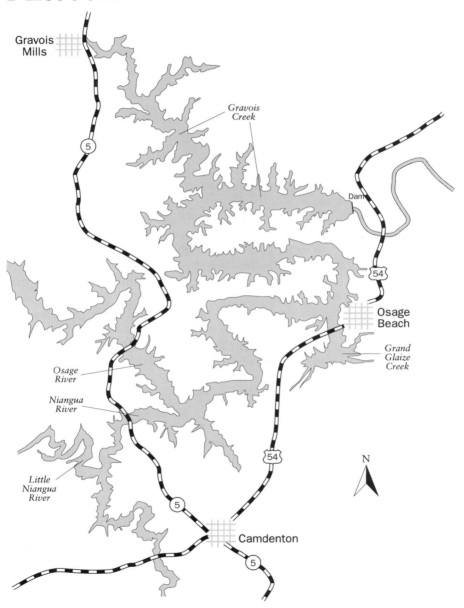

Gravois
Mills

*Gravois
Creek*

5

Dam

54

Osage
Beach

*Grand
Glaize
Creek*

*Osage
River*

*Niangua
River*

*Little
Niangua
River*

54

N

5

Camdenton

5

the Niangua and Little Niangua warm earliest, he concentrates in them. During the summer, the mid-lake region of the main Osage River and the Grand Glaize arm are his favorites, while in the autumn he concentrates in the upper part of the lake in the Gravois Creek area.

"Really," says Brauer, "there are no bad areas on the lake, and certainly not a lot of 'dead-looking' water. No matter which area of the lake or which tributary an angler may want to fish, he's going to find cove after cove with boat docks or rocky gravel bluffs and points, and bass could be on any of them."

Brauer himself has experienced a number of days when he caught 25 large-mouths over 5 pounds, and one morning years ago when he was still guiding on the lake, he and his clients caught three bass over 8 pounds and lost another over 10, all from a single rocky point. During national tournament competition here, an average weight of 4 pounds per bass is frequently required to win.

Action like this comes on several different lures, including jigs, crankbaits, spinnerbaits, jerkbaits, and buzzbaits. The jigs are generally the top producer around the boat docks, the crankbaits and jerkbaits cover the gravel coves and points, and spinnerbaits take care of flooded brush. In the autumn months when shallow baitfish bring bass up on rocky points, buzzbaits also draw a lot of strikes. Some anglers have also discovered the effectiveness of weightless floating plastic worms.

Many boat docks can be explored by flipping or skipping, as the bass hide around pilings or farther underneath the structures. Rod holders on the docks often indicate the possibility of brush piles underneath (the dock owners are fishermen and the brush serves to attract fish), and if this is the case, jerkbaits or buzzbaits may also be used. Interestingly, however, these brush piles are sometimes farther out in front of the docks rather than directly beside them.

This is the lake where suspending jerkbaits were first developed, as enterprising fishermen drilled holes in their lures, added small lead weights, and then covered them with epoxy; today, manufacturers add the weights themselves. These lures are particularly effective in the spring when bass move into the coves for spawning.

One autumn pattern that does not involve the boat docks and which Brauer himself has helped popularize is one he describes as "burning the bluffs." He uses a spinnerbait with a large size 6, 7, or 8 blade, and makes his casts parallel to the face of a long bluff. His retrieve buzzes the lure just under the surface as fast as he can turn the reel handle to bring up suspended bass.

In the summer, bass here tend to move to deeper water in the coves or off long points, depending on water clarity. The Glaize, especially, is known for its clear water, while the upper Osage tends to have more stained conditions. Big bass, however, can come anywhere, and at any season.

Striped bass and hybrid stripers have been stocked in Lake of the Ozarks since 1985. Both have done reasonably well, with 40-pound striped bass and 20-pound hybrids having been caught. Both species migrate up the Osage and Niangua Rivers in the spring, where they can be caught casting plastic minnow-imitation grubs in the current.

RESOURCES

Gearing Up: Depending on the style of fishing to be done, bass fishermen here may use light- to medium/heavy-action rods, but rarely do lines stronger than 14-pound test see much action except when the technique is flipping. Favorite lures include crawfish-pattern crankbaits, white buzzbaits, jerkbaits, jigs, spinnerbaits, and plastic worms.

Accommodations: More than a dozen communities surround the lake, offering a wide variety of motel and restaurant services. Numerous resorts are open, and Ha Ha Tonka, Missouri's largest state park, offers camping.

Additional Information: Lake of the Ozarks Convention and Visitors Bureau, P.O. Box 1498, Osage Beach, MO 65065; 573-348-1599.

26 TRUMAN RESERVOIR

Location: Osage River impoundment in West-central Missouri near Clinton and Warsaw.
Short Take: 55,600 acres; flooded timber, brushy flats, clear and dingy water areas, major river tributaries.
Primary Species: Largemouth bass.
Best Months: April through June.
Favorite Lures: Jigs, deep-diving crankbaits, spinnerbaits, large plastic worms.
Nearest Tourist Services: Clinton, Warsaw.

ANGLERS WHO FISHED TRUMAN RESERVOIR in the mid to late 1980s generally described the lake as a forest with a little water added so bass could live there. At first glance, the 55,600-acre Osage River impoundment seemed better suited for birds or squirrels than fish because the flooded timber was so thick.

The bass fishing, however, was excellent once an angler figured out where the bass were located. This wasn't always easy because every flooded hardwood looked as if it should hold a fish, and there were literally miles and miles of them.

Today, many of those trees have rotted at the waterline, and while Truman's outward appearance may have changed, the quality of bass fishing remains very good. There are still hundreds of acres of visible flooded cover standing above the water, but down below, the habitat is still nearly as dense as it was when the lake was impounded in 1979.

Truman's main tributary is the Osage River, the same river that forms Lake of the Ozarks, which actually begins immediately below the Truman Dam in Warsaw. Other tributaries include the Pomme de Terre and Grand Rivers, and Tebo Creek. A smaller river, the Sac, flows into the Osage. Thus, when anyone describes fishing in Truman, the reference is always to one of these five waterways.

Each of them provides essentially riverine-type conditions but with a myriad of small coves, points, bends, and flats. Water conditions vary greatly in the different arms—Tebo Creek is clear while the Osage and Grand Rivers range from dingy to muddy, for example—which translates into an increased number of fishing options. Even though much of the timber is no longer visible, virtually all the fishing techniques still relate to this cover in one way or another.

In the summer, both the Osage and Pomme de Terre Rivers are favorite fishing areas. Crankbaits and large 10-inch plastic worms worked across the brushy flats produce well in the Osage, while jigs and plastic worms fished through the trees near the main channel produce in the Pomme de Terre.

In the spring, the clearer water in Tebo Creek and the lower part of the Grand River draw the most attention. In both areas, some of the bass actually spawn in the forks of the flooded timber, during which time they can often be taken on plastic

TRUMAN RESERVOIR
MISSOURI

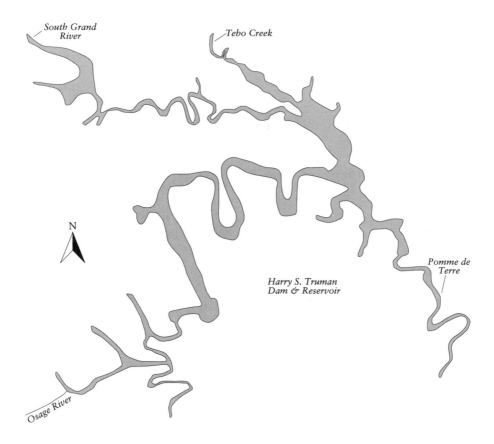

South Grand
River

Tebo Creek

N

Pomme de
Terre

Harry S. Truman
Dam & Reservoir

Osage River

worms slowly worked through the underwater limbs. One of Truman's heaviest bass ever, a 13-pound, 9-ounce giant, came from Tebo Creek.

Both the Grand and Osage have wide, shallow flats covered with brush that can be fished in spring with plastic worms and jigs, and again in the fall with deep-running crankbaits. Because of the brush and the predominantly dingy water color, jerkbaits are seldom effective lures here.

The technique of swimming a plastic worm through underwater timber is not an easy one to master, but anyone fishing Truman needs to be at least faintly familiar with it because it really is one of the most productive fishing methods on the lake. On Truman anglers prefer a 10-inch plastic worm Texas rigged with a 3/8-ounce sinker pegged on heavy line.

Because the bass are generally suspended between 10 and about 15 feet deep, the first step is counting the lure down for several seconds rather than starting an immediate retrieve. On subsequent casts this count can be extended to allow the worm to fall progressively deeper. Once the retrieve is started, the worm is slowly brought back so it appears to be swimming over the limbs and through the brush. Strikes are usually very strong, so there is no difficulty telling when a bass has hit; the important part is remembering the depth count when a bass does hit so the worm can be fished at that depth again.

Another problem frequently encountered at Truman is failing to realize the timber in itself is rarely the only factor—or even the most important factor—in determining where bass may be. Depth, especially an abrupt change from shallow to deep such as a creek or river channel, is normally more important. Anglers at Truman learn to key on depth changes within the flooded timber.

Very often depth changes can be identified by the growth pattern of the trees. For example, a change in the type of trees, such as from cedar to oaks, often signifies a depth change. Another indication may be the timber growing at an angle rather than straight, which frequently happens along the edge of a channel. Trees growing atop higher ridges of course are taller than those growing in a valley or flat, while at other times, a depth change might be located simply by slowly cruising through the timber and watching a depthfinder.

A word of warning to springtime anglers here is that Truman will rise very quickly during a heavy, prolonged rain, and at the same time it will also muddy very fast. A few years ago a three-day national bass tournament was conducted on Truman during which time it rained hard throughout the entire event. Fishermen could seldom work the same cover twice because it was going underwater so quickly! When the lake does rise rapidly, bass tend to move shallow toward the shoreline but during that particular tournament anglers could never pinpoint the fish because they were moving and spreading out just as fast as the water was coming up.

RESOURCES

Gearing Up: Because of the flooded timber and brush, bass fishermen use medium/heavy- and even heavy-action rods here, with lines testing 20 to 25 pounds. Even in the clearer water of Tebo Creek, fairly stout tackle is used. Lures include 10-inch plastic worms, 1/2-ounce jigs, and deep-diving crankbaits. Spinnerbaits can be effective in spring.

Accommodations: Motel and restaurant facilities are available in Clinton and Warsaw. Camping is available at several Corps of Engineers recreation areas around the lake.

Additional Information: Clinton Chamber of Commerce, 200 South Main Street, Clinton, MO 64735; 660-885-8166.

27 GRAND LAKE O' THE CHEROKEES

Location: Northeastern Oklahoma near the cities of Grove, Afton,and Miami, approximately 80 miles northeast of Tulsa.
Short Take: 59,200 acres, lower lake is open water with rocks, ledges, and deeper depths; upper lake includes more flats and river-type conditions.
Primary Species: Largemouth and spotted bass, limited smallmouth population in tributary rivers.
Best Months: March through May, September, October.
Favorite Lures: Jigs, spinnerbaits, crankbaits, Carolina-rigged grubs.
Nearest Tourist Services: Afton, Grove.

EACH YEAR THE OKLAHOMA DEPARTMENT OF WILDLIFE CONSERVATION ranks the state's lakes for productivity using a number of criteria tabulated from 12 months of bass tournament results, and each year Grand Lake (properly known as Grand Lake O' the Cherokees) consistently ranks at or near the top of the list.

When the average weights of winning tournament catches, the average weight per individual fish, and the number of fishing hours needed to catch a bass weighing 5 pounds or heavier are compiled, it is no wonder this scenic impoundment in the Ozark Mountains near the Arkansas and Missouri borders has become such a popular fishing destination for all of mid-America.

Created in 1940 by a mile-long dam across the Neosho River, the 59,200-acre lake has a 1,300-mile-long shoreline and an average depth of 35 feet. Other major tributaries include the Elk and Spring Rivers, as well as numerous smaller creeks.

Despite the abundance of deep water, Grand Lake looks—and fishes—more like a shallow water impoundment. That's because there are a lot of sand and rock flats, long tapering points, and gravel-bottom coves where bass can be caught less than five feet deep. The lower lake between the dam and Sailboat Bridge (U.S. Highway 59) does offer more rocky ledges and deeper water, but the upper lake from the bridge to the Elk River has shallow flats and river current.

Despite these normally productive features, most Grand Lake bass fishermen are immediately attracted to the lake's flooded willow trees. Many of the main lake points as well as some of the tributary creeks are lined with hundreds of acres of these trees. Between March and June and again in September and October, bass can usually be found somewhere in this cover, depending on the water level.

One mistake many visiting anglers make is fishing only the outside edges of the treelines, the way they might fish a grassline. On Grand Lake the bass are often much farther back in the willows. The key is staying in the right position to make long spinnerbait or jig casts into the trees, covering the entire area.

Grand Lake O' The Cherokees
Oklahoma

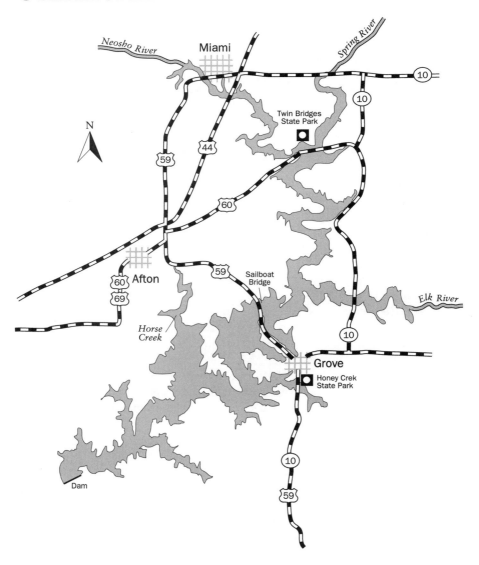

Angler John Sappington holds a nice Grand Lake largemouth caught on a jerkbait.

Among the favorite fishing spots on Grand are the Elk River, Horse Creek, and the Sailboat Bridge area. Each has not only willows but also a variety of other cover and structure, as well.

Sailboat Bridge is by far the most well-known section of the lake, and when a fisherman learns this area, he seldom needs to go anywhere else. Here there are deep coves, long points, two shallow bays filled with stumps and timber, and of course, the main river channel. Much of the bottom is covered with large rocks, too, which helps attract baitfish and keep bass in the area.

"Because the depth and cover are so varied around the bridge, you can take your pick of lures," notes former guide John Sappington. "I like to fish the rocky points with crankbaits or plastic grubs on a Carolina-rigged, but if the baitfish are active you can catch bass with spinnerbaits and even buzzbaits. Several years ago a winter

123

bass tournament was won around Sailboat Bridge with a total weight of nearly 45 pounds, and that was during three days of cold rain, wind, and sleet."

Another well-known spot is Horse Creek, a large tributary that flows into the lake south of Sailboat Bridge. If you want to throw jigs or spinnerbaits around flooded willows, this an excellent place to do it. Another technique is hopping jigs or Carolina-rigged grubs and lizards down the stair-stepping drop-offs around Blackberry Island, located in the mouth of the creek.

The Elk River flows into Grand not far above Sailboat Bridge and provides practically unlimited boat house fishing. Flooded willows line the rocky points that drop into the deeper river channel, but most anglers concentrate on the boat houses, either with a jerkbait, spinnerbait, plastic worm, or occasionally a topwater popper. Generally, the shallow-water houses hold more largemouth bass while the deeper ones have spotted bass.

The unusual configuration of Grand Lake, with its open water in the lower end and river tributaries in the upper end, helps contribute to year-round fishing possibilities in the lake. By March the bass begin moving up from deep main lake points into more shallow water, especially the flooded willow and stump-filled flats. Spawning normally occurs in April and May as the bass move farther back into shallow coves or into the brush.

This can be an excellent summer lake, too, especially if water is being released at the dam. This creates current around the main lake points and pulls fish up on top of those points. Sometimes aiming a few casts at the dam itself, where brush has washed in around some of the concrete structures, also results in some big fish.

"A friend of mine who needed a quality bass for a press photographer one summer day ran all the way to the dam from Sailboat Bridge," remembers Sappington, "and in five casts brought in three bass over 6 pounds. It can be that spectacular."

All in all, for a lake that's as old as it is, Grand Lake produces a lot of spectacular fishing, but then, the Oklahoma Department of Conservation has known that for years.

RESOURCES

Gearing Up: Everything from light-to medium/heavy-action spinning and baitcasting tackle is used here, although most bass fishermen opt for baitcasters and 12-to 20-pound test lines. Lure choices include topwaters, willowleaf spinnerbaits, both medium-and deep-diving crankbaits, soft plastic lizards and grubs, and 3/8-ounce jigs. Carolina rigs are especially productive in deeper water. Casting and pitching are favorite presentations.

Accommodations: Complete motel and restaurant services are available in Grove and Miami. Because this is a popular destination area, numerous resorts are located along the lake. Camping is available in Honey Creek Park and Twin Bridges State Park.

Additional Information: Grand Lake Association, 6807 Highway 59 North, Grove, OK 74344; 918-786-2289. Grove Area Chamber of Commerce, 104-B West Third, Grove, OK 74334; 918-786-9079.

28 Lake Eufaula, Oklahoma

Location: South-central Oklahoma in McIntosh County near McAlester and Eufaula.

Short Take: 102,000 acres; three major river tributaries, flooded timber, rocky shoreline, no vegetation.

Primary Species: Largemouth and smallmouth bass.

Best Months: March, April, September, October.

Favorite Lures: Spinnerbaits, plastic worms, jerkbaits, jigs.

Nearest Tourist Services: Eufaula, McAlester.

MANY OF THE COUNTRY'S LARGE IMPOUNDMENTS are often described as "two lakes in one," meaning water conditions in one section of the lake are completely different than conditions in another section. Oklahoma's Lake Eufaula, however, is often described as "three lakes in one." The largest impoundment in the state, one quick look at a lake map shows how accurate this description really is.

The lower part of the lake, for example, is made up of the South Canadian River and Gaines Creek with its own tributaries; the upper part of the lake consists of the North Canadian and Deep Fork Rivers; and the huge, open section of the lake where all these rivers join forms a third distinct area of the impoundment.

Overall, the lake is fairly shallow, and each of the three sections includes a lot of brush-covered shoreline, flooded willows and stumps. The bottom ranges from rock and boulders to sand and mud.

The sheer size of the lake and the variety of cover and structure combine to create many different fishing opportunities. Without question, one of the best overall areas is what is known as the Triangle, where the South Canadian River comes in from the west and meets Gaines Creek from the south not far from the city of Eufaula. The area is defined roughly by three highways, U.S. Highway 69, Oklahoma 9, and Oklahoma 9A.

Anglers here will find flooded willow flats, a long, rocky shoreline, and the riprap of the U.S. 69 bridge. Gaines Creek itself is not that popular with fishermen because much of it is filled with stumps, mud bars, old bridge pilings, and chunks of concrete, all potentially dangerous hazards for navigation.

Continuing up the lake and swinging east toward the dam, anglers have the option of fishing two extremely productive areas, Brooken Cove or Duchess Creek. Both of these spots are especially noteworthy in that they're likely to remain clear when heavy rains might muddy much of the rest of the lake.

Duchess Creek has several large coves and a lot of flooded timber, and is one of the places where bass spawn first on Eufaula. It's always a good place to swim a plastic worm or grub through the brush and stumps. Brooken offers similar flooded brush and stumps. This entire section of the lake has dozens of small coves that offer plenty of boat docks as well as brushy banks to fish.

In late April 1999, when heavy rains swept across Oklahoma and caused Lake Eufaula to rise seven feet in two days, a number of anglers learned just how productive Duchess

LAKE EUFAULA
OKLAHOMA

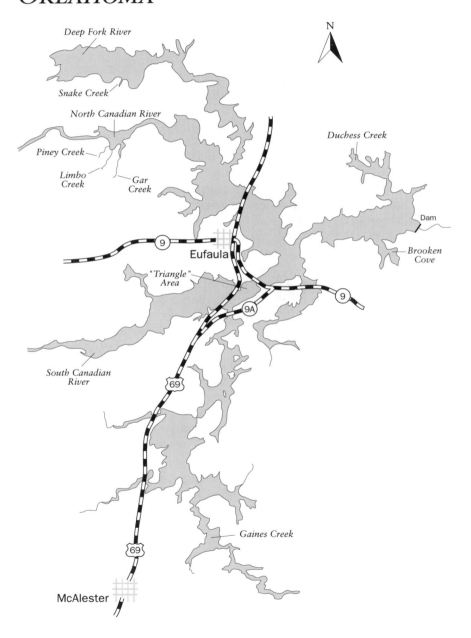

Deep Fork River

Snake Creek

North Canadian River

Duchess Creek

Piney Creek

Limbo
Creek

Gar
Creek

Dam

N

9

Eufaula

Brooken
Cove

"Triangle"
Area

9

9A

South Canadian
River

69

Gaines Creek

69

McAlester

Creek can be. Even though the water was high, the creek remained clear, and over the course of a three-day national bass tournament conducted by the Bass Anglers Sportsman Society, both first and second place finishers caught their fish here. Winner Leo Osborne weighed in an even 50 pounds, while runner-up Gary Yamamoto, literally fishing within sight of Osborne at times, weighed in 42 pounds, 13 ounces. That's more than 92 pounds of bass (a total of 27 fish) from the same area.

What happened during that particular tournament may be of interest to any anglers visiting Lake Eufaula (or any other bass lake, for that matter), in that lure presentation appeared to be more important than lure choice. On the third and last day of competition, Yamamoto caught more than 20 pounds of bass before Osborne had his first strike. He was slowly swimming a large plastic worm through the flooded bushes while Osborne, a veteran Lake Eufaula angler, was letting his plastic worm fall straight into the bushes. Once Osborne changed his presentation to a swimming one, he caught more than 17 pounds of bass in just over two hours.

The upper lake's North Canadian and Deep Fork Rivers offer thousands of acres of popular, highly productive bass water, as well. When the lake was impounded in 1964, literally miles of timber were flooded along these two rivers, and today the remaining stumps just below the surface provide that much habitat for bass. Three small tributaries of the North Canadian—Piney, Limbo, and Gar Creeks—are especially popular, while Snake Creek is a well-known tributary of the Deep Fork River.

In March and April Lake Eufaula is normally off-color from spring rains, but it certainly is not unfishable. Instead of looking for specific fish in shallow water, anglers use shallow-diving crankbaits around flooded willows, and spinnerbaits and jigs around the rocky banks.

Motorists heading north or south along U.S. 69, which crosses Eufaula several times, often get the wrong impression of this lake. From the highway, the water tends to look muddy, and indeed, it often is in these areas. What's important to remember is that only a very small part of the lake is visible from these bridges and that plenty of clear water is just a short distance away.

The water is clear enough, in fact, to support a viable smallmouth bass population. In recent years, the smallmouth have grown to as heavy as 5 pounds (largemouth here average 2 to 6 pounds). The smallmouth have spread throughout the impoundment, and are often caught on crankbaits and jerkbaits fished around some of the riprap and rocky shorelines.

RESOURCES

Gearing Up: Medium- to medium/heavy-action baitcasting rods with lines testing 14 to 25 pounds are preferred by many Lake Eufaula anglers, due to the generally off-colored water and thick cover. Favorite lures include 3/8- and 1/2-ounce jigs, plastic tube jigs and larger plastic worms, and medium-running crankbaits.

Accommodations: Lodging and restaurant facilities are available in Eufaula and McAlester as well as at Arrowhead and Fountainhead State Parks located on the lake. Campgrounds are located at these two state parks, as well as at several other locations around the lake.

Additional Information: Lake Eufaula Association, P.O. Box 792, Eufaula, OK 74432; 918-689-7751.

Fishing flooded brush is one of the most popular and productive techniques on Oklahoma's Lake Eufaula. Plastic worms, tube jigs, and spinnerbaits all produce well.

29 SAM RAYBURN RESERVOIR

Location: East Texas near Jasper.
Short Take: 114,500 acres; shallow hydrilla, underwater ridges, large tributaries and bays.
Primary Species: Largemouth bass.
Best Months: December through March, but lake open all year.
Favorite Lures: Spinnerbaits, Carolina-rigged lizards, lipless crankbaits.
Nearest Tourist Services: Jasper, Lufkin.

YOU CAN'T SEE IT, even when you launch up the lake at Caney Creek, but if you head north from there around the flooded buck brush and button willows and then cut through the remnants of the Black Forest to a little place called Peckerwood Point, you'll be about two casts away from one of the best fishing spots in all 114,500 acres of Sam Rayburn Reservoir.

Rayburn veterans like guide David Wharton say a stickup once marked the exact spot, but it's gone now, so you have to locate the precise place with electronics—two small creeks merging to form a point two feet below the surface, falling into eight and 12 feet and surrounded by hydrilla.

Wharton pulled up to the spot one February morning not long ago; his first bass weighed 12 pounds, 10 ounces and his second weighed over 7. While he was busy unhooking his first fish, his partner caught one weighing 10-8—all within a span of five minutes. The next morning Wharton returned and caught another bass over 10 pounds.

Peckerwood Point isn't the only big bass hole on this massive east Texas impoundment, of course. There's the fabled Black Forest, where a 14-plus-pounder left visiting Florida bass guide Chet Douthit's knees shaking; Harvey Creek, where South Carolina angler Carl Maxfield landed a 13-plus-pounder; and Easley Flats, which once produced more than 70 pounds of bass in two days from a 20-yard long stretch of underwater grass.

Catches like this make it easy to understand why bass fishing at Sam Rayburn is the lifeblood of the five counties the lake touches, so much so that restaurants in nearby Jasper regularly open early and motels provide late check-outs to allow fishermen a few extra hours on the water.

One of the primary influences for the lake's fishery has been the spread of hydrilla, which first appeared about 1978. In two years Rayburn went from zero vegetation to 25 percent hydrilla, which, combined with a heavy stocking of Florida-strain largemouth bass at the same time, set the stage for the future. The lake record largemouth in mid-1999 stood at 15 pounds, 8 ounces.

Here's a quick look at some of the lake's most famous fishing spots:

Black Forest: Many believe the Black Forest is a large area, but it is actually quite small and only about a third of it produces quality fish regularly. One key spot is

Sam Rayburn Reservoir,
Texas

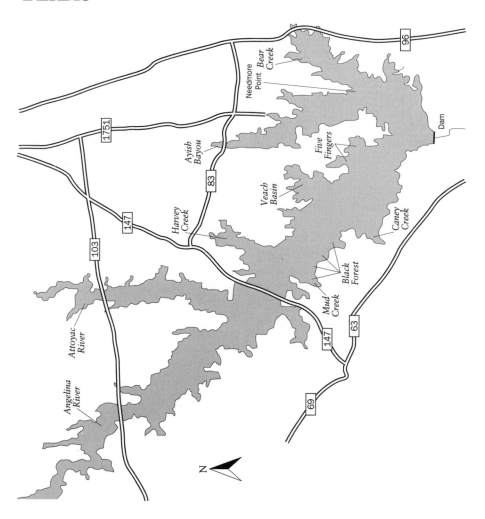

Mud Creek. Very little of the flooded timber that once characterized the forest is still standing, but it's still present underwater. Much of the better fishing is actually behind the Forest, in the shallow bays and sloughs along the shore.

Needmore Point: This is the point in the southeastern portion of the lake separating Bear Creek and Ayish Bayou. It is basically one long point that drops off, comes up, and drops again. There is no standing timber but plenty of hydrilla, as well as several small ditches that give good depth variations.

Veach Basin: Two major creek channels plus several smaller ones meet and crisscross here. Everything a fisherman could want is present: flooded timber, hydrilla, shoreline willows, and depth changes.

Harvey Creek: One of the larger tributaries, Harvey Creek provides hydrilla as well as flooded willows and shoreline brush. You could spend three days in here and not fish it all.

Lure selection for most of Rayburn is easy. The best overall choice is a tandem willowleaf spinnerbait, ranging from 3/4 ounce in spring when the vegetation is still deep, to as light as 1/8 ounce in summer when the vegetation is closer to the surface. Other favorites include Texas-rigged worms, jigs, crankbaits, and Carolina-rigged lizards.

With each, the technique is the same: work the hydrilla, either the inside edge, outside edge, or top of it, depending on the season and water level. In early spring, anglers fish both the inside edge and top; as the water warms they move to slightly deeper water and the outside edges. In the fall the inside edge usually produces best.

Access to the different parts of Sam Rayburn is easy, because 19 of the 21 parks and recreation sites constructed around the lake have launching facilities. These sites include the four marinas on Rayburn—Twin Dikes and Powell Park on the southern end, Jackson Hill just above the Texas Highway 147 bridge on the Attoyac River tributary, and Shirley Creek Marina farther up the Angelina River.

"As big as this lake is," says Wharton, "the best advice I can give is to study a lake map and pick one area and then fish it thoroughly. Don't try to run from one part of the lake to the other because it's just too big if you don't know where you're going. Besides, all of the well-known areas are well-known because they have fish."

Especially that little creek junction behind the Black Forest called Peckerwood Point.

RESOURCES

Gearing Up: Medium- to medium/heavy-action baitcasting rods with lines testing 15 to 30 pounds are used by most. Willowleaf spinnerbaits, plastic worms and lizards, lipless swimming plugs, and medium-running crankbaits are favorite lures. Several excellent tackle stores are located near the lake.

Accommodations: Complete motel and restaurant services are available in the small community of Piney Point (Highway 1007) on the southern end of the lake as well as in Jasper 12 miles away. Camping is offered at 14 Corps of Engineers and U.S. Forest Service recreation areas around the lake.

Additional Information: Jasper Chamber of Commerce, 246 East Milam, Jasper, TX 75951; 409-384-2762.

30 LAKE FORK

Location: Wood and Rains counties near Quitman in east Texas.
Short Take: 27,690 acres; shallow hydrilla, standing timber, deep ridges.
Primary Species: Largemouth bass.
Best Months: February through April, September through December.
Favorite Lures: Spinnerbaits, jigs, Carolina-rigged plastics, spoons.
Nearest Tourist Services: Alba, Quitman, Sulphur Springs.

HER NAME WAS ETHEL, AND SINCE NOVEMBER OF 1986 she has ranked as one of the most famous females in Texas.

Most famous among bass fishermen, at least, for Ethel is the name Lake Fork guide Mark Stevenson gave to the 17-pound, 10-ounce largemouth bass he caught from the 27,690-acre impoundment near the small city of Alba. Ethel was the first bass weighing more than 17 pounds ever caught in Texas, and she immediately established Lake Fork as one of the nation's premier trophy bass fisheries.

The reputation was well deserved, for Stevenson's fish, which was later put on exhibit in the aquarium at Bass Pro Shops in Springfield, Missouri, stood as the state record until January 24, 1992. That's when angler Barry St. Clair landed a Lake Fork bass weighing 18 pounds, 2 ounces, a record that still stands as this is written. In the

Lake fork unquestionably ranks as one of the nation's top trophy bass lakes. Numerous fish in the 15 to 17 pound range have been caught in recent years.

LAKE FORK
TEXAS

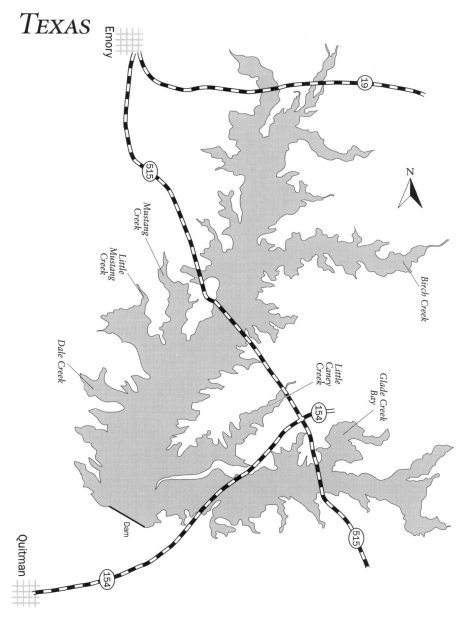

Emory

19

515

Mustang
Creek

Little
Mustang
Creek

Dale Creek

Birch Creek

N

Little
Caney
Creek

Glade Creek
Bay

154

515

Dam

Quitman

154

meantime, however, Lake Fork had also produced four other bass topping 17 pounds and five over 16 pounds. In addition, a bass weighing more than 19 pounds was found floating dead in the lake in March, 1988.

Today, big fish production has slowed slightly—only one largemouth topping 16 pounds was reported in 1999—but the lake still produces many 10-to 13-pounders each year. On anyone's list of America's trophy bass lakes, Fork ranks very near the top.

A number of factors have contributed to Lake Fork's amazing productivity, not the least of which has been a trophy management plan that has been closely monitored since the lake opened in 1980. The initial length and limit restrictions here— five bass daily, 14-inch minimum size—were soon changed to a 14- to 18-inch protective slot (bass that size must be released immediately). Current regulations have the slot increasing up to 24 inches on September 1, 2000, with only one bass over the slot to be kept.

At the same time, when Lake Fork was being developed by the Sabine River Authority, thousands of acres of standing timber were left in place, rather than bulldozed and burned. This was and continues to be valuable habitat for the bass.

"When you add hydrilla, along with the excellent water quality and heavy cover, you really do have the right recipe for big bass," notes veteran Lake Fork guide Richard McCarty, who has caught three bass over 13 and one topping 14 pounds here. "Even though the national attention the lake has received has increased fishing pressure, many of the same areas continue to produce well year after year."

Among the better-known areas are Mustang and Little Mustang, Dale, Little Caney, and Birch Creeks, and Glade Creek Bay. Bass here follow the same general movement patterns as on other lakes, but the abundant cover and vegetation allow them to spread out more.

In the summer, for instance, McCarty and other guides catch a lot of bass in the 25-to 35-foot range where they're holding in channels or along ridges. Some schooling action begins in open water in August. By September and October, surface schooling action peaks around the mouths of the large bays and creeks as both baitfish and bass gradually migrate to the backs of the tributaries, and as the water becomes colder in winter, many fish move into deeper channels.

Not all of them move to deep water, however. The heavy hydrilla in places like Mustang and Little Mustang Creeks keeps a lot of bass shallow throughout the winter. On some of the coldest days limits of 5-and 6-pound fish can be taken by retrieving shallow-running crankbaits over the vegetation, a technique that has produced more than one of Lake Fork's giants.

The best part about fishing Lake Fork is that big bass can come at any time and any place. In fact, one of McCarty's trophy bass came in a totally unexpected manner. He and two clients had located a school of surface-feeding bass, which are normally not larger fish, near Dale Creek. Because he had a spinnerbait already tied on, McCarty made a long cast, let the lure settle, and pumped his rod once. A 4-pounder hit, but on his next cast the fish weighed 11 pounds.

By February the bass are preparing to spawn, and this is when many of the heaviest fish are caught, although they may still be 20 to 25 feet deep (St. Clair caught his 18-pounder in water more than 40 feet deep). In March and April, however, spawning is in full swing in shallow water, and this is when Lake Fork sees the heaviest angler visitation of the year. Gradually the action slows and the bass migrate back to deeper summer structure.

Anglers coming to Lake Fork should always be prepared for the possibility of catching a bass weighing 10 pounds or more. To that end, the preferred lure choices include such big-fish favorites as 1/2-and 3/4-ounce jigs, Carolina-rigged lizards, and deep-diving crankbaits. Topwater fishing is popular early during the summer months, and spoons work well in winter.

Which lure is used depends on the type of cover and time of year, but at Fork much of the action centers either along the edges of the hydrilla with jigs or along channel banks and deep ridges with the Carolina rigs and crankbaits. Spinnerbaits can be fished over the top of the greenery or through shallow stumps and flooded timber.

Although it's been a number of years since Mark Stevenson caught his famous 17-pounder, this is one lake where big-fish dreams frequently do come true, and both he and McCarty believe there's another female swimming out there that could become even more famous than Ethel.

RESOURCES

Gearing Up: Medium/heavy- to heavy-action baitcasting rods with lines testing at least 20 pounds are recommended by most guides, although lighter tackle is occasionally used. Spinnerbaits (tandem willowleaf), plastic lizards, 1/2-ounce jigs, and large deep-diving crankbaits account for the most fish, with some occasionally falling to early morning topwaters. Pitching jigs along the edge of the hydrilla or casting to the deeper ridges and channels where timber is present are the primary fishing techniques.

Accommodations: Motel and restaurant services are available at many marinas around the lake, as well as in Sulphur Springs.

Additional Information: Lake Fork Area Merchants Council, Route 1, Box 22-A1, Emory, TX; 903-473-3367. Sabine River Authority, Lake Fork Division, P.O. Box 487, Quitman, TX 75783; 903-878-2262.

31 RICHLAND-CHAMBERS RESERVOIR

Location: Navarro and Freestone Counties near Corsicana in East Texas.
Short Take: 44,752 acres, filled with shallow standing timber and well-defined creek channels.
Primary Species: Largemouth bass.
Best Months: February through June.
Favorite Lures: Spinnerbaits, jigs, Carolina-rigged plastics.
Nearest Tourist Services: Corsicana, Fairfield.

IT WAS MID-AFTERNOON ON A WARM JUNE DAY, and while Alton Jones and a friend had enjoyed moderate success fishing since daybreak, they were still looking for what Jones labels a "magic spot" where the bass are big and they're all hungry at the same time.

The two anglers pulled up to an underwater hump near the mouth of a small creek named Long Arm Branch where the water is 22 feet deep, and Jones made a long crankbait cast so his retrieve pulled the lure down the hump toward deeper water. An 8-pounder slammed the diving plug before he had cranked his reel half a dozen times.

His partner made a nearly identical cast and matched Jones in his success; his bass was a 9-pounder.

The two caught 14 more bass there on consecutive casts with the crankbaits, and not a fish weighed less than 5 pounds. Then they switched to Carolina rigs and caught 20 more, including two over 10 pounds. It was the kind of day anglers everywhere dream about.

A spectacular day, but not unique on Richland-Chambers Reservoir, a 44,752-acre impoundment in east Texas near the city of Corsicana. Impounded in 1987, the lake immediately established itself as a quality bass fishery capable of producing plenty of double-digit largemouths; biologists have recorded a faster growth rate for bass here than on any other lake in Texas. The experience enjoyed by Jones has been duplicated by numerous other anglers who fish Richland-Chambers often.

The lake was formed by impounding Chambers and Richland Creeks. Both in themselves offer excellent fishing (Chambers muddies faster), but each has numerous smaller tributaries, flooded pond dams, underwater roadbeds, and literally thousands of acres of flooded timber and brush. The water quality is excellent—both drain rich, productive farmland—and larger-growing Florida bass have been stocked since 1988.

In addition to providing practically unlimited cover for the fish, the standing timber offers another benefit to the bass in that it is still so thick in places it makes

RICHLAND-CHAMBERS RESERVOIR

TEXAS

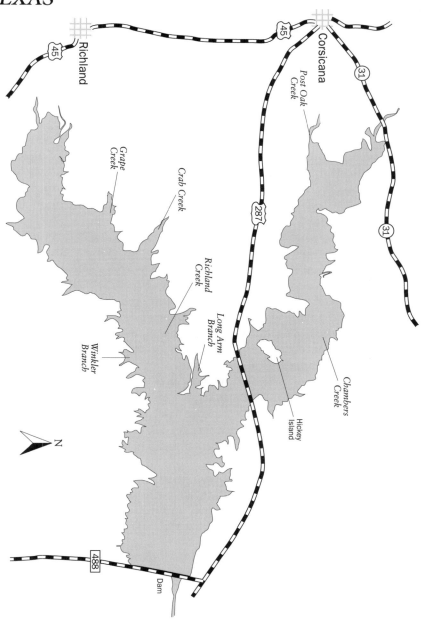

Richland

45

45

Corsicana

31

Post Oak Creek

31

Grape Creek

Crab Creek

287

Richland Creek

Long Arm Branch

Winkler Branch

Chambers Creek

Hickey Island

N

488

Dam

certain areas of the lake unreachable and unfishable. Every lake in America that consistently produces trophy-class bass has natural sanctuaries like this that protect the fish during the critical spring spawning season. Surprisingly, vegetation is not a primary factor on Richland-Chambers like it is on many other east Texas impoundments.

Most veteran anglers here agree there are two primary ways to fish Richland-Chambers. One is to cast spinnerbaits and jigs to the standing timber in water less than five feet deep, and the other is to work crankbaits and Carolina rigs over humps, ledges, and natural points in deeper water down to about 30 feet.

In either instance, however, the key is concentrating on creek channels. The most productive shallow-timber spots on this lake are always along the edges of a channel, and the best underwater structure will always be close to a deep channel.

The best-known tributary creeks include Grape, Crab, and Post Oak Creeks and Winkler Branch. All are similar in that each features a very well-defined channel that bends and turns through a maze of shallow flooded timber. Sometimes, especially in the winter months, better fishing takes place in the mouths of these tributaries rather than farther back in them; local anglers Ron Speed and his son Ron Jr., who have fished Richland-Chambers often, still remember a January day at the mouth of Grape Creek where they caught one 9-pounder and two over 8 in a just few minutes of casting.

Another locally famous spot is Hickey Island, a large island in Chambers Creek surrounded by brush and timber where the sandy bottom slopes gradually down to 10 feet, then falls quickly to 25 feet into the Chambers Creek channel. Sunken roadbeds around the eastern and southern sides of the island, as well as the mouth of nearby Little Cedar Creek, offer additional structure and changing depth.

This is not really a lake where someone can move down a shoreline and expect to catch a lot of bass like they may do on other impoundments. The reason is because of all the timber and the sharp channel drops. Even in the middle of the flooded timber, depth changes are critical.

Because of the heavy cover, favorite lures on Richland-Chambers include 1/2-ounce willowleaf spinnerbaits that can be slow-rolled through the brush without much danger of snagging; 3/8-and 1/2-ounce jigs that can be flipped and pitched to individual trees; and lizards and french fry-type soft plastic lures that can be Carolina-rigged over deeper structure. With all of these lures, lines testing 20 to 30 pounds are standard.

Many fishermen here use deep-diving crankbaits because they will cover a lot of deep water in a hurry. In the summer and again in the early winter, bass often gather in big schools but sometimes only in a small area the size of a truck. An angler can spend a lot of time searching for schools like that, and a crankbait makes it much easier.

Which is exactly why Jones always has at least one of the deep divers tied on his rods. He hasn't forgotten that magical spot he found near the mouth of Long Arm Branch.

Crankbaits, spinnerbaits and jigs are among the preferrred lures at Richland-Chambers, and when fished carefully around all the standing timber, big bass like this are often the result.

RESOURCES

Gearing Up: Medium to medium/heavy-action baitcasting rods with lines testing 20 to 30 pounds are preferred here, due to the heavy cover. Jigs, spinnerbaits, deep-diving crankbaits, and plastic lizards and crawfish imitations cover deep and shallow water year-round; pitching and short casting to visible cover are the primary presentations.

Accommodations: Complete motel and restaurant services are available in Corsicana and Fairfield. Camping is available at Oak Grove Campground as well as at the lake's two marinas, Clearview and Midway Landing.

Additional Information: Corsicana Area Chamber of Commerce, 120 North 12th Street, Corsicana, TX 75110; 903-874-4731.

32 LAKE AMISTAD

Location: Rio Grande River impoundment along the Texas/Mexico border near Del Rio.
Short Take: 67,000 acres; large rocky canyons but only one major tributary; widespread hydrilla.
Primary Species: Largemouth and smallmouth bass.
Best Months: February through April, October, November.
Favorite Lures: Spinnerbaits, crankbaits, large plastic worms, topwaters.
Nearest Tourist Services: Del Rio.

THE LAST THING SERIOUS FISHERMEN WOULD EXPECT TO SEE IN A DEEP, clear-water lake is hydrilla, but at Lake Amistad this fast-growing Asian weed has become widespread, and as a result, the bass fishing has improved dramatically. In fact, since it first appeared about 1994, the hydrilla has totally changed how anglers fish the 67,000-acre impoundment.

Located along the Texas/Mexico border, Amistad has been often described as a blue gem in a brown desert, a description referring to the beautiful blue lake set in a semi-arid countryside characteristic of this part of Texas. In addition to the Rio Grande, the primary tributary is the Devils River. The Pecos River, also considered a tributary by some, does not flow into the major part of the lake, but rather enters the Rio Grande more than 60 miles above the dam. Several smaller creeks feed both the Rio Grande and Devils Rivers.

The entire area has been designated the Amistad National Recreation Area, and is administered by the National Park Service. This means there is no residential and extremely limited commercial development along the shorelines. At Amistad, there are just three full-service marinas, although launching ramps and picnic areas are located around the lake. A Mexican fishing license, available at the marinas, is required to fish the Mexican side.

"Lake Amistad is more of a shallow-water spinnerbait fishery now," notes south Texas resident Mike Hawkes, who has fished Amistad practically since its impoundment in 1969. "Before the hydrilla, we fished the deeper water with crankbaits and jigs because there weren't many fish in the shallow water. Now, virtually all our fishing centers around the hydrilla, because that's where the fish stay."

What makes Amistad unusual is the way the hydrilla pinpoints the primary fishing areas. The vegetation requires soft dirt/mud for its roots, but because most of Amistad has a hard rock bottom, the hydrilla grows only in areas where silt has washed in and covered that rock. The result is long, often isolated rows of hydrilla with distinct edges. In the clear water, these edges are quite visible, allowing anglers not only to make precise, accurate casts but also to occasionally even see the fish they're casting to.

LAKE AMISTAD
TEXAS

Although the hydrilla— probably introduced from the boat or trailer of a bass fisherman coming from another lake—is now widespread throughout the lake, several areas have established themselves as key fishing spots. Among the best known of these are Castle Canyon, Tlaloc (Rain God) Canyon, Marker 17 (three canyons on the Mexican side of the lake), and the Devils River itself if you're specifically interested in smallmouth bass.

Castle Canyon is actually considered part of the Devils River, since it opens into the main lake near the mouth of the river. Here anglers find slightly stained water, particularly in the back reaches where California and Evans Creeks enter the canyon. The main part of the canyon is characterized by long hydrilla points, and there is a deep channel near the ends of those points. Frequently the water is slightly off-color in this area, which usually brings the bass more shallow.

Tlaloc, or Rain God Canyon, is the first major bay or canyon upstream from the dam on the Mexican side of the lake. Here the hydrilla tends to be more broken because of the rock/mud bottom, and there are wide, shallow flats. The water is also dingy in the back of this cove.

At Marker 17, anglers have their choice of three major canyons on the Mexican side—Zorro, Tule, and Caballo. Grass-covered flats drop into the main Rio Grande channel here, and seem to create a type of gathering or staging area for largemouths, especially around the long point separating Caballo and Tule Canyons. Caballo also has several smaller coves and canyons along its western shore that frequently hold fish.

Historically, the Devils River has been the best area of Amistad for smallmouth bass, probably due to the river's cooler, clearer water. Depending on water levels, as little as 10 miles of river may be navigable by boat, but even that short distance will put an angler into good bronzeback country. Rocky bluffs and mid-river boulders form excellent habitat here.

The preferred smallmouth lures are crankbaits and jigs worked anywhere around the rocks. Although there is a lot of deep water in the Devils River, the bluffs do not always fall straight into bottomless depths; there are usually some ledges or shallow rocky bottom structure to hold the fish, especially near Rough Canyon.

For largemouth around the hydrilla, slow-rolling spinnerbaits along the edge of the vegetation often results in good catches. The lake record stands at over 15 pounds, and each spring numerous bass over 10 pounds are caught with this technique. Larger 10-inch plastic worms are also popular and effective, either on standard Texas rigs or with a longer leader and Carolina-rigged. Again, the most effective method is working the lure along the edges and points of vegetation.

In Rain God Canyon where the hydrilla is frequently more broken, anglers do well by pitching jigs into the open-water holes within the hydrilla. The best places, of course, are on the shallow flats but close to the deeper channel. Topwater fishing is also productive around this scattered vegetation, especially in early spring and again in the autumn.

Lake Amistad, located on the Texas/Mexico border, is highly unusual in that hydrilla has become established in the lake, but only in areas where heavy silt has covered the generally rocky bottom.

RESOURCES

Gearing Up: Anglers here use medium- and medium/heavy-action rods and lines ranging from 10- to 20-pound test, depending on the type of fishing. Heavier lines are usually the norm when concentrating in and around the hydrilla. Productive lures include 1/2- and 3/4-ounce willowleaf spinnerbaits, 10-inch plastic worms, deep-diving crankbaits, and topwater chuggers.

Accommodations: Complete motel and restaurant services are available in Del Rio, where several motels cater specifically to fishermen. Camping is available at several designated National Parl Service campgrounds around the lake, but primitive boat camping is allowed along most of the shore.

Additional Information: Del Rio Chamber of Commerce, 1915 Avenue F, Del Rio, TX 78840; 210-775-3551.

33 TOLEDO BEND RESERVOIR

Location: Louisiana/Texas border between Hemphill, Texas and Many, Louisiana.
Short Take: 186,000 acres; filled with brush, standing timber, hydrilla and eelgrass; shallow flats.
Primary Species: Largemouth bass.
Best Months: October through April.
Favorite Lures: Lipless crankbaits, spinnerbaits, Carolina-rigged lizards.
Tourist Services: Hemphill, Texas; Many, Zwolle, Louisiana.

ONE NOVEMBER DAY IN 1967, Hemphill, Texas resident Tommy Martin and a friend launched their small aluminum boat in the new lake being built just out of town on the Sabine River. For weeks Martin had been watching the bulldozers—sometimes counting as many as 21 at a time—pushing down trees and brush around the Highway 21/6 bridge leading into Louisiana, and being an avid fisherman, he could hardly wait for the reservoir to fill.

"All I had that day was one lure," remembers Martin, "but it was enough. My friend and I caught 113 bass that day, and as you can see, 32 years later I'm still here and still fishing the same lake."

The lake is Toledo Bend, at 186,000 acres one of the largest man-made impoundments in the United States. It is also one of the most famous in that it helped usher in the growing sport of bass fishing, not only to Texas and Louisiana but to the entire United States. Martin went on to become one of the premier guides on Toledo and later a top-ranked professional tournament competitor. Today, he still competes and guides regularly.

Toledo is like a number of other southern lakes in that thousands of acres of standing timber were flooded during impoundment so the bass had plenty of cover and habitat. Then, in 1975, hydrilla first appeared in the lake, and it added to the habitat.

Larger-growing Florida-strain bass were first stocked in 1985 and have been stocked regularly ever since, so not only does the lake produce a lot of fish, it's producing a lot of big fish. The lake record stands at over 15 pounds.

Toledo Bend stretches more than 65 miles from end to end, and with all its bays and tributary creeks embraces more than 1,200 miles of shoreline. The lake is characterized by wide, shallow flats where the water is seldom deeper than 10 feet; bays and tributary creeks choked with standing timber, stumps, and hydrilla; rolling ridges where the depth may drop abruptly from three to over 30 feet; and well-defined creek channels that wind for miles through the Texas and Louisiana countrysides.

The Highway 21/6 bridge at Pendleton Harbor between Milam, Texas and Many, Louisiana, is considered mid-point of the lake.

TOLEDO BEND RESERVOIR
TEXAS/LOUISIANA

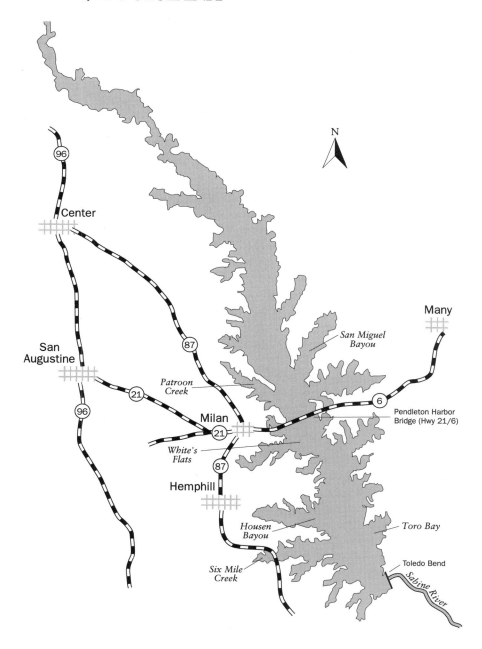

Because it is too far to run from one end to the other, most fishermen concentrate either above or below the bridge. In the fall and winter months, the lower end south of the bridge tends to produce better fishing while in the spring and summer the upper part of the lake is better.

The following areas are among the better-known fish producers on the lake:

White's Flats: This is a large, shallow, hydrilla-filled flat located just south of the Pendleton Harbor Bridge on the Texas side. Water depth ranges from two to about 10 feet deep with a few deeper ditches, but most of the brush has been cleared. It produces excellent crankbait fishing in the fall.

Housen Bayou: This is another large bay on the Texas side located south of White's Flats. Hydrilla is present, but the bay is also filled with stumps and flooded timber. The river channel cuts along the outer edge of the bay, which may be why this is a good big bass area.

Toro Bay/Pirates Cove: Located near the dam on the Louisiana side, Toro Bay offers underwater ridges, islands, vegetation, flats, and some of the clearest water on the lake. It's a major spawning area in the spring.

San Miguel Bayou: A large bayou on the Louisiana side just north of the bridge, local anglers and even some maps call this "Sammy Gill Bayou." It opens into another equally well-known area, the 1215 flats, named for the old flooded roadbed here. It's a stumpy area with hydrilla and a lot of five-to eight-foot water that drops into 12-to 15-foot ditches. This is one of the best-known areas of the entire lake and provides good jig and worm fishing.

Patroon Creek: There's a well-known story on Toledo about one guide who never left this creek with his clients for a full year because it's that good. Located north of the Pendleton Bridge on the Texas side, it produces a lot of big bass on plastic worms, jigs, and spinnerbaits.

Despite its huge size, Toledo Bend is actually a friendly lake for first-time anglers, especially if a fisherman chooses one of the better-known areas and stays in it. The boat lanes through the timber are buoyed and cleared, and in many instances, it takes hours to thoroughly fish a single wide flat or one of the creeks anyway.

Lure choices include 1/2-ounce red/crawfish-colored lipless crankbaits for the shallow flats, 1/2-ounce willowleaf spinnerbaits for the brush, and both Carolina-rigged and Texas-rigged lizards for the ridges and ditches. Jigs are excellent choices for fishing the edges of the hydrilla.

Martin, in fact, is the angler most often credited with developing the technique of deep-jigging in the hydrilla. When the Asian weed began appearing in the lake and matting on the surface, he donned diving mask and flippers to see what it looked like underwater. What he found was that while the vegetation was thick on top, it was actually open a few feet below the surface. Not only that, the open water was full of bass.

No manufacturer made a jig heavy enough to break through the hydrilla mat, so Martin added sinkers to his own jigs and began catching enormous fish, including one tournament-winning stringer of more than 83 pounds. Today, fishing heavy jigs through matted hydrilla is a common technique on lakes wherever the grass is found.

RESOURCES

Gearing Up: Medium to medium/heavy-action baitcasting and pitching rods with lines testing 12 to 25 pounds are the most popular. Lipless crankbaits are excellent spring lure choices, as are willowleaf spinnerbaits. Texas-rigged plastic worms and lizards still catch a lot of bass here, but Carolina rigging is increasing in popularity.

Accommodations: Lodging is available at more than two dozen marinas around the lake, many featuring kitchenettes or cabins. Restaurants are also available in Hemphill, Milam, and Many. Some marinas also have campgrounds; additional camping opportunities are available in the nearby Sabine National Forest on the Texas side.

Additional Information: Toledo Bend Tourist Information Center, 15091 Texas Highway, Many, LA 71449; 800-259-5253.

34 LAKE TEXOMA

Location: Texas/Oklahoma border near the cities of Pottsboro and Denison, Texas, and Kingston, Durant, and Madill, Oklahoma.
Short Take: 89,000 acres; fairly deep open water, rocky points and ridges, several large tributaries, little shoreline cover, no vegetation.
Primary Species: Largemouth, smallmouth, and striped bass.
Best Months: March through May, September through November.
Favorite Lures: Crankbaits and topwaters for largemouth and smallmouth bass, plastic grubs for striped bass.
Nearest Tourist Services: Pottsboro, Kingston, Durant, Madill.

JIM MORTON HAS FISHED LAKE TEXOMA LITERALLY HUNDREDS OF TIMES over the past 45 years, but one September trip not long ago stands out. In less than eight hours, Morton and his partner Bob Myers boated more than 50 largemouth bass, all on topwater lures, and the fish were still biting when they had to leave.

What makes Morton's day so special is that Lake Texoma, created by a dam across the Red River in 1944, is certainly well past what most would consider its prime. Nonetheless, the huge, sprawling lake continues to provide not only excellent largemouth fishing but also fine action for smallmouth and striped bass.

The lake backs up both the Washita and Red Rivers and forms the boundary between Texas and Oklahoma along much of its length. Two major highways, U.S. Highway 70 between Kingston and Durant, and Oklahoma 99 between Whitesboro, Texas, and Madill, Oklahoma, cross the lake and provide easy access. More than a dozen marinas and fishing camps dot the 580-mile shoreline.

Texoma's early fame revolved around striped bass, which were originally stocked in 1965. At one time as many as 200 guides offered fishing trips to visiting sportsmen, and the fish were plentiful enough that skilled guides could take out two separate parties in a single day. This is one of the few lakes where striped bass reproduce naturally, and fish weighing more than 35 pounds have been taken here. Today, most stripers caught weigh less than 10 pounds, but they are still plentiful and a popular attraction.

Texoma's deepest water is located near the dam, and it is in this deeper water where much of the striped bass action takes place. In the mid-1970s when striped bass fishing was in its heyday here, this open water was known as Striper Alley, and guide boats literally lined up to troll their deep-diving crankbaits—the famous Hellbender lure was developed in nearby Sherman just for Texoma stripers—but today the guide boats work throughout the lake and use either live bait or soft plastic lures.

Over the decades, Texoma's once plentiful shoreline cover has rotted away and left the banks largely barren of suitable habitat for largemouth bass. Thus, nearly all serious fishing for them takes place in several large tributary creeks or on main lake points.

LAKE TEXOMA
TEXAS/OKLAHOMA

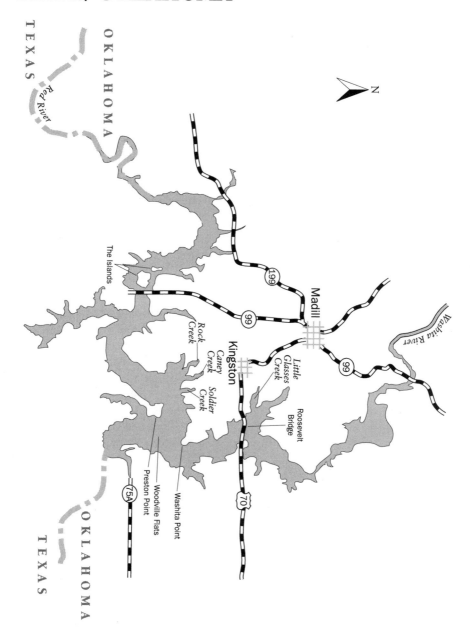

The four most popular tributaries are Little Glasses, Rock, Caney, and Soldier Creeks on the Oklahoma side of the lake. Each offers not only rocky shoreline points and dropoffs, but also some shallow water with brush and laydowns. Equally important, these tributaries also offer protection from the wind, which can be a serious problem in spring and fall.

Other well-known fishing spots include Washita Point, a long, jutting peninsula on the Oklahoma side where the Washita River, flowing in from the north, joins the Red River coming in from the west; and Preston Point, a tall, rocky promontory on the Texas side across from Washita Point. Between these two points is an excellent fishing area known as the Woodville Flats, where the depth rises suddenly from 80 to 15 feet. The channel of the Red River runs very close to Preston Point while the Washita River channel cuts close to Washita Point, all of which combine to provide the classic shallow-water/deep-water combination bass love.

Still another popular area is known as The Islands, which consists of two major islands, North and Treasure, and a stump field that lies behind them. The Red River channel runs between these stumps and the shoreline and provides deep water adjacent to shallow water. It's a great summer and fall fishing area because bass school here in the shallow water.

Smallmouth bass, which have attained weights of over 7 pounds in Texoma, have spread throughout much of the lake. In years past, most smallmouth activity centered along the steeper, rocky shoreline on the Texas side of the lake near the dam, but today the fish are caught throughout Texoma. One especially well-known area that tends to produce larger smallmouths is Bowman Point, located on the Oklahoma side of the lake a short distance up the Washita arm.

Lure choices for largemouth and smallmouth include crankbaits, topwater lures, and soft plastic grubs rigged on jigheads. Some spinnerbait fishing is productive in spring when water levels tend to be higher and flood some shoreline cover, but overall, this is a lake where a lot of casting will be to unseen underwater targets.

Perhaps the most popular above-water casting targets are the unusual floating tire barriers put out in front of many marinas for protection from wind-driven waves. These long rows of automobile tires are especially attractive to largemouths, and rare is the day when someone doesn't catch at least one fish by dropping a jig or plastic grub around them. The marinas themselves also offer excellent fishing at times because they provide both shallow-water structure and shade.

Spring is a good season on Texoma, but many others prefer autumn because it's when bass hit topwater lures the best. After all, Morton and Myers aren't the only anglers who have enjoyed some of Texoma's 50-bass-on-topwaters days.

RESOURCES

Gearing Up: In winter and early spring if bass are sluggish, anglers may use 8-pound-test line here with light spinning outfits; at other times 12-to 20-pound test lines are standard, as are medium-and medium/heavy-action rods. Medium-and deep-diving crankbaits along with soft plastic grubs and crayfish imitations work well for all three species of fish. Topwater chuggers and poppers produce well in the autumn months.

Accommodations: Complete motel and restaurant services are available in Kingston, Madill, and Durant, as well as in Pottsboro on the Texas side.

Additional Information: Lake Texoma Association, P. O. Box 610, Kingston, OK 73439; 405-564-2334.

WEST

ARIZONA

CALIFORNIA

NEVADA

NEW MEXICO

UTAH

WASHINGTON

35 LAKE HAVASU

Location: Colorado River impoundment along the Arizona/California border at Lake Havasu City, approximately 200 miles northwest of Phoenix.
Short Take: 25,000 acres with 50 additional miles of river; clear and dingy water, rocky points, shoreline vegetation, weeds, current, one tributary.
Primary Species: Largemouth and striped bass.
Best Months: September through May.
Favorite Lures: Jigs, plastic worms, crankbaits, topwaters; plastic grubs for stripers.
Nearest Tourist Services: Lake Havasu City.

VISITORS COME TO THIS SCENIC COLORADO RIVER impoundment for many reasons: to see the original London Bridge, reconstructed here as the centerpiece of the city; to fish for striped bass that may weigh as much as 50 pounds; or simply to enjoy the dry, high desert sunshine. More and more, however, they're coming to fish for largemouth bass.

That's because the bass fishing at Lake Havasu is slowly but steadily improving, due in no small part to an ongoing fish habitat improvement project in which artificial cover is being placed throughout the lake. Natural vegetation continues to spread as well, and while a 5-pound largemouth is still a very nice fish here, more and more of them are being caught.

Lake Havasu is somewhat unusual in that while the impoundment stretches more than 85 miles between the Davis Dam in the north and Parker Dam in the south, less than 30 miles of this is really considered a lake. For most of the upper 57 miles the Colorado is contained within its banks and has an average depth of just 10 to 12 feet. Beginning at Lake Havasu City and extending southward to the Parker Dam, Havasu becomes a true lake with deeper open water.

Although the river section looks somewhat featureless on most maps, the bass fishing here can be surprisingly good. The shoreline offers hundreds of small, rocky coves, shifting sandbars, and literally miles of shoreline bulrushes and cattails (nearly always described as tules and pronounced "TOO-leez").

Fishing techniques range from crankbaiting the points and sandbars to pitching and flipping jigs and plastic worms along the edges of the bulrushes. The best spots seem to be those where the depth drops quickly out from the vegetation. When current is particularly strong, anglers often do well by pitching back into the vegetation, or by casting upstream and letting the water flow bring the lure down along the edge of either the greenery or the rocks.

The best-known upriver fishing area is Topock Bay, located just north of the Interstate 40 bridge approximately 25 miles above Lake Havasu City. Sometimes described as a big field filled with tule islands, Topoc is a shallow, off-river marsh that provides excellent largemouth habitat throughout the year. It's a favorite spot for

LAKE HAVASU
ARIZONA/CALIFORNIA BORDER

N

0   5   10
Miles

Davis Dam

163   68

NEVADA

Colorado River

40

Needles

Topock Bay

ARIZONA

Topock

95

Windsor Beach
State Park

Lake Havasu City

Friendly Island
Goose Bay

Red Rock Point
Power Line
Cove

California
Bay

Question Mark
Cove

Bill Williams
River

Parker Dam

Heron Island Cove

In the Bill Williams River arm of Lake Havasu, anglers usually concentrate on fishing the tules that grow along the shoreline

flipping plastic worms and tube jigs, and occasionally throwing a topwater buzz bait. In addition to the vegetation, Topoc also has boat docks and riprap.

In the lower part of the lake, good fishing begins in Lake Havasu City just out from Windsor Beach State Park. A lot of bass tournaments are conducted at the park, and bass are released right at the launch ramp. From there the bass can swim just a short distance either up or downriver and hide in the deep vegetation and brush that lines both sides of the main river channel, or in the artificial cover placed closer to the shore. This is a popular area for crankbaits as well as Carolina-rigged worms and tube baits.

One of the key fishing spots here is known as the Windsor Beach Flats, where the water drops abruptly from eight to 22 feet. Along one spot on that breakline there is a single huge tree (not visible from the surface) that tournament bass fishermen have been known to stay on for several days because it is so dependable.

From Windsor Beach southward the lake offers numerous coves and bays, many of them with gravel/sand bottoms and reasonably shallow depths that can all be fished with crankbaits or Carolina rigs. Some will also have vegetation and can be flipped with plastic worms.

Lake Havasu's only tributary is the Bill Williams River, which flows in just above the Parker Dam. While water remains clear in the lake and upper river most on the time, the Bill Williams arm tends to be dingy, thus making it one of the most popular fishing areas of the entire lake. Both shorelines are fairly irregular and are lined with bulrushes, and a number of places like Power Line Cove, Question Mark Cove, and Heron Island have additional fish attractors.

Although the Bill Williams River offers only three to four miles of fishable water, many prefer to concentrate on the lower end of the river around the Interstate 95 bridge crossing. Here the bullrushes are even thicker along the shorelines, and flipping is basically the only workable presentation. As in the upper river, water depths often drop quickly away from the bulrushes, and the fishing is usually better where this occurs.

Striped bass fishing takes place year-round in the open water south of Lake Havasu City, although it is probably least enjoyable during the summer when air temperatures may top 115 degrees. Trolling plastic minnow-imitation jigs is a favorite technique during the summer when the fish tend to be deeper. Beginning in early September, however, when the stripers begin schooling on the surface, and continuing throughout the autumn, anglers may catch and release several dozen stripers a day by casting to breaking fish. Because they are roaming constantly as they follow threadfin shad, the stripers are liable to be anywhere, anytime, and while some real heavyweights have been taken here, the average size is 3 to 4 pounds.

Some of the known striped bass areas include Red Rock Point, a long, narrow point of land about 15 miles south of Lake Havasu City along the eastern shoreline; behind Friendly Island in Goose Bay, about four miles south of the city; and California Bay, a large embayment on the western shore about two miles south of the city.

The Lake Havasu Fisheries Improvement Project, which began in 1993 and will continue for a decade, has designated more than 40 sites up and down the lake for habitat improvement. Several different types of artificial structures are being anchored to the bottom, and many sites cover 10 acres or more. Virtually all are located in fairly shallow water near the shorelines and are pinpointed on lake maps. The project is being done cooperatively by several different governmental agencies and is one of the largest of its type ever undertaken.

In the future, as more and more habitat is put into place, the fishing is almost certain to improve, and as that happens, more and more visitors will definitely add bass fishing as their reason for coming to the lake.

RESOURCES

Gearing Up: Everything from light-action spinning rods to medium/heavy-action baitcasters are used, depending on the technique, time of year, and species of fish. Likewise, lines can range from 8- to as heavy as 20-pound test. Favorite lures include1/4- to 1/2-ounce jigs, plastic worms and tube baits, and medium-running crankbaits. Some topwater buzzbaits are also used in the autumn. For striped bass, plastic grubs are very successful.

Accommodations: Complete motel and restaurant facilities are available in Lake Havasu City. Camping is permitted at numerous Bureau of Land Management locations around the lake as well as at commercial campgrounds near the city.

Additional Information: Lake Havasu Tourism Bureau, 314 London Bridge Road, Lake Havasu City, AZ 86403; 520-453-3444.

36 Lake Oroville

Location: Feather River impoundment 70 miles north of Sacramento, California, near Oroville.
Short Take: Approximately 15,500 acres; deep, clear water with both steep canyon walls and sloping sandy banks, rocky points, flooded timber.
Primary Species: Spotted and largemouth bass.
Best Months: April, May, September, October.
Favorite Lures: Spinnerbaits, jerkbaits, small plastic worms.
Nearest Tourist Facilities: Oroville.

IF EVER A FISHERMAN IN THE WESTERN UNITED STATES wanted to catch spotted bass, he need look no farther than Lake Oroville. This 15,500-acre impoundment in northern California offers fine spotted bass action throughout the year, and although the fish are not of record size, they're plentiful enough to keep anyone happy. No one has caught a 7-pounder here, but 2- to 5-pounders are certainly not uncommon. And, if for some reason the spotted bass aren't cooperating, anglers can change tactics and try for largemouths, which, while not as plentiful, do attain weights of over 12 pounds on this lake.

What makes Lake Oroville so interesting is its configuration, which allows anglers to try for either spotted bass or largemouths in specific areas. The lake is formed by four very large tributaries of the Feather River, the West, North, Middle, and South Forks. The West Fork and North Fork form the upper end of the reservoir while the Middle and South Forks flow in on the lower end. These four arms are where most of the fishing takes place, and each has its own personality.

The South Fork, for example, offers sloping banks, sandy flats, and an abundance of flooded oak and pine trees, which makes it an excellent area for largemouths, especially in McCabe's Cove and around the Enterprise Bridge, where spinnerbaits dominate the lure choice. The Middle Fork, by contrast, has steep, vertical walls, big boulders, and only a little flooded timber, so it's better for spotted bass and small plastic worms.

The North Fork has features of both the South and Middle Forks and provides excellent fishing in its own tributary, Berry Creek; the West Fork is characterized by rocky points, sloping banks, and large shallow coves with flooded timber, which makes it one of the most popular fishing areas for both species on the entire lake.

The two most productive areas in the West Fork are Lime Saddle Cove and Spring Valley Cove, and if you're having trouble deciding where to start fishing on the lake, or even which species you prefer, either of these well-known areas is a good place to start. Spotted bass can be found on the deeper points while largemouths live back in the timber.

Lake Oroville
California

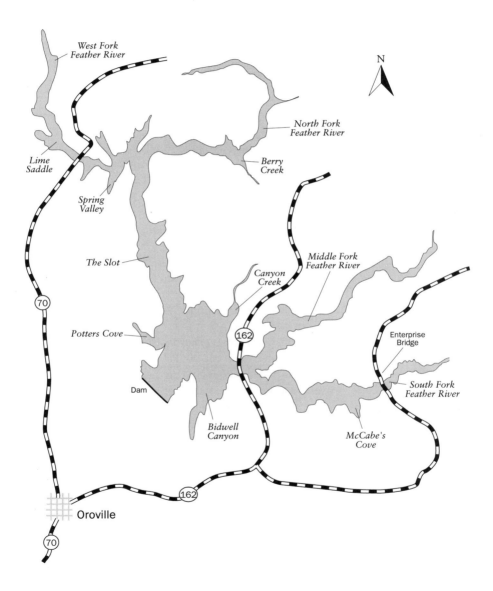

West Fork
Feather River

North Fork
Feather River

Lime
Saddle

Berry
Creek

Spring
Valley

The Slot

Middle Fork
Feather River

Canyon
Creek

70

Enterprise
Bridge

Potters Cove

162

South Fork
Feather River

Dam

Bidwell
Canyon

McCabe's
Cove

162

Oroville

70

The main body of the lake itself is relatively small, but two good fishing areas stand out for largemouths, especially in the spring. These are Bidwell Canyon, a large shallow embayment on the lower end of the lake; and Potters Cove, located up the lake along the western shore. Both of these areas offer large shallow-water areas with standing timber. The rule of thumb on Oroville is that if you're searching for largemouths, look for flooded timber, but if you're after spotted bass, stay close to the rocks.

A number of fishing techniques are used for spotted bass on Oroville, but the favorite is known as shaking a plastic worm. Thin, short finesse-type worms are rigged on 1/8-ounce leadheads and 8-pound-test line, cast to rocky points or sloping bottom in 10 to 15 feet of water, and then retrieved with a rod-shaking action. Instead of crawling along the bottom, the shaking action makes the worm appear much more erratic and keeps it slightly above the bottom. This technique is also used with a vertical presentation; the worm is counted down to a preferred depth, then simply held at that depth and shaken until a bass grabs it. Some fishermen add small glass beads to their worm rigs to increase the noise the worm makes.

Not surprisingly, the favorite plastic worms for Lake Oroville are those that are hand poured rather than injection molded. California has long been an innovator in hand-pouring, and while it is slower and more costly, the process allows manufacturers to produce textures and color combinations not ordinarily possible by machine-driven injection molds. Although both techniques produce lures of nearly identical shapes and sizes, anglers firmly believe hand-poured plastic worms are more realistic looking to the bass because of their colors.

While a lot of largemouth bass are taken here on plastic worms, two other favorite year-round techniques are spinnerbaiting around the flooded timber and fishing jerkbaits along sloping banks. Most spinnerbaiting is with the technique of slow-rolling, in which the lure is reeled slower so it stays deeper. Some skilled anglers will actually work their lures down to 20 feet through the flooded timber. Jerkbaits, fished on 8- or 10-pound-test line, cover depths down to five or six feet, and bring fish up from even deeper water.

Because this is such a deep lake, a lot of angling is done with jigging spoons on which fishermen routinely catch bass at depths of 40 and 50 feet. The key is locating schools of pond smelt, the primary forage here, and then dropping a spoon down through them. One way to locate the smelt is by slowly crisscrossing the mouths of some of the larger coves like Potters or Spring Valley, and watching a depthfinder until the schools of baitfish show up. Another way to find the smelt is by moving up on one of the long rocky points in any of the rivers and then crisscrossing it out to deeper water; somewhere along the point, baitfish will probably be found.

Lake Oroville also has a large population of crayfish, which normally makes jigs highly productive lures, but for some reason jigs are not all that popular on the lake. The reason is probably because spotted bass tend to hit plastic worms a little more reliably, and spinnerbaits cover the water faster for largemouths.

RESOURCES

Gearing Up: The clear water on Lake Oroville generally dictates the use of lighter tackle for both largemouths and spotted bass. Lines testing 8 to 10 pounds and medium-action rods are standard. The main exception is for spinnerbaiting in the timber when heavier 14- to 20-pound-test lines are used. Lure choices here include 1/2-ounce tandem willowleaf spinnerbaits, four-inch plastic worms with 1/8-ounce leadheads, 1/2-ounce jigging spoons, and jerkbaits.

Tourist Facilities: Complete motel and restaurant facilities are available in Oroville. Camping is permitted at several campgrounds located around the lake.

Additional Information: City of Oroville, 1735 Montgomery, Oroville, CA 95965; 530-538-2401.

37 LAKE SHASTA

Location: Northern California in the Whiskeytown-Shasta-Trinity National Recreation Area just north of Redding.
Short Take: 30,000 acres; unusual mountain lake with abundant shallow flats and flooded timber, four major river tributaries, no vegetation.
Primary Species: Spotted, smallmouth, and largemouth bass.
Best Months: March through May, September, October.
Favorite Lures: Plastic worms, spinnerbaits, jigging spoons, topwaters.
Nearest Tourist Services: Redding.

BASS FISHERMEN COMING TO NORTHERN CALIFORNIA'S LAKE SHASTA will find a welcome change of pace, for it isn't often that an extremely popular boating and skiing lake also happens to be such a prolific bass fishery. At 30,000-acre Lake Shasta, however, anglers will find a lake dominated by spotted bass that have topped 8 pounds, largemouths over 15 pounds, and even smallmouth bass in the 5-pound class.

"The spotted bass totally dominate the lake," notes veteran angler Gary Dobyns, who has fished Shasta for more than 20 years. "In the early 1980s before the California Department of Fish and Game stocked spotted bass here, the lake had an excellent smallmouth fishery, but now the spotted bass have taken over.

"That's not bad, by any means. The spotted bass here are extremely aggressive and provide plenty of excellent fishing all year long. And I personally believe there may be a world-record spotted bass in the lake" he adds.

California's largest impoundment, Lake Shasta is formed by four tributary rivers, the Pit, Squaw, McCloud, and Sacramento. Each of these has numerous smaller tributary creeks, as well as a wide variety of structure that includes an unusually high amount of shallow water.

"This is certainly one of the main reasons Lake Shasta supports such a high fish population," notes Dobyns. "The backs of a lot of coves are filled with standing timber or have a hard gravel bottom that provides excellent spawning habitat and high survival rates. Although the lake has plenty of big bass, Lake Shasta is not really a trophy fishery. It's much better known for its sheer numbers of fish."

Much of the bass fishing takes place in the lower end of the lake in the Pit River, which anglers generally consider one of the premier largemouth areas. Within the Pit River, the Jones Valley area is best known. The largest cove on the river with several smaller coves and tributaries of its own, Jones Valley offers excellent flats with a lot of shallow water and flooded timber. It's prime spinnerbait country. Other excellent fishing spots in the Pit include Dead Horse, Arbuckle, and Reynolds Creeks, also with timber and shallow flats.

The Squaw River (often referred to as Squaw Creek by local anglers like Dobyns) meets the Pit at, appropriately, Squaw Point. The Squaw offers excellent smallmouth

LAKE SHASTA
CALIFORNIA

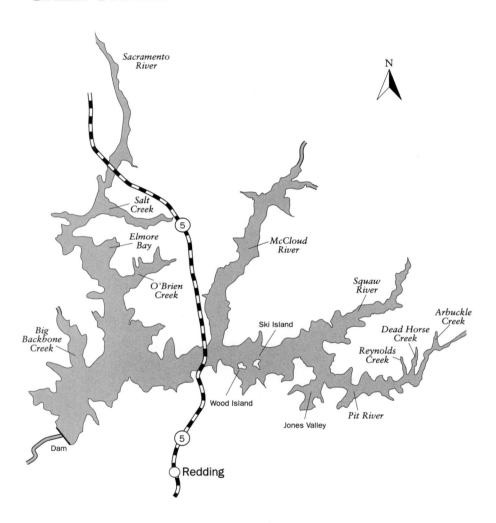

fishing, primarily because of its combinations of deep tributaries and shallow flats. During the summer and fall months this area often provides good topwater action.

Not far from the junction of the Pit and Squaw are two prominent angling landmarks, Ski and Wood Islands. The islands aren't as important as what's between them—a long underwater ridge or hump that seems to produce quality bass year-round. The lake record largemouth (over 15 pounds) was caught on this hump, and numerous other big fish have been taken here, as well.

The McCloud River, which flows in from the north not far from these islands, does not have the timber of the Pit River but instead offers more rocks and greater depth. Anglers can fish miles of rocky shoreline here, dropping plastic worms along the ledges and boulders or jigging spoons farther offshore, and stay busy enough that they never have to visit any other part of the lake.

The Sacramento River, the primary tributary of Lake Shasta, has two major tributaries of its own that have well-deserved reputations as fish producers. These are Salt and Big Backbone Creeks. Salt Creek offers rolling flats split by a deep creek channel, while Big Backbone and its smaller adjoining tributary, Little Backbone (known collectively as the Backbone area), have rocky points, deep drops, and extremely clear water but excellent spotted bass fishing.

Several lures and techniques are popular on Lake Shasta. Probably the most popular lure is a small plastic worm, fished with light line as a Carolina-rigged or split-shot setup. Wherever they are found, spotted bass seem to prefer plastic worms over any other lure, and Lake Shasta is no exception. Largemouth hunters like Dobyns often use spinnerbaits and jerkbaits around the flooded timber.

Lake Shasta has a huge shad population, and locating schools of these baitfish with a depthfinder is one of the surest ways to find spotted bass. The baitfish gather in large schools for their own protection while the bass hover below them. Whenever one of the shad—or a lure—appears to be leaving the school, it gets hit almost instantly by one of the spots.

In September and October the bass frequently drive the shad to the surface, and this is when topwater fishing takes over. Chuggers, poppers, and even buzzbaits will all take fish, especially back in the coves and around the timber.

Surprisingly, perhaps, some of the year's best fishing takes place in the winter months. Even when water temperatures drop to 45 degrees, the spotted bass remain aggressive and can often be caught on plastic worms or spinnerbaits in less than 10 feet of water. Other fish may be taken deeper by jigging spoons off the rocky bluffs or around bridge pilings where they suspend.

Lake Shasta is part of the Whiskeytown-Shasta-Trinity National Recreation Area, and as such is often described as one of the most scenic impoundments in the entire West. From some parts of the lake, it is even possible to see the 14,162-foot summit of Mount Shasta, about 60 miles away. Bass fishermen, however, while certainly recognizing the scenic beauty of the area, know Lake Shasta as one of the best spotted bass fisheries in the nation.

RESOURCES

Gearing Up: Light- to medium-action rods with lines testing 6 to 10 pounds are popular at Lake Shasta, but heavier tackle may be used successfully in the dingier water in the back reaches of the Squaw and Pit Rivers. Finesse-type four- and six-inch plastic worms, 1/2- and 3/4-ounce tandem willowleaf spinnerbaits, topwater chuggers, and 1/-ounce jigging spoons will all catch bass.

Accommodations: Complete motel and restaurant facilities are available in Redding along Interstate 5, which also crosses the lake. Literally thousands of acres of surrounding mountainous wilderness are open to camping, as are numerous campgrounds along the lake shore.

Additional Information: Redding Convention & Visitors Bureau, 777 Auditorium Drive, Redding, CA 96001; 800-874-7562.

38 CLEAR LAKE

Location: Northern California approximately 2 and a half hours north of San Francisco near Clearlake.
Short Take: 43,000 acres; shallow, natural lake with milfoil, tules, boat docks, rock, one small tributary.
Primary Species: Largemouth bass.
Best Months: March through June, September, October.
Favorite Lures: Spinnerbaits, plastic worms, jigs, crankbaits.
Nearest Tourist Services: Clearlake.

WHENEVER THE ROLL OF PREMIER CALIFORNIA BASS LAKES IS CALLED, Clear Lake is usually among the first mentioned. While not as famous as some of the state's other lakes that have produced fish in the 15- to 20-pound class, Clear Lake definitely can hold its own with bass in the 5- to 10-pound range. It is the sheer number of fish of this size that has put Clear Lake on the angling map.

"Without question, Clear Lake ranks as one of the better bass fisheries in the entire West," notes California angler Skeet Reese, who has fished Clear Lake for well over a decade. "It is the largest natural lake in the state, but it is basically shallow with a variety of cover that provides plenty of habitat for the fish.

"If Clear Lake were located in southern California instead of where it is north of the Napa Valley, I'm pretty sure it would already have produced some truly monstrous bass."

That is extremely high praise, indeed, for any body of water, but it is also totally appropriate for Clear Lake. The lake record is 17.52 pounds, and five-fish, 30-pound stringers are taken each spring.

The spring spawning months, beginning as early as March and continuing through early June, are generally considered the best big bass months at Clear Lake, but local anglers like Reese have made big catches during the summer and autumn seasons, too. The heaviest fishing pressure does occur in the spring, however, which is why September and October are preferred by some.

The lake has a somewhat unusual configuration in that the larger, upper portion is generally round or saucer shaped, which necks down into a channel (appropriately named the Narrows) that splits into two smaller but separate arms. There are two major islands located in these arms, and a number of small canals, known as Clear Lake Keys, are accessible off one of these arms.

Clear Lake is largely spring fed. The only tributary, Redman Slough, is a small, winding creek located on the far northern end of the lake. Overall, the lake is about 25 miles long and has an average depth of perhaps 12 feet. The lake is extremely fertile, and visibility ranges down to about five feet.

A number of fishing areas throughout the lake seem to produce well in all seasons. One of the best known is in the smaller arm around Rattlesnake Island. The

CLEAR LAKE
CALIFORNIA

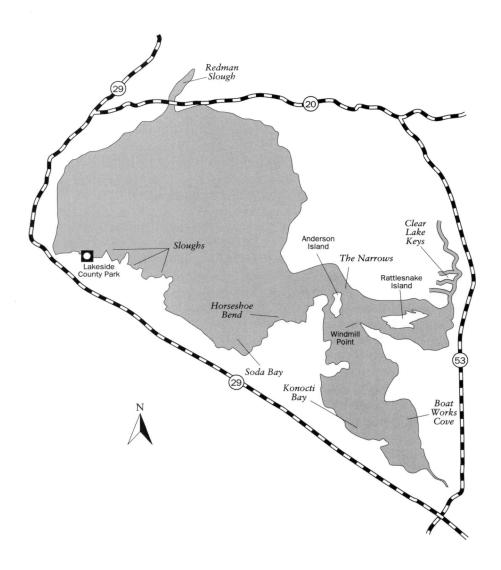

bottom here has become a dumping area for old slot machines, refrigerators, and other odds and ends that only add to the bass habitat. It's an excellent place to drop a Texas-rigged plastic worm, or, if you like to live dangerously, a smaller finesse-type worm.

From Rattlesnake Island many fishermen continue into the series of shallow, weedy canals known as Clear Lake Keys. Flipping bottom-bumping lures like plastic worms or tube jigs often works well in this area, since the water is shallow. Another popular spot nearby is Windmill Point, which separates this arm from the larger arm to the south.

Clear Lake's larger arm contains a small embayment named Konocti Bay that often produces well, while others like a cove on the other side known as the Boat Works. In either area, fishing choices are varied; the Boat Works cove has both rock and gravel on the bottom and probably holds the warmest water on the lake, which makes it a favorite early spring area.

A deep channel runs through the Narrows around Anderson Island, and it is here that some of Clear Lake's deepest water is found. Just around the corner, however, are two other fishing spots that certainly deserve mention, Horseshoe Bend and Soda Bay. In both areas, anglers can go straight along the shoreline fishing tules with jigs or soft plastics, throw a spinnerbait around some boat docks, detour offshore to crankbait some deeper rocks and dropoffs, then return to the shore and fish more tules, then more docks.

Several miles farther up the lake, at Lakeside County Park, anglers have a large, almost marsh-like habitat of sloughs, tules, and other vegetation to consider. Some consider this the best area of the entire lake because of the generally shallow water and heavy cover.

Redman Slough, located at the upper end of the lake, is a long, narrow, slightly dingy creek lined with brush and tules. This is where fishermen who like to flip jigs and plastic worms often do the best, because other lure presentations seldom reach the fish very successfully. In the Slough, the bridge area is always worth fishing.

During the summer months, night fishing can be productive, especially with large topwater poppers and chuggers and even buzzbaits. With all the boat docks around the lake, as well as the vegetation, there is certainly no shortage of casting targets.

At the same time, other Clear Lake fishermen target some of the lake's deeper, open-water rock ridges with crankbaits. The lake has a large crawfish population (as well as shad) that makes this technique particularly effective during the summer. The Windmill Point area, locally famous for its bream and sunfish concentrations, is another favorite crankbait spot.

RESOURCES

Gearing Up: Because heavy cover and big bass are to be expected here, anglers use medium- to medium/heavy-action baitcasting rods and lines testing 12 to 20 pounds. Flipping is usually done with stronger lines. Favorite lures are 1/2-ounce willowleaf spinnerbaits, 1/2-ounce jigs, plastic worms, medium- and deep-diving crankbaits, and topwater chuggers. Favorite colors are blue and black for soft plastics, crawfish/brown for crankbaits and jigs.

Accommodations: This is an extremely popular tourist area, and complete motel and restaurant facilities are available around the lake in Clearlake, Lakeport, and Kelseyville. Camping is popular at Clear Lake State Park as well as in the nearby Mendocino National Forest.

Additional Information: Clear Lake Chamber of Commerce, P.O. Box 629, Clearlake, CA 95422; 707-994-3600.

39 SAN JOAQUIN RIVER DELTA

Location: West-central California between Stockton, Sacramento, and San Francisco.

Short Take: 1,000 miles of navigable, fishable, man-made waterways; tule-lined canals, rock riprap, laydowns, tidal fluctuations, five major rivers.

Primary Species: Largemouth bass.

Best Months: April, May, October through December.

Favorite Lures: Plastic worms, jigs, spinnerbaits, lipless crankbaits.

Nearest Tourist Services: Stockton.

OF ALL THE PLACES IN AMERICA where an angler can catch largemouth bass, perhaps none is as unusual as California's San Joaquin River Delta. In the 50-odd miles between Stockton and San Francisco, five major, nutrient-rich rivers flow together to form a huge, shallow delta, which in turn has been diked and dammed and channeled into more than 1,000 miles of canals and sloughs that eventually empty into San Francisco Bay.

Construction of the canals and levees began as long ago as 1869 and continued for more than 60 years, during which time some 700,000 acres of land were reclaimed. Today, this land continues to be some of the richest farmland in the state. The canals have become a major source of boating recreation, for it is possible to travel from Stockton to San Francisco by boat, and many do just that, especially when the pro football 49ers have a home game.

Over time, many canals have become lined with tules and other types of vegetation. Wave erosion has broken other dikes to create small, shallow lakes, and in still other places the dikes have formed brush-covered islands. Water depths are seldom more than 20 feet, but daily tidal fluctuation can be four to five feet.

In short, the San Joaquin River Delta (the other rivers are the Sacramento, Cosumnes, Calaveras, and Mokelumne) ranks as one of the finest bass fisheries in the United States because of the abundant cover and the quality of the water. The region has produced individual bass weighing more than 15 pounds; five-bass daily limits of over 34 pounds; and three-day catches (15 bass) weighing more than 78 pounds.

"The Delta has tremendous fishing," says California angler Mark Tyler, who, in the spring of 1999 caught bass weighing 8 and 14 pounds on consecutive casts. "The area has some unusual features, such as the huge tidal fluctuations, but overall, I think it's comparable to any bass lake anywhere for the quality of fish it produces."

The problem, of course, is finding those fish in the 1,000 or so miles of canals. Tyler caught his two big bass in April just as the fish were preparing to spawn, certainly one of the best times to fish the Delta, but big bass can come from practically anywhere and at any time of year.

SAN JOAQUIN RIVER DELTA
CALIFORNIA

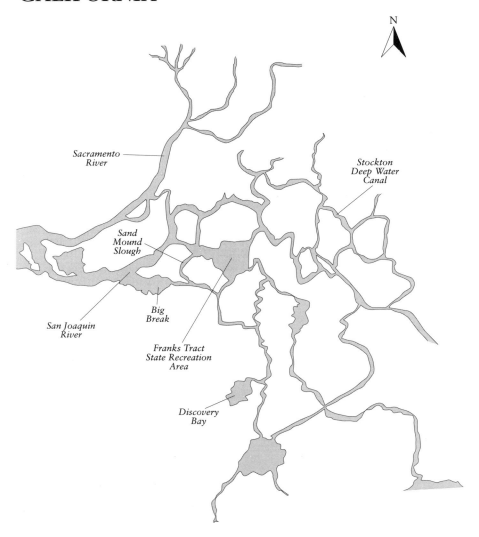

N

Sacramento
River

Stockton
Deep Water
Canal

Sand
Mound
Slough

Big
Break

San Joaquin
River

Franks Tract
State Recreation
Area

Discovery
Bay

Mark Tyler of Concord, California, holds a 14 pound, 9 ounce largemouth he caught in the San Joaquin River Delta. On his previous cast, Tyler caught an 8 pounder.

One of the most well-known areas is Franks Tract State Recreation Area, located about 15 miles west of Stockton by way of the Stockton Deep Water Channel. This is the largest "lake" in the Delta, covering more than four square miles. It is very shallow and like the other lakes, has tules, stumps, and brush around much of its shoreline. This is a good place to flip plastic lizards and worms, or perhaps throw lipless crankbaits.

Other areas that are likely to produce good fishing include Sand Mound Slough, a winding, tule-filled canal that edges Franks Tract to the south; Big Break, a smaller, shallow lake lined with tules; and Discovery Bay, a development/resort complex in the south-central Delta filled not only with the ever-present tules but also boat docks.

It is difficult to describe bass fishing in the Delta without discussing the tules, the dominant shoreline vegetation of many western waters. In the Delta, they quickly take over the muddy islands in the canals, and the best fishing normally is at the ends of the islands where the tide sometimes washes out deeper holes. Pitching plastic worms and jigs around these tule islands is probably the most reliable fishing technique throughout the Delta.

Another productive tactic, especially in the open-water lakes, is casting lipless crankbaits. Sometimes this may seem like an endless exercise in casting and winding, but it can very easily pay off with one of the Delta's monsters. Angler Gary Howell, like Tyler a veteran Delta angler, never changed lures during a national bass tournament on the Delta one spring, and in three days weighed in more than 60 pounds of fish, including one over 12 pounds. The key to this type of fishing is simply making a lot of casts and covering a lot of water.

A third fishing tactic is fishing jigs or crankbaits along the rock riprap that reinforces many of the dikes. In the spring bass migrate to these rocks to spawn because they offer a hard bottom, but the fish generally remain close to the riprap at all times of the year.

The tides may fluctuate as much as four or five feet, and are something every Delta angler must learn to understand. Normally, most fishermen prefer an outgoing tide because it pulls bass out of the flooded tules to the tips of the points where they're more accessible. Others, however, prefer the higher tide because it pushes fish into the tules where they can be caught by flipping. During a full moon, the tides may be a foot higher than normal.

Is there any easy way to fish this vast labyrinth of canals, islands, and lakes? Actually, there is. Just head down any of the smaller canals so you can stay out of the boat traffic, and start fishing a plastic worm or jig around any of the tule islands you find. There are enough bass here that eventually you'll catch one, and it very well may be one of the Delta's giants.

RESOURCES

Gearing Up: Medium- to heavy-action baitcasting rods with lines testing 14 to 25 pounds are standard in the Delta, although some enjoy using lighter spinning rods with lines as light as 10-pound test. Favorite lures include 3/8-ounce jigs, Texas-rigged plastic worms, and lipless crankbaits.

Accommodations: Complete motel and restaurant facilities are available in Stockton, and some of the marinas also have accommodations. Camping is also available at numerous marinas.

Additional Information: Stockton/San Joaquin Convention & Visitors Bureau, 46 West Fremont Street, Stockton, CA 95202; 209-943-1987.

40 LAKE MEAD

Location: Southern Nevada and western Arizona approximately 25 miles from Las Vegas.
Short Take: 163,000 acres; high desert lake with clear and muddy water, large tributaries, canyons, coves, rocks, aquatic vegetation, flooded trees and bushes.
Primary Species: Largemouth and striped bass.
Best Months: April, May, September, October.
Favorite Lures: Spinnerbaits, crankbaits, jigs, plastic worms and tube jigs, topwater lures.
Nearest Tourist Services: Boulder City, Nevada.

MORE AND MORE, IT SEEMS, VISITORS ARE COMING TO LAKE MEAD to take their chances with largemouth bass, rather than travel to nearby Las Vegas to take chances there in the casinos. That's because this winding, scenic Colorado River impoundment has been completely rejuvenated as a bass fishery by the introduction of several different types of aquatic vegetation in recent years.

Today in the spring and fall it is possible to catch 25 to 30 bass per day, something extremely difficult, if not unheard of, just a few years ago. The lake has even produced largemouth bass over 10 pounds, again something definitely unheard of in the past.

In fact, bass fishermen coming to Lake Mead today probably won't recognize the lake if it's been more than 10 years since their last visit. In 1987 the first efforts at restoring Lake Mead's fishery—creating new habitat and adding fertilizer to the water—were initiated and have been continued ever since. Today, thanks to the Lake Mead Fertilization and Cover Enhancement Projects initiated largely by personnel at the University of Nevada, Las Vegas, there are bulrushes, willows, and cattails along many parts of the shoreline, and pondweed grows in coves all over the lake.

The result has been not only a dramatic change in the lake's largemouth population, but also a change in how anglers fish the lake, because now instead of being gin clear, the water is slightly dingy. Spinnerbaits are popular and productive lures in the spring, and buzzbaits produce well in the autumn.

Lake Mead's primary tributary is the Colorado River, which flows out of the Grand Canyon and into the eastern end of the lake. Two other tributaries are the Muddy and Virgin Rivers, which join and form a section of the lake known as the Overton Arm. The rest of the lake is generally described by its various basins—large, fairly open areas several miles long that are separated by shorter narrow canyons. The primary basins include Boulder Basin on Mead's western end, Virgin Basin in the middle, and Gregg Basin on the eastern end. The Overton Arm empties into Virgin Basin from the north.

LAKE MEAD
NEVADA

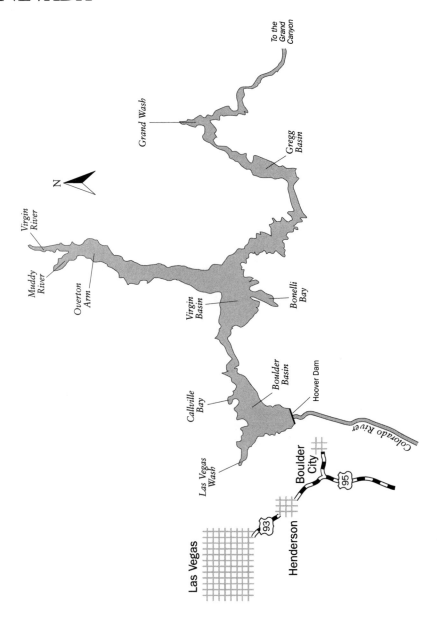

The lake itself is only part of the 1.5-million-acre Lake Mead National Recreation Area, and as such, is part of the National Park System. The entire region is not only scenic but also unique in that three of America's four desert ecosystems meet here. More than a million visitors come to Lake Mead annually, not only to fish but also to dive, hike, and camp.

Anywhere in the different basins anglers will find coves and points to fish. In the spring if the water is high, the backs of coves will have flooded brush, willows, and salt cedars as casting targets for spinnerbaits, crankbaits, and jigs. Sightfishing for visible bass will also be possible, particularly in the Virgin Basin area.

Virgin Basin presents the most open water of any part of Lake Mead, and many fishermen concentrate along its southern shoreline in Bonelli Bay. The islands in the mouth of the bay as well as the rocky points all along the shoreline offer excellent jig and spinnerbait fishing. In the fall, this area produces some of the lake's largest bass on big topwater plugs and buzzbaits. Because of the flooded timber in the backs of these coves, baitfish are always present, which is why the bass are here, too.

Another popular area is the Overton Arm, primarily because the water here has always been more off-color than anywhere else on the lake. The Overton Arm continues for more than 20 miles and contains not only points and islands but also numerous areas with weeds and vegetation. In the spring of 1999, a 10-pound largemouth was caught in the Overton.

Grand Wash, a large bay at the far end of Gregg Basin, is popular with some fishermen. By the time you get here, you're 60 miles from the Hoover Dam, but if you've made the run from Callville Bay Marina (in Boulder Basin) where many anglers launch, you have some excellent points, coves, and plenty of stair-stepping ledges to fish. The water is often a little cooler here and may be more dingy.

On the opposite end of the lake in Boulder Basin, many anglers head from Callville Bay straight across the basin to the opposite shoreline. Here the depth change is not nearly as dramatic as it is in other parts of the lake, and there is flooded brush and aquatic vegetation to go along with the more gentle ledges and points. Other bass fishermen continue to Las Vegas Wash, a narrow canyon at the far western end of Boulder Basin that offers some off-colored water as well as flooded brush and tumbleweeds.

Anglers at Lake Mead should be aware that this lake, like many others in the western states, can become extremely rough because of the way the canyon walls funnel the wind. While there are many coves and bays that offer shelter from the rough water, there are not very many launch ramps where a rescue trailer can be taken. Getting stuck on this lake can last as long as a storm lasts.

RESOURCES

Gearing Up: Although the lake is now more dingy than before the vegetation was established, visibility still averages 10 to 12 feet. That means most fishermen use medium- or medium/light-action rods with lines testing between 8 and 14 pounds. Productive lures include 1/2-ounce willowleaf spinnerbaits, 3/8- and 1/2-ounce jigs, large topwater chuggers, buzzbaits, and plastic worms used on both Texas and Carolina rigs.

Accommodations: The nearest accommodations are in Boulder City and Henderson, both of which have complete motel and restaurant facilities. Las Vegas is only slightly farther away with additional accommodations. Camping is permitted at several National Park Service campgrounds around the lake.

Additional Information: Lake Mead National Recreation Area, 601 Nevada Highway, Boulder City, NV 89005; 702-293-8907.

41 ELEPHANT BUTTE RESERVOIR

Location: Sierra County in south-central New Mexico near the town of Truth or Consequences.

Short Take: 36,558 acres; desert reservoir with both shallow and deep water, rocky points, coves, flooded timber, limited vegetation, no tributaries.

Primary Species: Largemouth, smallmouth, and striped bass.

Best Months: March through May, September, October. Striped bass also good November through January.

Favorite Lures: Jigs, jerkbaits, shallow crankbaits, plastic worms and grubs, topwaters. Live bait is also popular for striped bass.

Nearest Tourist Services: Truth or Consequences.

OF ALL THE THINGS A BASS FISHERMAN WOULD LEAST EXPECT to see in a lake in the desert, flooded trees probably top the list, but at Elephant Butte Reservoir in south-central New Mexico, the unusual is common. This 36,558-acre Rio Grande River impoundment offers superb largemouth and smallmouth fishing, and has produced striped bass of more than 54 pounds.

The main reason the uncommon is common here lies in Elephant Butte's configuration: it is comprised of two completely distinct basins joined by a narrow, four-mile canyon. The upper basin, or lake, contains shallow, dingy water; rocky flats and bays filled with flooded salt cedar and mesquite; and has an average depth of perhaps 20 feet. In contrast, the lower basin offers deep, clear water with limited timber and vegetation and averages nearly 80 feet deep, although it also contains some shallow, brushy points and coves. The connecting canyon, known as the Narrows, is four miles long and has both shallow and deep water. The lake's name comes from a rock formation on the lower lake.

Elephant Butte is somewhat unusual in that other than the Rio Grande, the lake has no tributaries. There are numerous canyons and arroyos leading into the lake from the surrounding countryside, but they remain dry all but a few weeks of the year when they're channeling rain runoff from the nearby mountains.

Largemouth bass are found in both the upper and lower lakes, while smallmouth are much more common in the lower, deeper lake. Striped bass, as expected, inhabit both the lower lake as well as the Narrows.

Dennis Hoy, a veteran angler who lives near Elephant Butte and who has fished the impoundment for many years, describes the lake as probably one of the most underrated lakes in the Southwest. New Mexico is not known for either largemouth or smallmouth, and while Elephant Butte is the largest lake in the state, most visitors come here to try for a big striped bass.

"Striped bass fishing is really good in the winter months when anglers fish live shad under balloons in the Narrows," explains Hoy. "Shad move into this area as water in the upper basin begins to get cold, and the stripers really gorge themselves.

ELEPHANT BUTTE RESERVOIR
NEW MEXICO

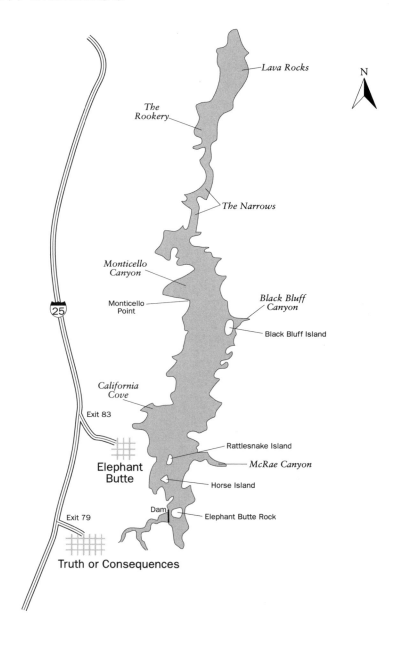

Lava Rocks

The Rookery

N

The Narrows

Monticello Canyon

Monticello Point

Black Bluff Canyon

Black Bluff Island

California Cove

Exit 83

Rattlesnake Island

Elephant Butte

McRae Canyon

Horse Island

Exit 79

Dam

Elephant Butte Rock

Truth or Consequences

25

Elephant Butte, the largest reservoir in New Mexico, consists of two distinct basins. The upper basin is shallow and slightly dingy while the lower basin is deeper and has clear water. Both largemouth and smallmouth bass are present.

Guides use a technique known as balloon fishing, in which a plastic balloon is inflated and clipped to the line to keep the bait at a certain depth.

"The balloon floats on the surface and gets blown around by the wind so the shad is actually moving through the water. The lake record for stripers is 54 pounds, 8 ounces, but fish over 40 pounds are caught every year."

For largemouth bass fishing, two primary areas stand out in the upper lake. These are Lava Rocks and the Rookery. The Rookery is a large, timber-filled bay on the western side of the lake just above the Narrows, while Lava Rocks is much farther up the lake along the eastern side. The name comes from shoreline rock formations; the place itself is a large, shallow flat with flooded brush and trees.

Flipping and pitching plastic worms, grubs, and jigs are the primary fishing techniques in these two areas, although spinnerbaits and occasionally topwaters also work well. Lava Rocks is exposed to the wind and quickly becomes unfishable, and it will also turn muddy after a heavy rain. Those types of conditions usually push anglers into the Rookery, which offers more protection.

Lower lake hotspots include Monticello and McRae Canyons and California Cove. They're good because all are large areas and each contains rocky points with scattered brush, shallow flats, and of course, nearby deep water. Because the cover is not nearly as thick here as in the upper lake, crankbaits, jerkbaits, spinnerbaits, and topwaters can all be used.

On the lower lake, anglers are just as likely to catch smallmouth bass as they are largemouths, although the fish are usually slightly deeper. While largemouth may be found around the secondary points or perhaps even in the backs of the canyons, smallmouth are frequently closer to the mouths. Small plastic worms and grubs and light 8- and 10-pound-test lines may be used in the clear water, even though fish of 4 and 5 pounds might be encountered.

Although threadfin and gizzard shad migrate into the Narrows in November, some baitfish are present in the area throughout the year. The Narrows is not a steep-walled canyon at all, but rather, a long, narrow part of the lake formed by fairly low hillsides. Because of better-known hotspots in both the upper and lower lakes, the Narrows probably receives the least fishing pressure of anywhere on the Butte, with the exception of striper fishing in the winter. Jerkbaits, jigs, and Carolina-rigged plastic worms can all be used to probe the rocky shorelines for fish.

Because Elephant Butte has no active tributary creeks, some of the bass patterns commonly found on other reservoirs don't always work here. In the autumn months, for example, when shad migrate to the backs of creeks and bass follow them, on Elephant Butte shad might be in the back of a canyon one day, out on the point the next, and possibly halfway back again on the following day.

There is schooling activity here in September and October, but it frequently occurs in the middle of the day, not early and late as so often happens on other lakes. When an angler can find schooling bass, the topwater action is superb. The heaviest largemouths are usually caught in April and May as they begin moving shallow to spawn.

RESOURCES

Gearing Up: Light- to medium/heavy-action rods are used here for largemouth and smallmouth bass; choices depend not only on lures and fishing techniques, but also on water clarity. Striper fishermen use medium/heavy- and heavy-action rods, with lines to match. Favorite lure choices include everything from small finesse worms to 5/8-ounce jigs, both shallow and deep-diving crankbaits, jerkbaits, and topwater plugs.

Accommodations: Motel and restaurant facilities are available in Truth or Consequences. Campgrounds are located nearby at Elephant Butte Lake State Park.

Additional Information: Truth or Consequences/Sierra County Chamber of Commerce, Box 31, Truth or Consequences, NM 87901; 505-894-3536.

42 LAKE POWELL

Location: Colorado River impoundment on the Arizona/Utah border near Page, Arizona, approximately 150 miles north of Flagstaff.
Short Take: 161,390 acres; deep clear water, steep-walled canyons, rocky points, some flooded brush, no vegetation.
Primary Species: Largemouth, smallmouth, and striped bass.
Best Months: March through May, September, October.
Favorite Lures: Plastic worms, tube jigs, and grubs, spinnerbaits, topwaters.
Nearest tourist Services: Page.

OF ALL THE BASS LAKES IN THE UNITED STATES, none truly compares to Lake Powell, the huge, clear-water impoundment on the Colorado River in northern Arizona and southern Utah. It is not a spectacular fish producer, but it is spectacularly beautiful. Stretching 186 miles northward from Glen Canyon Dam in Page, the lake offers a kaleidoscope of steep canyons and unusual rock formations along both shorelines. There are 96 major canyons along the lake's nearly 2,000 miles of shoreline, all encompassed within the National Park Service's Glen Canyon National Recreation Area.

Named for John Wesley Powell, the famed explorer of the Grand Canyon (which begins just a few miles below Glen Canyon Dam), the rugged, undeveloped countryside surrounding the lake looks little different today than when Powell came down the river in 1869. The hills and canyons are dotted with ancient Anasazi ruins, pictographs, and natural stone arches—many reachable only on foot or by four-wheel-drive vehicle.

Most of the real travel here, however, is by water. For bass fishermen that translates into a run of more than 100 miles from Wahweap Marina near the dam up to the San Juan River, where the majority of bass fishing takes place. Here the water loses its clarity and becomes stained to muddy, is much richer in nutrients, and contains some of the highest baitfish (shad) populations in the entire lake. This is not to say bass are not caught anywhere else on Lake Powell, because they are, but for years the most consistent action and the largest bass have come from the San Juan River arm.

Although the San Juan offers nearly 50 miles of fishable water, bass anglers usually begin fishing in the vicinity of Piute Canyon, about 20 miles up the river from its junction with the Colorado. From Piute Canyon, good bass water extends another 25 miles upriver to Copper Canyon. This entire section is characterized by hundreds of small pockets, coves, and points as well as boulders, sandbars, and flooded brush.

Techniques vary according to the season, but three of the most popular include pitching jigs, plastic worms, or tube jigs around the rocks and boulders; bouncing a crankbait through deeper rocks; or burning a spinnerbait as fast as possible over the

LAKE POWELL
UTAH/ARIZONA BORDER

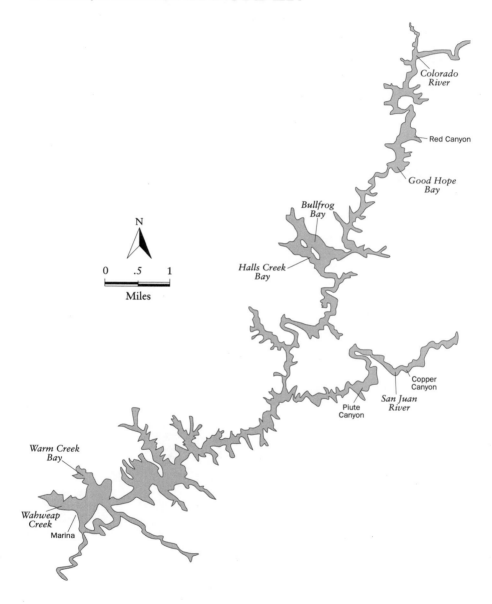

Colorado
River

Red Canyon

Good Hope
Bay

Bullfrog
Bay

N

0   .5   1

Miles

Halls Creek
Bay

Copper
Canyon

San Juan
River

Piute
Canyon

Warm Creek
Bay

Wahweap
Creek

Marina

Anglers at Lake Powell often find themselves fishing around unusual rock formations and occasionally even natural rock arches. Much of the bass fishing takes place in the San Juan River arm of the lake.

flooded brush in the backs of the canyons. In the spring when bass have moved shallow to begin spawning, anglers are often amazed at how many fish are present in relatively small areas; a national tournament was won with nearly 45 pounds of bass (15 fish), all of which were caught along a single 20-yard stretch of shoreline near Piute Canyon.

Another technique that may produce well here is known as "dead-sticking," which is best described as pitching a plastic worm or tube jig to the boulders and just letting it lie motionless on the bottom. When bass are on this pattern, it may take 15 to 30 seconds of nerve-wracking waiting, but suddenly a bass just clobbers the lure. It's as if the fish are waiting to see just what the lure is going to do, then they decide to attack before it does anything.

Because the San Juan River is so well known for bass fishing and thus receives the heaviest pressure, some fishermen continue up the Colorado to Halls Creek Bay, Bullfrog Bay, and even farther to Good Hope Bay and Red Canyon, about 125 miles from the dam. Here the water remains relatively clear except in the very backs of the canyons where it turns greenish with nutrients, but these areas are relatively small and cannot withstand a lot of fishing pressure. The main reason to fish them at all is to escape the heavy traffic in the San Juan.

There is some bass fishing on the lower end of the lake not far from Wahweap Marina in Warm Creek Bay and also in Wahweap Creek. Both areas have scattered flooded brush in shallow water, but the water is so shallow the fish have shadows. A good technique here is pitching a small jig on light line to the base of the steeper bluffs and just letting it fall to 10 or 12 feet around the broken rocks. Because the water is clear and the bass population not nearly as numerous as farther up the lake, these lower canyons do not receive much attention from serious fishermen.

Although spring fishing can be extremely enjoyable, Lake Powell's fall fishing is equally well known because this is when bass hit topwaters well. The fish move to shallow gravel points near the mouths of the upriver canyons, particularly along the points within the first several miles of the San Juan before the water really changes color.

Lake Powell has long been known for its striped bass population, and fish of nearly 50 pounds have been caught over the years. Historically, September and October are two of the best months to catch them, as the stripers, just like the largemouths, tend to be more shallow. If baitfish are abundant, some topwater action may be possible, but more often the fish are located with depthfinders and fished with spoons or plastic grubs. Sometimes largemouth fishermen catch stripers when they're using crankbaits in the San Juan, but not regularly. Stripers are caught up and down the lake, but the majority will be found close to the baitfish in the upper end.

Lake Powell is also world famous for houseboating, and indeed, thousands of houseboats may take to the water on a summer weekend. Anglers who have time to spend on the lake often pull their bass boats behind the houseboats so they can camp near their favorite fishing areas—and there isn't a prettier lake anywhere in which to do it.

RESOURCES:

Gearing Up: Because of the predominantly clear water, lighter rods and lines are the rule rather than the exception on Lake Powell. Light- to medium-action rods with lines ranging from 8-to 14 pound test are best. Popular lures include 1/2-ounce spinnerbaits, plastic worms and tube jigs, 3/8-ounce regular jigs, medium-running crankbaits, and topwater poppers.

Accommodations: Complete motel and restaurant facilities are available near the dam in Page as well as at both Wahweap and Bullfrog Marinas. Campgrounds are located at these same two marinas, but primitive camping is permitted anywhere around the shoreline.

Additional Information: Page-Lake Powell Chamber of Commerce, 644-C North Navaho, Page, AZ 86040; 520-645-2741.

43 COLUMBIA RIVER

Location: Kennewick, Pasco, and Richland, Washington.
Short Take: 32,000 acres; rocks, gravel, some hydrilla, river current, clear water, tule banks.
Primary Species: Smallmouth and largemouth bass.
Best Months: April, May, June, September.
Favorite Lures: Finesse-type plastic worms, buzzbaits, jigs, crankbaits.
Nearest Tourist Services: Tri-Cities area of Kennewick, Pasco, and Richland.

IN THE PACIFIC NORTHWEST THE COLUMBIA RIVER ENJOYS a reputation as one of the finest smallmouth bass fisheries in the entire region, and it is a well-deserved compliment. The river, which for part of its length forms the border between Washington and Oregon, flows for hundreds of miles but is contained and controlled by a series of dams and pools all along its length. Only one of the pools or "lakes" as they are described on maps, the Wallula Pool (Lake Wallula), is the part of the river described here.

The Wallula Pool covers some 32,000 acres and stretches more than 60 miles between the McNary Dam on the lower end and Priest Rapids Dam on the upper end. Fishing options include both gravel and grass flats, island points, underwater shoals, tule-covered banks, and mid-river rock piles. In addition, both the Snake and Yakima Rivers flow into the Columbia in this pool and provide additional opportunities, although bass fishermen seldom venture very far up either waterway. Overall, the water in the pool is fairly clear, generally dictating the use of lighter lines and smaller lures.

While both largemouth and smallmouth bass are present, smallmouth dominate. This is primarily because of the current and the generally rocky habitat found throughout the river; smallmouth fishing is really quite productive all the way down the river to the coast. In the Wallula Pool, smallmouth topping 5 pounds are caught regularly, although most are slightly smaller. The largemouths also top 5 pounds and tend to stay in the shallow water closer to the hydrilla or tules.

The major consideration for bass anglers here is river current, because it dictates fish activity. When the current is flowing, meaning water is being released at one or both dams, the bass tend to be more active, but too much current makes boat control difficult. At the same time, current flow in the upper end of the pool may be strong, but by the time the water reaches the Kennewick area, it may be hardly noticeable if water is not also being released downstream simultaneously.

One of the best-known smallmouth areas in the Wallula Pool, Hanford Reach, is about 50 miles up the Columbia from Kennewick. The key here is staying in the rocky pools and sloughs near the edge of the river rapids and bouncing small plastic worms and grubs on light line around the rocks and into the eddy areas. Just getting to Hanford Reach is a challenge, for this part of the Columbia is not a pool at all but a fairly fast-flowing, unmarked river filled with underwater shoals. The Hanford Reach area, incidentally, is the source of the plutonium used for the first atom bomb.

COLUMBIA RIVER
WASHINGTON

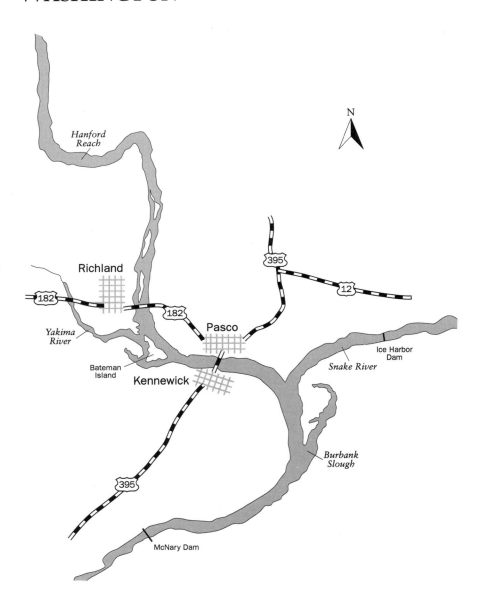

The massive Columbia River has gained a reputation as one of the top smallmouth bass fisheries in the Pacific Northwest. The fish readily hit crankbaits fished around the rocks.

Another favorite fishing spot for both smallmouth and largemouth is around the mouth of the Yakima River, not far upstream from Kennewick. Bateman Island sits in the middle of the bay at the mouth of the Yakima, and many anglers fish right around the island itself; there are both shallow gravel flats as well as a steep drop into the Columbia River channel off one edge. Others fish the grassy points of the Yakima because the water there is filled with brush washed down the river.

Fishing techniques in this area are largely dictated by the mood of the fish as well as the current. Slowly crawling small plastic worms on drop-shot and Carolina rigs works well when the fish are not particularly active, but crankbaits can be used when the bass are biting well.

South of Kennewick, the Snake River enters from the northeast. Only about eight miles of the river is fishable before anglers are stopped by the Ice Harbor Dam. Locking through Ice Harbor to enter Lake Sacajawea is possible, but few bass fishermen do. That's primarily because just below the Snake, anglers find Burbank Slough, a quiet, hydrilla-filled bay where largemouth bass hit buzzbaits rattled over the vegetation. The shorelines are covered with tules here, too, which can flipped with jigs.

This is one of the widest areas of the Wallula Pool, and there is good fishing just below the mouth of Burbank Slough along the shallow flat edging the river channel, as well as along the shorelines. Downriver the banks are very rocky, and there are actually several short sections of submerged railroad along the western shoreline that can be fished with plastic worms or jigs.

Some bass fishermen lock through the McNary Dam where another 60 miles of river is open to the John Day Dam. In this pool anglers will find much the same habitat as in the Wallula Pool—rocks, shoals, and scattered vegetation.

While current may be the overriding factor in how an angler fishes this part of the Columbia, wind is frequently the factor that determines where he fishes. Between the McNary Dam and Kennewick, the Columbia makes a huge 180-degree bend, while at the same time becoming quite narrow where the river crosses from Washington into Oregon. Here the wind is funneled through a canyon, and fishermen heading downriver from Kennewick in calm water suddenly find themselves facing huge waves as they round this bend. At the worst of times, merely trying to navigate just the few miles to the McNary Dam is all but impossible.

RESOURCES

Gearing Up: Because of the clear water, most fishermen along this section of the Columbia use light- or medium-action spinning rods with 8- or possibly 10-pound-test lines. When fishing for largemouths around the vegetation, medium/heavy-action rods and stronger lines are used. Favorite lures include four-inch finesse-type plastic worms and grubs, 3/8- and 1/2-ounce jigs, medium-diving crankbaits and buzzbaits.

Accommodations: Complete motel and restaurant facilities are available in the Tri-Cities area of Kennewick, Pasco, and Richland. Camping is also available in the immediate area.

Additional Information: Tri-City Area Chamber of Commerce, P.O. Box 6986, Kennewick, WA 99336; 509-736-0510

MIDWEST

MICHIGAN

MINNESOTA

SOUTH DAKOTA

44 LAKE ST. CLAIR

Location: Near Detroit about midway between Lake Huron and Lake Erie on the Michigan/Ontario border.
Short Take: 420 square miles; clear, shallow, weedy reservoir with sandy bottom, heavy shoreline development, several large tributaries.
Primary Species: Smallmouth and largemouth bass.
Best Months: May through October.
Favorite Lures: Spinnerbaits, plastic tube jigs, grubs, shallow crankbaits.
Nearest Tourist Services: Mount Clemens, Michigan.

YEARS AGO, the general consensus among anglers tended to be that the farther north one traveled, the less productive the bass fishing became. Today's fishermen know this simply is not true, and Michigan's Lake St. Clair is a perfect example. This huge, open-water lake offers superb smallmouth fishing and very good largemouth action, and the fishing appears to be improving each year. Smallmouth topping 6 pounds are caught annually.

That's because zebra mussels, a small bivalve now present throughout the lake, have cleaned the water through their internal feeding/filtering system and thus opened the door to increased vegetation growth. That, in turn, has allowed the forage base of crayfish and spottail minnows to expand, and the bass population has grown accordingly.

Lake St. Clair is fed primarily by the St. Clair River, which flows southward from Lake Huron. Other smaller tributaries include the Clinton River entering from Mount Clemens along the western shore, the Thames and Sydenham Rivers that come in on the Canadian side, and several others. In May the smallmouth begin moving shallow to spawn, but the actual fishing season does not open until the third week of June.

The lake's average depth is less than 15 feet, although a 30-foot-deep dredged navigation channel between the mouth of the St. Clair River and the beginning of the Detroit River (leading out of the lake to Lake Erie) cuts straight across the lake.

This channel, which is lined with vegetation along much of its length, and the lower portions of the St. Clair River itself, provide some of the primary fishing opportunities. Strong current in the river, however, tends to position the smallmouth here very specifically—often behind the vegetation—so just locating the bass is not always easy. At the same time, once the fish are located, they are often gathered in large schools.

This channel/river fishing pattern works best in late summer when spottail minnows begin migrating from the lake up the river. Shad-colored crankbaits and smoke-colored plastic grubs are among the best lures to use. Ironically, perhaps, local anglers report that this river migration is not as extensive as it once was, possibly due to the increased growth of vegetation.

Lake St. Clair
Michigan

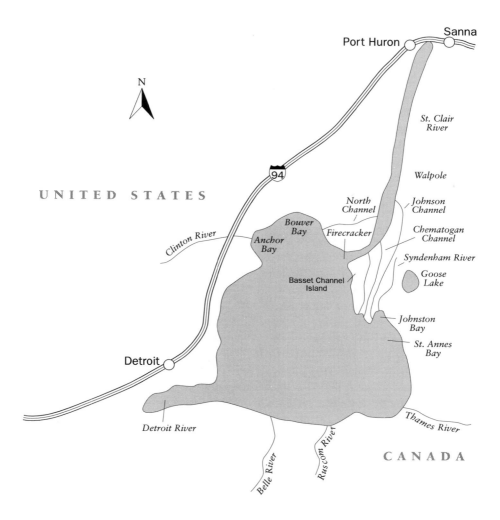

The navigation channel is marked with lighted buoys, and has several larger lighted towers that are frequently used as fishing reference points. Probably the most well known of these is a tower known as the Firecracker, located at the mouth of a channel leading into the St. Clair River. The water around the Firecracker drops from two to perhaps eight and then to 13 feet on the flats behind the tower, and then into the 30-foot channel itself.

The scattered weedbeds in other parts of the lake can produce smallmouth throughout the spring, summer, and autumn months. Vegetation is heaviest in Anchor and Bouvier Bays in the northern portion of the lake, and also along the eastern shoreline south of the mouth of the St. Clair River. This latter area is part of the Walpole Island Indian Reserve and requires not only an Ontario fishing license but also an Indian fishing permit.

In any of St. Clair's shallow, grassy flats, one major key to locating bass often depends on finding some type of deeper water breakline. Several such deeper creeks bisect the Walpole Reserve and are always worth exploring for their smallmouth potential. Among the better-known areas are the Bassett Channel, Johnson Channel, and Chematogan Channel. In each of these, small crankbaits, plastic worms and grubs, and tube jigs can be used for smallmouths.

Several other areas in the preserve are also worth noting, including Goose Lake, Johnston Bay, and St. Annes Bay, all of which feature shallow water with broken clumps of vegetation. Here, spinnerbaits can often be the best lure choice.

In the northern section of St. Clair, particularly Bouvier Bay, bass fishermen have a number of fishing options open to them. Boat docks line the shoreline and can be fished with plastic worms and grubs for both largemouth and smallmouth; the North Channel itself offers a depth change with vegetation and current that can be crankbaited; and the various small islands (especially Grass Island) offer grassy points that can be fished with spinnerbaits or plastic worms.

Along the lake's southern shore, scattered weedbeds around the mouths of the Thames, Ruscom, and Belle Rivers traditionally provide good to excellent smallmouth fishing during the spring and summer. One reason these three areas produce well is that there is a distinct breakline around the shoreline here, where the water drops fairly abruptly from as shallow as two and four feet down to eight and 10 feet. Depending on the size and configuration of the weedbeds along the breakline, anglers have a choice of using spinnerbaits, shallow crankbaits, or plastic worms.

All in all, Lake St. Clair might be compared to Florida's Lake Okeechobee, since both are very shallow, weed-filled natural lakes. While Okeechobee is famous for its largemouths, however, St. Clair unquestionably ranks as one of the nation's premier smallmouth fisheries, and many of the southern anglers who have experienced the fishing here come north again year after year.

RESOURCES

Gearing Up: Because of the overall clear water conditions, most bass fishermen here use light- to medium-action spinning rods, and lines testing 6 to perhaps 12 pounds. Some heavier lines may be used when dingy water is located. Both single and tandem willowleaf spinnerbaits are popular, although these lures are frequently hit by northern pike and muskie. Other lure choices include shallow running shad and crawfish-colored crankbaits, plastic tube jigs and grubs, and jerkbaits.

Accommodations: Complete motel and restaurant facilities are located in Mount Clemens and Detroit along Interstate 75 and Interstate 94. Limited camping is available.

Additional Information: Central Macomb County Chamber of Commerce, 58 Southbound Gratiot, Mount Clemens, MI 48043; 810-463-1528.

45 LAKE MINNETONKA

Location: Southern Minnesota near Minneapolis and Wayzata.
Short Take: 14,310 acres; series of small lakes connected by short canals, heavy milfoil, boat docks, rocks, deep water.
Primary Species: Largemouth and smallmouth bass.
Best Months: June through September.
Favorite Lures: Jigs, spinnerbaits, deep crankbaits, Carolina-rigged lizards.
Nearest Tourist Services: Wayzata, Minneapolis.

RARE, INDEED, IS A LAKE SITUATED PRACTICALLY WITHIN THE CITY LIMITS of a major metropolitan area that ranks as one of the nation's better bass fisheries, but Lake Minnetonka, located only a dozen miles from Minneapolis, can be classified just that way. Both largemouth and smallmouth bass are present in huge numbers and very respectable sizes here; in fact, largemouth weighing 6 pounds are not at all unusual.

The reasons for Minnetonka's success can undoubtedly be linked primarily to the lake's heavy growth of Eurasian milfoil, and secondly, perhaps, to the lake's unusual configuration. Actually, Minnetonka's 14,310 acres spread across more than a dozen separate lakes (most are actually named bays on the lake maps), all connected by short canals. The entire complex fits within an area just 11 miles long and six miles wide, and embraces 110 miles of shoreline. The lakes are natural, and were formed some 15,000 years ago by glaciers.

The milfoil is spread throughout the shallows of most of the lakes, but as an added attraction, Minnetonka's shorelines are dotted with boat docks, and much of the deep water outside the grassline is filled with rocks. Thus, bass fishermen have a variety of fishing options immediately available.

The largest individual body of water in the Minnetonka complex consists of Lower Lake North and Lower Lake South, and each has one or more large embayments branching off the main body. These two lakes are separated by Big Island, behind which one enters Lafayette Bay, and then by canal into East Upper Lake. From here one can go either to West Upper Lake or South Upper Lake, or by canal to Halsted Bay or Black Lake and so on. Eventually, a fisherman can get right back to Lower Lake North after having visited virtually all of the different bays and lakes without ever taking his boat out of the water. The most confusing part to anyone not completely familiar with the lakes is getting the names straight!

Initially, most fishermen begin by working the milfoil. Depending on the time of year and the height of the vegetation in the water, spinnerbaits or jigs are the primary lures. If the vegetation has not grown to the surface, slow-rolling 3/4- and even 1-ounce spinnerbaits over the top of the greenery eight to 10 feet deep produces excellent action. Later in the summer when the milfoil is matted on the surface, dropping heavy jigs through the vegetation works well.

LAKE MINNETONKA
MINNESOTA

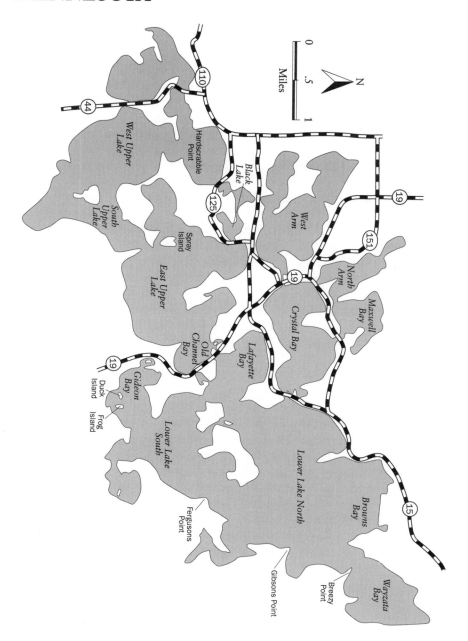

West Upper Lake

South Upper Lake

East Upper Lake

Hardscrabble Point

Black Lake

West Arm

Spray Island

North Arm

Maxwell Bay

Crystal Bay

Old Channel Bay

Lafayette Bay

Gideon Bay

Duck Island

Frog Island

Lower Lake South

Lower Lake North

Browns Bay

Fergusons Point

Gibsons Point

Breezy Point

Wayzata Bay

0 .5 1

Miles

N

What many seasoned Minnetonka anglers try to do is combine the milfoil with the rocks. There are numerous rocky reefs as well as man-made rock piles throughout the lake, and when the location of the rocks coincides with the outside edge of the milfoil, the result is almost guaranteed. While most of the rocks are natural, each year a few more get added by local anglers. In the winter when these lakes are frozen, ice fishermen put out rocks over their favorite fishing spots, and when the ice melts in spring, the rocks fall to the bottom and become that much more fish habitat.

This is really what makes the Minnetonka lakes so much fun to fish—the rock/milfoil combination exists all through them, and most lake maps show the locations of the underwater reefs. Crankbaits are popular for this type of fishing, as are Carolina rigs, especially when the rocks are deeper than about 15 feet.

The boat docks offer another fishing opportunity, and there is no shortage of them, since this is primarily a residential area. Flipping and skipping jigs and soft plastic worms, and sometimes slow-rolling spinnerbaits are the favorite techniques.

Lower Lake North and Lower Lake South form an excellent starting place to fish, as both provide several proven rock/milfoil locations. At Breezy Point, located on the eastern end of Lower Lake North where it enters Wayzata Bay, anglers frequently do well fishing deep crankbaits or Carolina-rigged lizards around the rocky dropoff outside the grassline. The same condition exists just across the lake in Browns Bay, and down the lake at Gibsons Point, Fergusons Point, and at the eastern tip of Big Island. In each of these areas, shallow, grassy water falls steeply into deeper depths.

In Lower South Lake's Gideon Bay, both Duck and Frog Islands are lined with rocky underwater reefs that normally provide good smallmouth fishing. The water drops very quickly from five to 30 feet allowing anglers to cover all the magic depths on a single cast.

East Upper Lake, South Upper Lake, and West Upper Lake offer many of the same types of fishing choices. Rocks in Old Channel Bay, off the edge of Spray Island, and around Hardscrabble Point (all shown on maps) are just a few of the known fishing spots worth a visit. These three lakes are actually a single large body of water, and these particular areas are all within a six-mile radius; visiting fishermen need not worry about making long runs through open water at Minnetonka.

The larger the lake or bay, the more clear the water tends to be. Overall, there certainly is not a shortage of places to fish, and should the wind make conditions rough, there are plenty of escape routes. There is no fishing in the canals, and a strict boating speed limit (maximum of 40 mph) is in force throughout.

When all conditions are right—water level, milfoil height, stable weather—which generally occurs in late summer—the fishing in this unusual series of lakes can truly be amazing. The State of Minnestoa describes itself as the "Land of 10,000 Lakes," and many would put Minnetonka at the top of that list.

RESOURCES

Gearing Up: Medium- and medium/heavy-action baitcasting rods, especially pitching and flipping rods, are preferred here because of the vegetation and rocks. Lines testing 12 to 25 pounds are standard. Favorite lures include jigs ranging from 1/2- to 3/4-ounce, willowleaf spinnerbaits of the same weight, deep-diving crankbaits, and plastic lizards.

Accommodations: Complete motel and restaurant facilities are available in Wayzata, Excelsior, Navarre, and Minneapolis. Camping is also available nearby.

Additional Information: Wayzata Chamber of Commerce, 402 East Lake Street, Wayzata, MN 55391; 612-473-9595.

46 LAKE OAHE

Location: Missouri River impoundment stretching from Bismarck, North Dakota to Pierre, South Dakota.
Short Take: 371,000 acres; large tributary rivers and creeks, shallow canyons, rocky points and flats, pockets and coves, limited vegetation, some flooded sloughs in upper end.
Primary Species: Smallmouth bass.
Best Months: May through October.
Favorite Lures: Topwaters, crankbaits, jigs, spinnerbaits.
Nearest Tourist Services: Pierre and Mobridge, South Dakota; Bismarck, North Dakota.

LAKE OAHE STRETCHES 231 MILES ACROSS THE TWO DAKOTAS, and while its primary claim to fame rests as one of the nation's most outstanding walleye fisheries, the lake's growing smallmouth bass population cannot be ignored. For now, the smallmouth are basically confined to the lower half of the lake, but as has been the case in many other impoundments, the fish are almost certain to expand their range up the lake in the years ahead. There is also limited largemouth fishing in the upper end closer to Bismarck.

Oahe was created between 1948 and 1962, and is one of six major impoundments along the upper Missouri River. Oahe's earth-filled dam is one of the largest of its type in the world, and has created one of the largest man-made lakes in the United States. The lake has 2,250 miles of basically undeveloped shoreline.

Overall, Oahe can be described as rocky and sandy with moderate to clear water. There is extremely deep water close to the shoreline in many areas, but most of the canyons become shallow enough for excellent topwater, jig, and crankbait fishing. On the lower end, the only vegetation to be found is scattered shoreline grass in the very backs of the canyons. Forage is abundant and includes the spottail shiner, goldeneye, perch, and emerald shiner.

The upper part of the lake is essentially a river-type environment, although with a number of backwater sloughs that are filled with standing timber, brush, reeds, and other vegetation. This is where the largemouth are caught. These shallow backwaters are out of the current and somewhat reminiscent of what bass fishermen find on some southern waterways. Spinnerbaits and even buzzbaits can be used here throughout the spring and summer.

At the city of Mobridge, South Dakota, the lake gradually begins to widen although still retaining the overall appearance of a huge river. While the primary source of water for Oahe is the Missouri, other major tributaries include the Grand, Moreau, and Cheyenne Rivers, along with numerous other creeks. The Grand enters the Missouri at Mobridge from the west; the Moreau and Cheyenne flow in from the west between Mobridge and the dam at Pierre.

LAKE OAHE
SOUTH DAKOTA/NORTH DAKOTA
BORDER

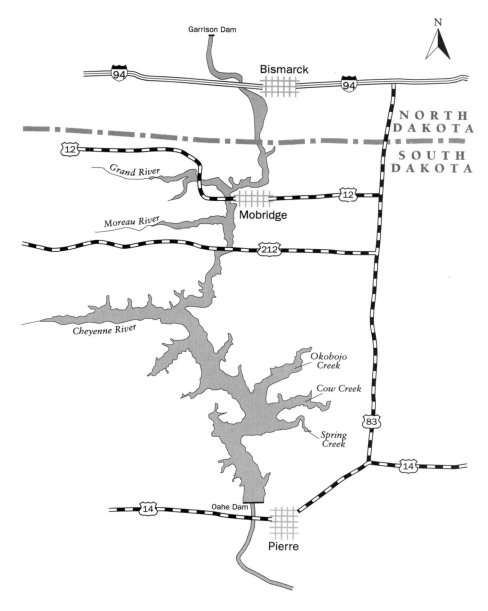

Smallmouth were first stocked in 1985 in the deepest water at the dam, and this is still where the best fishing is found. This lower end of the lake offers hundreds of rock and gravel pockets, primary and secondary points, and shallow coves around either shoreline above the Oahe Dam. This structure can be fished with a variety of lures for the smallmouth, and it is not unusual, in fact, for three fishermen in the same boat to be using three different lures—a topwater, a crankbait, and a jig, for example—and all three be catching bass.

Because Lake Oahe is rated as one of America's premier walleye fisheries, the smallmouth bass have been largely neglected. At the same time, the lake's chinook salmon fishery has also blossomed, even further reducing fishing pressure on the smallmouth. Still a third reason the bass fishing does not receive strong attention is because overall the fish average just 1 to 3 pounds in size. For an angler who would rather catch numbers of fish rather than trophy-sized fish, Oahe definitely deserves consideration.

Spring and Cow Creeks are two lower-lake tributaries that anglers can pinpoint for smallmouth action. Both offer a variety of shallow habitat, including not only flats but also gravel shorelines and even some submerged timber. Like the other tributaries, however, depths in both of these creeks quickly change.

The prime time to fish for Oahe smallmouths is during the late spring and throughout the summer. The bass start biting soon after ice-out in early spring. Spring and Cow Creeks warm quicker than other areas and start producing smallmouth in early May. The fishing continually improves as the water warms, and remains dependable until October.

In the early spring, slow, suspending jerkbaits and jigs are probably the best lures to use, but as spring moves into summer, topwater chuggers become more effective. The bass spawn in June at depths as shallow as three feet, then gradually move toward the deeper drops where plastic worms and tube jigs can be used successfully.

Even though the smallmouth gradually move toward deeper water, much of the time this does not necessarily mean a move into the main lake. Most of Oahe's tributaries, including Spring and Cow Creeks, have deep water suitable for the fish. Many times the smallmouth simply suspend at various depths, or hold over a ledge along the edge of a sharp drop. This can be as shallow as 12 to 15 feet, which is why topwater lures still work in July and August; the bass can still be attracted by a surface commotion.

When the topwater bite slows, anglers can change to small tube jigs, drop-shot rigs fished vertically, or possibly even some Carolina rigs, although the steepness of the bottom contours may make these less effective in places. After the spawning season, the trick to locating smallmouth here is simply working deeper water.

A special word of warning is in order for fishermen, however, which relates to the rapidly changing weather in the region and its effect on this huge lake. In a word, Lake Oahe, as well as its upstream sister lake, Lake Sakakawea (also known as Garrison Reservoir), both become extremely rough when winds begin rolling across the prairies, as they frequently do this time of year. It pays to keep an eye on the weather and to study forecasts carefully.

Anglers visiting Oahe for the first time will probably appreciate the wilderness-type setting of the lake, since very little shoreline development has been permitted. In addition, the Standing Rock and Cheyenne River Indian Reservations are located along portions of the western shoreline.

RESOURCES

Gearing Up: Because of the generally clear water, most smallmouth fishermen here choose medium-action rods with lines testing 10 or 12 pounds. Lighter spinning tackle can also be used quite successfully. Favorite lures include 3/8-ounce jigs, topwater chuggers, jerkbaits, and medium-diving crankbaits.

Accommodations: Motel and restaurant facilities are available on the lower end of the lake in Pierre, in the mid-section in Mobridge, and on the northern end in Bismarck. Camping is allowed along the shoreline and at several developed Corps of Engineers campgrounds.

Additional Information: Pierre Area Convention and Visitors Bureau, Box 548, Pierre, SD 57501; 605-224-7361.

NORTHEAST

NEW HAMPSHIRE

NEW YORK

WASHINGTON D.C.

47 LAKE WINNIPESAUKEE

Location: Eastern New Hampshire near the cities of Center Harbor, Laconia, and Wolfeboro.

Short Take: 44,000 acres; clear water with sand/gravel/rock points and shoals, underwater vegetation, no major tributaries.

Primary Species: Largemouth and smallmouth bass.

Best Months: May through September.

Favorite Lures: Topwaters, jerkbaits, plastic tube jigs and lizards, spider jigs, and spinnerbaits.

Nearest Tourist Services: Laconia, Center Harbor, Wolfeboro.

THIS GLACIER-BORN LAKE ON THE EDGE OF New Hampshire's famed White Mountains has been filled with smallmouth bass for more than a hundred years, but only during the past decade or so have bass fishermen discovered what a gem this New England lake really is. With its 274 separate islands and generally wooded shoreline, it is pretty enough to have been chosen for some of the filming of Henry Fonda's famous film *On Golden Pond* (the rest was filmed at Squam Lake just eight miles north), and the lake's trout and salmon fishing has been productive enough to have attracted anglers since colonial times.

"Today, thanks to some of the national publicity it has received, Winnipesaukee is probably even better known for its smallmouth fishing," notes Rick Lillegard, who has been guiding on Winnipesaukee for 15 years. "The fish aren't really that big but there are just an incredible number of them. The average smallmouth here weighs 2 to 3 pounds, but when you can catch them steadily all day long, their smaller size doesn't matter.

"Largemouth bass fishing is excellent, too," continues Lillegard, "with a lot of 3 to 5 pounders. There are a lot of tournaments on the lake now, and fishermen are targeting the largemouths more and more because they are larger. I've seen largemouths weighing as much as 8 pounds, which is a big fish in this part of the country."

Lillegard and others credit the lake's habitat for the successful bass fisheries. Sand, pea gravel, and boulders cover the bottom and form much of the shoreline. In the open water, numerous gravel shoals rise from depths of over a hundred feet to within six or eight feet of the surface to provide additional habitat, and if this isn't enough, much of the bottom is also covered by moss and grass. In the far backs of some of the shallow coves, there are even some lily pads.

"I have been able to fish throughout the United States," says Lillegard, "and I don't believe I have ever seen a lake with so much or such perfect rock and gravel habitat as we have on Winnipesaukee. What surprises me is that bass fishing did not become popular here sooner than it did."

Lake Winnipesaukee
New Hampshire

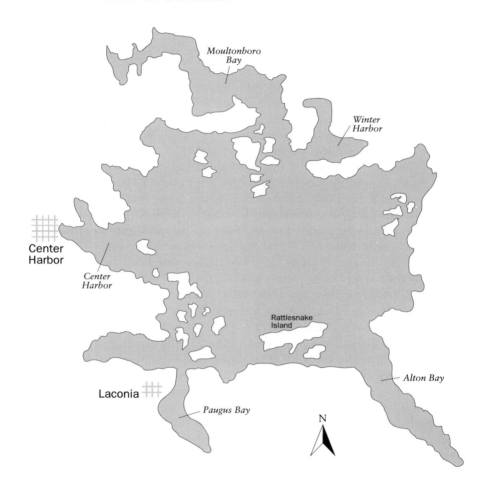

Moultonboro Bay

Winter Harbor

Center Harbor

Center Harbor

Rattlesnake Island

Alton Bay

Laconia

Paugus Bay

N

Two additional reasons for Winnipesaukee's success are the abundance of forage for the bass, which includes both crayfish as well as small white perch, and New Hampshire's strict catch-and-release fishing regulations, in which all bass caught between May 15 and June 15 (the spawning season) must be released immediately. Before May 15 there is a two-bass daily limit, while after June 15 the daily limit increases to five fish.

Winnipesaukee has no major tributaries (water level fluctuation is also very slight), so virtually all bass fishing is done in or near the large bays and small coves within those bays. Among the key areas are Center Harbor on the northern side, Paugus Bay near the city of Laconia on the western side, and Moultonboro Bay on the northeastern part of the lake. Each of these offers protected waters off the main body of the lake. Paugus Bay is particularly well known for producing excellent catches of both largemouth and smallmouth off the points, around the boulders, over the weedbeds, and from under the boat docks.

Bass fishing generally gets started here in early May, about two weeks after ice-out. Lillegard has observed smallmouth spawning as early as the first weeks of May when the water temperature is still in the 50s, but most years it's a little later. Because the water is so clear in Winnipesaukee—generally about 15 feet—sightfishing for bedding bass can be excellent, which is why the New Hampshire Fish and Game Department requires that fish caught during this time be released.

After spawning is completed and the bass gradually begin moving toward deeper water, topwater action takes center stage. Big chuggers and poppers worked over points and around the submerged islands are likely to get clobbered by either species, and this can last throughout the summer.

When the topwater bite slows, plastic spider jigs or Carolina-rigged lizards can be used around the sand and gravel shoals and especially along the edges of the vegetation. On Winnipesaukee there are several types of deep vegetation but the one most anglers key on is known simply as sand grass. It can be found as deep as 20 or 25 feet but it only grows about a foot high. Summer spinnerbaits are also excellent lure choices for largemouths in some of the shallow coves.

Boat docks are common all around the lake, and a favorite technique for them is fishing jerkbaits around the pilings in early spring, then changing to either tube jigs or spider jigs later. These docks are where many of Winnipesaukee's 3- to 5-pound largemouths are taken.

It is interesting to note that on January 1, 2000, New Hampshire became the first state to prohibit the use of lead in either fishing weights or jigheads. Visiting anglers should be aware of this law and be prepared to switch to either brass or steel, both of which are available in area tackle shops.

Winnipesaukee can become extremely rough very quickly, but fortunately it is well-buoyed to aid navigation. Additionally, all the shallow shoals that frequently pinpoint smallmouth hangouts are also marked. The lake is fishable in the wind because of the large embayments, all of which have launching ramps.

RESOURCES

Gearing Up: Because of the clear water, anglers here rely on light- or medium-action spinning and baitcasting rods with lines testing 6 to 10 pounds. Fast-moving spinnerbaits and jerkbaits can be fished with slightly heavier lines. Other productive lures include 1/4-ounce spinnerbaits, topwater poppers, plastic tube jigs, and spider jigs.

Accommodations: This is a favorite recreation/vacation area (it's less than three hours north of Boston), so motel and restaurant facilities are abundant around the entire lake. Camping is also available at numerous areas along the shore.

Additional Information: Greater Laconia/Weirs Beach Chamber of Commerce, 11 Veterans Square, Laconia, NH 03246; 603-524-5531. Northern Bass Supply, P.O. Box 698, Kingston, NH 03848; 800- 227-7032.

48 LAKE CHAMPLAIN

Location: Vermont/New York border and extending into Quebec.
Short Take: 271,000 acres; both clear and dingy water, weedy shallows, islands, rocky bluffs, open water.
Primary Species: Smallmouth and largemouth bass.
Best Months: May through October.
Favorite Lures: Spinnerbaits, buzzbaits, jigs, plastic worms and grubs.
Nearest Tourist Services: Burlington.

SOME BELIEVE THAT IF THE FRENCH EXPLORER SAMUEL DE CHAMPLAIN had stayed long enough to sample the bass fishing at the massive 125-mile-long lake he discovered and named after himself in 1609, he would never have left.

As it turned out, bass fishing at Lake Champlain remained largely undiscovered until the mid-1990s when it was suddenly found to be one of the best—if not the absolute best—smallmouth fisheries in the United States. Many anglers who fish this beautiful New England lake today honestly believe they're catching bass that have never seen an artificial lure, an astounding revelation in this day and age.

Champlain went relatively unnoticed in the bass fishing world for a number of reasons, perhaps the primary one being that local anglers in the region preferred to go after some of the lake's other species like walleye and northern pike, a feeling not unusual in this part of the United States. For example, it was not until about 1980 that the full extent of the smallmouth and largemouth fishery in New York's St. Lawrence River was recognized, and it took a multi-day professional bass tournament there, just as at Lake Champlain in 1997, to show local authorities what a fishing bonanza swam in their waters.

Lake Champlain is one of the largest lakes in North America, embracing some 435 square miles, or a stunning 271,000 acres. It is so big, and so divided by islands, points, and bays, that many actually consider this to be several different lakes. The easiest way to describe Champlain is by describing prominent features or landmarks.

One of the most well-known areas is Malletts Bay, a large embayment along the Vermont side just north of Burlington. This is a popular bass fishing area because it is well protected and offers miles of relatively shallow water filled with both rocks and vegetation. The fishing here is excellent, too, especially with jigs, spinnerbaits, and jerkbaits. There are a lot of small coves, rocky points, and wide flats in this area, along with very dramatic breaklines where the depths may fall from five to 50 feet in just a short distance.

About 20 miles south of Malletts Bay the lake begins to narrow, and many fishermen prefer this area for fishing because the water also begins to lose its clarity. One well-known spot is around the mouth of the Boquet River on the New York side, where the bottom forms a mile-wide flat less than 10 feet deep before falling into 150-foot depths. About 10 miles farther south on the Vermont side, the mouth

LAKE CHAMPLAIN
NEW YORK

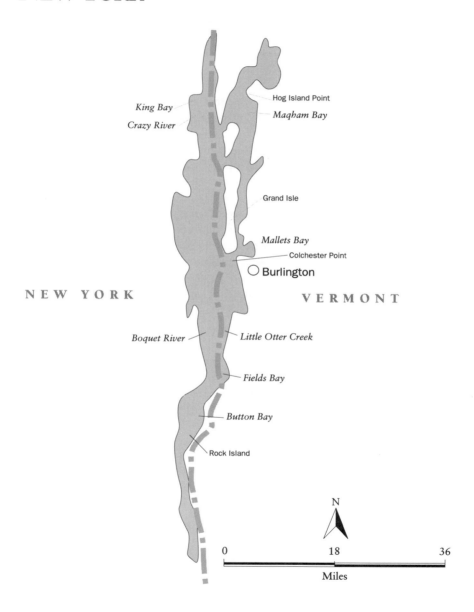

King Bay

Crazy River

Hog Island Point

Maqham Bay

Grand Isle

Mallets Bay

Colchester Point

◯ Burlington

NEW YORK

VERMONT

Boquet River

Little Otter Creek

Fields Bay

Button Bay

Rock Island

N

0   18   36

Miles

of Little Otter Creek forms a similar large flat; both of these areas are excellent large-mouth spots that can be fished with spinnerbaits, jerkbaits, and jigs.

Even farther south, as the lake continues to narrow, are Fields Bay, Button Bay, and Rock Island, all areas that provide shallow weedy cover or rocky structure that provides excellent largemouth fishing.

North and west of Malletts Bay, Lake Champlain features much more wide-open water. Here, Grand Isle (also known as South Hero Island), which actually helps form part of Malletts Bay, marks the beginning of the Lake Champlain Islands. From this point to the northern end of the lake more than 25 miles away, Champlain is filled with islands big and small. Because South Hero, North Hero, and the others lie mainly in a north-south direction, they effectively divide this part of Champlain into eastern (New York) and western (Vermont) sections.

Fishermen have literally thousands of options, ranging from island points, se-cluded bays, and more shallow flats, to steep cliffs and underwater ridges and shoals. Places that anglers might consider fishing include Maquam Bay and Hog Island Point on the Vermont side, and King Bay and the mouth of the Great Chazy River on the New York side.

Overall, this upper part of the lake has extremely clear water, but both small-mouth and largemouth are present in amazing numbers. Summertime catches of 50 to 60 fish per day are not unusual, with smallmouth averaging 2 to about 4 pounds, and largemouth slightly less. A 5-pound smallmouth and a 6-pound largemouth here are considered trophies.

Wherever an angler decides to fish here, he must pay attention to the weather. Lake Champlain quickly becomes extremely rough and dangerous in even a 10 mph north wind, due to its wide-open areas, and a 20 mph wind usually makes small boat navigation impossible.

The good part about fishing Champlain is that there are many protected coves and access points along its shoreline, and that the fishing can be so good long runs across open water may not be necessary. For example, just outside Malletts Bay around Colchester Point, shallow 10- to 12-foot grass-filled water extends more than a mile offshore. It's a highly productive area that can be fished for hours, and it is only minutes from a launching ramp.

Another aspect of this unusual lake is that fishermen can generally catch both smallmouth and largemouth on a variety of lures. It's not quite a case of trying to find something the bass won't hit, but at times it does seem like virtually any lure in the tacklebox will bring a strike. The fishing is just that good.

RESOURCES

Gearing Up: Anglers use everything from heavy-action flipping sticks to medium-action spinning rods here, depending primarily on the type of fishing and the water clarity. Line sizes also vary accordingly, ranging from as light as 8 to as heavy as 20-pound test. First-time visitors might consider medium-action baitcasting rods with 12-pound-test line as a starter. White spinnerbaits, black/brown jigs, soft plastic jerkbaits, topwater chuggers and buzzbaits, and plastic tube jigs will all catch bass here; it is often a case of fishing whatever lure the angler enjoys most.

Accommodations: Complete motel and restaurant facilities are available in Burlington. Campgrounds are located in numerous areas up and down the lake in both Vermont and New York.

Additional Information: Burlington Chamber of Commerce, 60 Main Street, Burlington, VT 05401; 802-863-3489.

49 ST. LAWRENCE RIVER

Location: Northwestern New York and southern Ontario.
Short Take: Approximately 45 miles of river; clear, rocky, weedy, islands, channels, bays.
Primary Species: Smallmouth and largemouth bass.
Best Months: Late June through mid-September.
Favorite Lures: Jigs, plastic tube jigs and worms, topwaters.
Nearest Tourist Services: Clayton and Alexandria Bay, New York.

THE SECTION OF NEW YORK'S ST. LAWRENCE RIVER between Cape Vincent and Morristown is often described as the prettiest 45 miles of bass water in America, and for good reason. This is the fabled 1,000 Islands region, where the river is filled with rocky, tree-covered islands both large and small. Even residential development on these islands (many are privately owned) does not detract from the area's natural beauty.

Add to this the clear, greenish-blue water of the St. Lawrence itself and truly wonderful twin fisheries for both largemouth and smallmouth bass, and it is little wonder this area has become one of America's best-known rivers. It is also one of Canada's favorite waterways, as the St. Lawrence forms the boundary between the United States and Ontario for part of its length. Anglers need both American and Canadian licenses when the fishing season for bass annually opens the third week of June.

Terry Baksay, a professional bass fisherman who lives in Connecticut, first visited the St. Lawrence in 1981 and was so enchanted by the area he's been returning ever since. During his early visits he concentrated on smallmouth, for that was the species for which the river was best known, but over the years he has seen the largemouth fishing continually improve.

"One of the reasons for this improvement has probably been the spread of zebra mussels throughout the river," notes Baksay. "It has made the water much clearer and caused the smallmouth to stay in deeper water where they're harder to catch.

"The clear water has allowed the vegetation and weed growth to improve, and that has definitely helped the largemouth. They're a shallow-water fish anyway, and it could be that bass fishermen are concentrating on them more now than ever before."

Whatever the reason or whatever the species, anglers have but one basic rule to remember when fishing the St. Lawrence: weeds hold the bass. Whenever a fisherman is casting or pitching lures around the milfoil, arrowroot, angel hair, or other vegetation, he is usually going to be close to fish.

Still, a number of places often tend to be more reliable as bass producers than others. These include the Admiralty Islands group near the Canadian city of Gananoque; Lake of the Isles; Goose Bay; and Chippewa Bay. There are, of course,

ST. LAWRENCE RIVER
NEW YORK

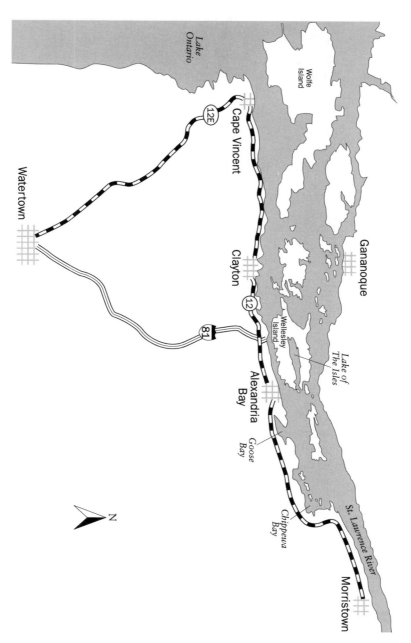

The St. Lawrence River is known as the Thousand Islands. Here a bass fisherman fishes in the shadow of Boldt Castle, which was built on one of the islands near Alexandria Bay.

hundreds of other places, but these four will certainly get any bass angler started. All are located within a short distance of Clayton and Alexandria Bay, two well-known river tourism communities, themselves only seven miles apart.

The Admiralty Islands group is reached by going up the river from Clayton, around large Grindstone Island, and across to the Canadian side. Before reaching the Gananoque community on the Ontario shore, a fisherman will be negotiating his way through the Admiralty Islands. Like most places in the 1,000 Islands, the fishing options here are widely varied; one of the best is working a black plastic worm down the rocky dropoffs of the islands and crawling it slowly through some of the darker, shadow-filled corners and crevices.

Lake of the Isles is a three-and-a-half-mile-long body of open water in Wellesley Island, several miles down the St. Lawrence from Clayton near Alexandria Bay. This is a narrow, shallow, weedy bay which usually provides the most consistent large-mouth action on the river. Here bass fishermen often skim and skitter topwater rats and frogs across the vegetation, just as on some southern lakes. Other lure choices include jigs, plastic worms, and occasionally spinnerbaits.

Goose Bay is located about three miles down the St. Lawrence from Alexandria Bay and on the same side of the river. It is an extremely shallow, rocky bay not quite as large as Lake of the Isles, and with both rocks and weeds it produces largemouth and smallmouth bass. Walking topwaters around the rocks and pitching jigs into the weeds are the two most reliable fishing techniques.

Chippewa Bay is the next large bay down the St. Lawrence on the New York side of the river; it also produces both largemouth and smallmouth, although small-mouth tend to move into the deeper water on the outside of the bay as summer progresses. Some may remember this bay as the site of Bo Dowden's 1980 Bass Masters Classic world championship victory, in which he boated more than 54 pounds of bass in three days. Dowden's technique that week was basically working a jig down around the rocks—the very same technique that works so well today.

Chippewa Bay is essentially the last large embayment of the river on the American side, and while it does not mark the end of the 1,000 Islands region, few bass anglers venture much farther down the river. Indeed, today many fishermen head up the river from Clayton and test the waters of Lake Ontario, which also offer an outstanding smallmouth fishery.

What is truly amazing about fishing in the St. Lawrence is that while it is a huge river, extending nearly a thousand miles from its headwaters at Lake Ontario through Montreal and finally to the Gulf of St. Lawrence and to the Atlantic, the best bass fishing by far is centered within a 15-mile area around Clayton and Alexandria Bay that can easily be enjoyed by anglers of all experience levels.

RESOURCES

Gearing Up: Largemouth fishermen working weedlines and rocks generally choose medium- or medium/heavy-action baitcasting rods with 15- to 20-pound-test lines. Smallmouth anglers often use lighter spinning rods with lines in the 8- to 14-pound-test range. Favorite lures include 1/2-ounce jigs, large topwater chuggers, plastic worms and tube jigs, and occasionally 3/8-ounce double willowleaf spinnerbaits.

Accommodations: Complete motel and restaurant facilities are available throughout the region, especially in Clayton and Alexandria Bay, as this is a popular summer vacation area. Camping opportunities are also readily available in numerous state parks along the shore and on Wellesley Island.

Additional Information: 1000 Islands International Tourism Council, P.O. Box 400, Alexandria Bay, NY 13607; 800-847-5263.

50 POTOMAC RIVER

Location: Washington, D.C.
Short Take: Approximately 50 miles fishable for bass; tidal influence, hydrilla, shallow underwater cover, large tributaries.
Primary Species: Largemouth and striped bass.
Best Months: April, May, September, October.
Favorite Lures: Jigs, crankbaits, spinnerbaits, plastic worms.
Nearest Tourist Services: Waldorf, Maryland

UNLESS THEY HAPPEN TO BE BASS FISHERMEN, tourists driving across the Woodrow Wilson Bridge (Interstate 95) just south of Washington, D.C. seldom realize that when they look down at the Potomac River they're seeing one of the finest bass fisheries in eastern America. Anglers who solve the twin puzzles of tidal influence and hydrilla usually have a busy day on the water.

As unlikely as it may seem, it is possible to follow the Potomac right into Washington, catching bass within sight of the Washington Monument or even in the Pentagon harbor. One of the best areas on the entire river, for example, is just a few casts north of the Wilson Bridge itself, where professional bass tournament angler Jay Yelas has won tens of thousands of dollars over the years. Just a few miles down the river, fishermen can look for bass in the shadow of Mount Vernon, which is visible high on the bluff above.

The Potomac is an ever-changing fishery, however, and while some areas do remain consistently productive year after year, others do not. That's because hydrilla covers much of the Potomac's shallow water areas, and its growth is dependent on water flow. Heavy saltwater intrusion from Chesapeake Bay or high, muddy water from north of Washington will totally change the hydrilla growth pattern each year. Large beds of the vegetation that are present one year may be completely gone the next.

Most bass fishing takes place along a 50-mile stretch between Washington and the U.S. Highway 301 bridge. Below the 301 bridge the saltwater influence is much stronger, and besides, there are many, many fishing options above the bridge.

The Potomac forms the boundary between Maryland and Virginia, and a number of large tributaries on both sides have produced good catches over the years. These include Piscataway, Mattawoman, and Nanjemoy Creeks on the Maryland side, and Occoquan Bay, Chopawamsic, Aquia, and Potomac Creeks on the Virginia side.

In all of these, anglers will encounter a variety of cover and structure, including not only hydrilla but also lily pads, boat docks, pier pilings, rocks, and even shoreline brush. Some of these tributaries, like Mattawoman and Aquia, are large and wind for miles so that a fisherman will usually have his choice of what he wants to fish. Mattawoman, especially, is popular because many fishing tournaments are held

POTOMAC RIVER
WASHINGTON, D.C.

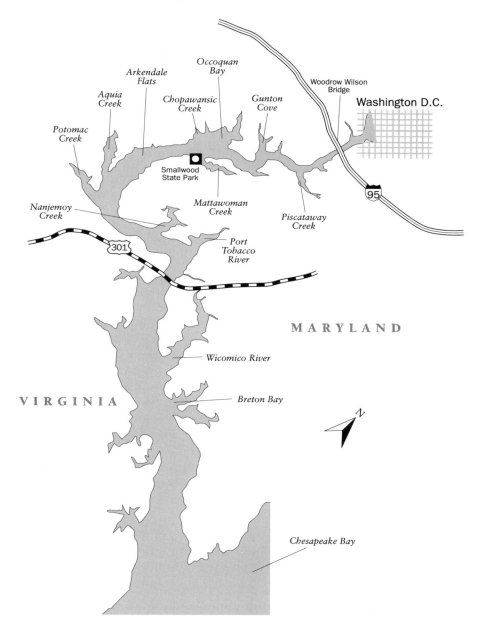

Arkendale
Flats

Occoquan
Bay

Woodrow Wilson
Bridge

Washington D.C.

Aquia
Creek

Chopawansic
Creek

Gunton
Cove

Potomac
Creek

Smallwood
State Park

95

Nanjemoy
Creek

Mattawoman
Creek

Piscataway
Creek

301

Port
Tobacco
River

MARYLAND

Wicomico River

Breton Bay

VIRGINIA

N

Chesapeake Bay

out of Smallwood State Park and the fish are released nearby; because the creek has so much cover available, the bass don't leave. Occoquan Bay, just across the river from Mattawoman, offers vast shallow flats edged by marsh filled with lily pads, stumps, logs, pilings, and rocks.

These big tributaries also provide calm water when the main river is rough. Whenever an incoming or outgoing tide meets a strong wind blowing from the opposite direction, the river can turn bad, with big rolling swells and whitecaps. When this happens, small boat navigation is extremely difficult and fishing is all but impossible.

In the main river itself, the Potomac has many sunken or grounded barges that provide excellent fish habitat and which are normally marked on maps. The best known of these graveyards is the Arkendale Flats, about two miles above the entrance to Aquia Creek on the Virginia side. Here fishermen not only have a dozen or so rotting barges to fish but also scattered hydrilla, which normally grows in this area.

Many Potomac anglers have encountered rock piles out in the river, and on occasion, these have produced amazing numbers of bass. There are more than 100 of these rock piles between the Wilson and US 301 bridges; they served as ballast for old sailing ships. When the ships were no longer needed, they were burned on the water, which allowed the rocks to fall to the bottom in a single large cluster. Many of these are well known and their locations are marked on better river maps.

Potomac tides, which may fluctuate two feet or more, have baffled bass fishermen here for years. In most instances, the outgoing tide is preferred by anglers because it pulls fish out from some of the thick cover where they become more accessible. Thus, the technique of "running the tide" evolved; starting at one end of the waterway, fishermen would run the river fishing the outgoing tide but still staying ahead of the incoming tide as long as possible.

Such tactics usually result in the loss of a lot of fishing time, however, and many anglers today now choose a single large fishing area, such as Occoquan Bay or Mattawoman Creek, and stay in it, regardless of the tide. Doing this usually requires different lures and casting presentations as the water floods previously visible cover, but the technique has proven successful in recent national tournaments and can just as easily be followed by any angler.

Spinnerbaits and jigs are two of the most popular lures on the Potomac—spinnerbaits for the shallow logs, stumps, and lily pads and jigs for the hydrilla and the sunken barges. Where the vegetation has broken into clumps, lipless crankbaits probably see more action than anything else.

The Chesapeake Bay area has long been known for its striped bass fishing, and in the spring the stripers provide good action in the Potomac, as well. A variety of lures are used, including large jigs, jerkbaits, and even topwater plugs at times.

RESOURCES

Gearing Up: Bass fishermen here normally chose medium- or medium/heavy-action rods with lines testing 12 to 20 pounds. Much depends on the fishing technique and type of cover. Favorite lures include 1/2-ounce spinnerbaits, 3/8- and 1/2-ounce jigs, lipless crankbaits, and plastic worms on either a Carolina or Texas rig.

Accommodations: Complete motel and restaurant facilities are available in Waldorf and La Plata, Maryland as well as in Washington, D.C. Camping is offered at Smallwood State Park near Waldorf and other sites along both sides of the river.

Additional Information: Charles County Office of Tourism, P.O. Box B, La Plata, MD 20646; 301-645-0558.

THE REST OF THE BEST

As mentioned earlier, a number of major lakes and rivers were not included simply because of editorial limitations. Herewith are brief descriptions of another dozen that could easily be included on anyone's list of favorite bass waters.

Red River, Louisiana—The Corps of Engineers has dammed the Red River in Louisiana to create a series of large pools and flooded backwaters filled with standing timber, hydrilla, lily pads, and other brush. The pools most often fished by anglers are Pool 4 and Pool 5, which extend downriver from Shreveport a total of about 60 miles. The next pool, Pool 6 is also fished, primarily by anglers launching in Alexandria and coming upriver. The spring and summer months are best.

Wheeler Lake, Alabama—Once reknown for superb largemouth action in and around its thick milfoil beds, this 68,300 acre impoundment immediately below Lake Guntersville on the Tennessee River still deserves some attention even though the vegetation has been eradicated. Catching good stringers is much more difficult now, but anglers still have tributary creeks, a vast network of underwater ditches and flats, and stumpy channel ledges in which to search for both largemouth and smallmouth.

Umpqua River, Oregon—If drifting down a big river in an oar-powered boat and casting to a seemingly endless supply of smallmouth bass interests you, then the Umpqua River near Elkton, Oregon should be on your calendar. The fish are frequently visible in the clear water and readily hit a variety of small soft plastics, topwaters, and crankbaits. The largest fish are caught during April and May, the most fish come during July and August. Package floats with guides, meals, and accommodations are the best way to fish the Umpqua, and they're available through the Big K Ranch in Elkton, which owns 10 miles of prime river frontage.

Lake Pleasant, Arizona—Since 1993 when Lake Pleasant began expanding from 3,000 to its present 10,000 acres, the fishing has been excellent, especially for trophy-class largemouths. Located about 35 miles northwest of Phoenix, the lake is best fished during the winter and spring when it's at full capacity. Unfortunately, Lake Pleasant's relatively small size, heavy drawdown during the summer, and fishing pressure have anglers a little uneasy about the lake's long-term future as a trophy fishery.

St. Johns River, Florida—The St. Johns River near Palatka, Florida, has certainly produced its share of trophy bass over the years, especially Lake George. Trophy bass guides often fish with live shiners, but others use soft plastic lures like tube jigs, worms, and flukes. Along the river there are banks of reeds, weedy coves, and even island points that can all be fished. The water is basically clear and shallow; in January sight-fishing for bedding bass is popular.

At Lake Ray Roberts, a 29,350 acre impoundment near Denton, anglers have thousands of acres of flooded timber to fish. Jigs, spinnerbaits, crankbaits, and plastic worms all work well during the year.

Smith Mountain Lake, Virginia—This scenic 20,000 acre impoundment on the Roanoke River is best known for its striped bass fishing, but smallmouth are also present. The stripers, which have topped 40 pounds here, can be caught on bucktail jigs as well as soft plastic grubs.

Lake Ray Roberts, Texas—The spread of hydrilla, combined with thick flooded timber and a decade of age have propelled this 29,350 acre lake into the limelight, not an easy task considering the competition from other Texas impoundments. This is unquestionably one of the lakes to watch in the years ahead for big bass; fish topping 10 pounds began showing up regularly during the spring of 1999, with three 14-pounders being caught in one day.

Arkansas River, Arkansas—This slow-flowing waterway offers a variety of fishing conditions, including stumpy backwater sloughs, flooded timber, rock wing dams, laydowns, sandbars and channel drops. Two bass fishing world championship events have been conducted near Pine Bluff, although it is possible to lock through various dams and fish a number of different pools. Current flow determines where and how the river should be fished, but overall quality is excellent.

Lake Sakakawea, North Dakota—This long, winding 368,000 acre impoundment on the Missouri River is better known for walleye than for smallmouth bass, but only because bass are not as popular here as in other parts of the country. The fish aren't as large as in other well-known smallmouth lakes, but the combination of rocky points, gravel banks, protected coves, and clear water ensures they'll always be here.

Dale Hollow, Tennessee—Dale Hollow's claim to fame, of course, is that this is the lake where the current world record smallmouth was caught. Many, including legendary smallmouth fisherman Billy Westmorland who lives near the lake, believe larger fish still swim in Dale Hollow's deep, rocky waters.

Norris Lake, Tennessee—If huge striped bass make your heart beat a little faster, this northeast Tennessee reservoir could easily be the place to make it happen. Long known as one of the finest striped bass reservoirs in America, fish over 50 pounds have been caught here. As with other lakes in this region, the water is deep and clear.

Lake Cumberland, Kentucky—This deep, clear 50,250 acre riverine impoundment near Somerset is another of the nation's better striped bass fisheries, although smallmouth, largemouth, and spotted bass are also present here. The heaviest smallmouth are taken in the winter months in deep water, while largemouths are caught shallow in the spring.

About the Author

Steve Price has been an award-winning writer and photographer for more than 25 years, specializing in outdoor recreation and travel. Formerly the Outdoor Editor of Southern Living Magazine and the South Regional Editor of Field & Stream, he has been a Senior Writer for Bassmaster Magazine for more than 21 years. He has written more than 2,500 magazine articles and sold thousands of photographs to many national and international publishers, including the National Geographic Society, Reader's Digest, and Time-Life. Assignments have taken him throughout the United States and much of Canada as well as to Africa, South and Central America, India and Asia. He has also written numerous video and television scripts and has served as the producer and host of a nationally syndicated radio show. This is his fifth book, his third about bass fishing. A graduate of the University of North Carolina at Chapel Hill, he lives in Granbury, Texas.

FALCON GUIDES® Leading the way™

FalconGuides® are available for where-to-go hiking, mountain biking, rock climbing, walking, scenic driving, fishing, rockhounding, paddling, birding, wildlife viewing, and camping. We also have FalconGuides on essential outdoor skills and subjects and field identification. The following titles are currently available, but this list grows every year. For a free catalog with a complete list of titles, call FALCON toll-free at 1-800-582-2665.

BIRDING GUIDES

Birding Illinois
Birding Minnesota
Birding Montana
Birding Northern California
Birding Texas
Birding Utah

PADDLING GUIDES

Floater's Guide to Colorado
Paddling Minnesota
Paddling Montana
Paddling Okefenokee
Paddling Oregon
Paddling Yellowstone & Grand

WALKING

Walking Colorado Springs
Walking Denver
Walking Portland
Walking St. Louis
Walking San Francisco
Walking Virginia Beach

CAMPING GUIDES

Camping Arizona
Camping California's
    National Forests
Camping Colorado
Camping Southern California
Recreation Guide to Washington
    National Forests

FIELD GUIDES

Bitterroot: Montana State Flower
Canyon Country Wildflowers
Central Rocky Mountain
    Wildflowers
Great Lakes Berry Book
New England Berry Book
Ozark Wildflowers
Pacific Northwest Berry Book
Plants of Arizona
Rare Plants of Colorado
Rocky Mountain Berry Book
Scats & Tracks of the Pacific
    Coast States
Scats & Tracks of the Rocky Mtns.
Southern Rocky Mountain
    Wildflowers
Tallgrass Prairie Wildflowers
Western Trees
Wildflowers of Southwestern Utah
Willow Bark and Rosehips

ROCKHOUNDING GUIDES

Rockhounding Arizona
Rockhounding California
Rockhounding Colorado
Rockhounding Montana
Rockhounding Nevada
Rockhound's Guide to
    New Mexico
Rockhounding Texas
Rockhounding Utah
Rockhounding Wyoming
Teton National Parks

HOW-TO GUIDES

Avalanche Aware
Backpacking Tips
Bear Aware
Desert Hiking Tips
Hiking with Dogs
Mountain Lion Alert
Reading Weather
Route Finding
Using GPS
Wilderness First Aid
Wilderness Survival
Zero Impact

MORE GUIDEBOOKS

Backcountry Horseman's
    Guide to Washington
Family Fun in Montana
Family Fun in Yellowstone
Exploring Canyonlands & Arches
    National Parks
Exploring Hawaii's Parklands
Exploring Mount Helena
Exploring Southern California
    Beaches
Hiking Hot Springs of the Pacific
    Northwest
Touring Arizona Hot Springs
Touring California & Nevada
    Hot Springs
Touring Montana and Wyoming
    Hot Springs
Trail Riding Western Montana
Wild Country Companion
Wilderness Directory
Wild Montana
Wild Utah
Wild Virginia

■ *To order any of these books, check with your local bookseller*
*or call FALCON ® at **1-800-582-2665**.*
Visit us on the world wide web at:
www.FalconOutdoors.com

FALCONGUIDES® Leading the Way™

FALCON®

FALCONGUIDES® Leading the Way

Come to America's wilderness areas and enjoy some of the most pristine hiking conditions you'll ever experience. With FalconGuides® you'll be able to plan your trip, including learning how to get there, getting a permit, if necessary, and picking your campsites. Types of trails, difficulty ratings, distances, maps, elevation charts, and backcountry regulations are covered in detail. You'll also learn "leave no trace" principles, safety tips, and other essential information specific to the wilderness area you visit. The following titles are currently available, and this list grows every year. For a free catalog with a complete list of titles, call FALCON toll-free at 800-582-2665.

Hiking the Beartooths
Hiking the Bob Marshall Country
Hiking Colorado's Weminuche Wilderness
Hiking Oregon's Central Cascades
Hiking Oregon's Eagle Cap Wilderness
Hiking Oregon's Mount Hood & Badger Creek Wilderness
Hiking Wyoming's Cloud Peak Wilderness
Hiking Wyoming's Wind River Range
Wild Montana
Wild Utah

Wilderness area FalconGuides® are published in cooperation with *The Wilderness Society*

To order any of these books, check with your local bookseller,
Or call FALCON at 1-800-582-2665.
Visit us on the world wide web at:
www.FalconOutdoors.com

FALCONGUIDES® Leading the Way™

■ *To order any of these books, check with your local bookseller
or call FALCON* ® *at* **1-800-582-2665**.
Visit us on the world wide web at:
www.FalconOutdoors.com

FALCON®

Going Somewhere?

Insiders' Guides offer 60 current and upcoming titles to some of the country's most popular vacation destinations (including the ones listed below), and we're adding many more. Written by local authors and averaging 400 pages, our guides provide the information you need quickly and easily—whether searching for savory local cuisine, unique regional wares, amusements for the kids, a picturesque hiking spot, off-the-beaten-track attractions, new environs or a room with a view.

Explore America and experience the joy of travel with the Insiders' Guide® books.

Adirondacks
Atlanta, GA
Austin, TX
Baltimore
Bend & Central Oregon
Bermuda
Boca Raton & the Palm Beaches
Boise & Sun Valley
Boulder & the Rocky Mountain National Park
Branson & the Ozark Mountains
California's Wine Country
Cape Cod, Nantucket and Martha's Vineyard
Charleston, SC
Cincinnati
Civil War Sites in the Eastern Theater
Colorado's Mountains
Denver
The Florida Keys & Key West
Florida's Great Northwest
Golf in the Carolinas
Indianapolis
The Lake Superior Region
Las Vegas
Lexington, KY
Louisville, KY
Madison, WI
Maine's Mid-Coast
Maine's Southern Coast
Michigan's Traverse Bay Region
Mississippi
Montana's Glacier Country

Monterey Peninsula
Myrtle Beach
Nashville
New Hampshire
North Carolina's Central Coast & New Bern
North Carolina's Southern Coast & Wilmington
North Carolina's Mountains
North Carolina's Outer Banks
Phoenix
The Pocono Mountains
Portland
Relocation
Reno & Lake Tahoe
Richmond
Salt Lake City
San Diego
Santa Barbara
Santa Fe
Sarasota & Bradenton
Savannah
Southwestern Utah
Tampa & St. Petersburg
Texas Coastal Bend
Tucson
Twin Cities
Virginia's Blue Ridge
Virginia's Chesapeake Bay
Washington, D.C.
Williamsburg
Yellowstone